DO-IT-YOURSELF
ADVERTISING

DO-IT-YOURSELF ADVERTISING

How to Produce Great Ads,
Brochures, Catalogs, Direct Mail,
and Much More

Fred E. Hahn

JOHN WILEY & SONS, INC.
New York • Chichester • Brisbane • Toronto • Singapore

Library of Congress Cataloging-in-Publication Data

Hahn, Fred E., 1925–
    Do-it-yourself advertising : how to produce great ads, brochures, catalogs, direct mail, and much more / by Fred E. Hahn.
       p. cm.—(Wiley small business series)
    Includes index.
    ISBN 0-471-55389-1 (cloth).—ISBN 0-471-55390-5 (pbk.)
    1. Advertising—Handbooks, manuals, etc. I. Title. II. Series:
Small business series (New York, N.Y.)
HF5823.H187   1993
659.1—dc20   92-29710

Printed in the United States of America.
10 9 8 7 6 5 4

Dedicated, with thanks, to Michael Snell, the literary agent who said "Write it!"; to John Mahaney, the John Wiley editor who said "We'll publish it!"; and to America's 6,983 booksellers, who, if they sell just one copy each per day for just a very few years (we'll tell them when to stop), will surely help make their customers happy, successful, and maybe even rich!

| Preface

Like most of you, the author of this book is not a creative genius. Unlike most of you, he has been fortunate in working for three decades with excellent coaches who shared their advertising and promotion know-how with him. It is as a thank you to them that he now shares that know-how with you. It wasn't his to begin with. It's only fair to pass it on.

This book is a step-by-step guide to the creation or supervision of the most widely used advertising and promotional activities. Four kinds of audiences will find it particularly helpful:

1. The business, corporation, or organization that must do its own advertising and promotion.
2. Persons newly appointed or promoted to positions in advertising, promotion, marketing, or marketing services with little or no experience in those fields.
3. Managers with supervisory responsibility for advertising and promotion.
4. Adult education and in-house training directors who find traditional textbooks unsatisfactory for their needs.

The book works equally well as a blueprint for the do-it-yourselfer, amateur or professional, or as a checklist for managers and supervisors. It is not a complete "course" in advertising. Each chapter covers a specific type of activity or project and is complete in itself. It focuses on just those things you must know and do to accomplish that specific objective—produce an ad, prepare a catalog, supervise a television commercial, etc. Ordinary English is used as much as possible. When technical terms are introduced, they are defined immediately, in context. Like every other profession, advertising has its own language, and certain "ordinary" words can prove confusing to the uninitiated. ("Light" for "short" in advertising copy was my first such experience.)

ADVERTISING AND PROMOTION

Since "advertising" and "promotion" are often used interchangeably, even by professionals, some definitions may be helpful.

In ordinary use, "promotion" is everything that is done to help sell a product or service in every step of the sales chain, from the presentation materials a salesperson uses during a sales call to the television commercial or newspaper advertisement that tries to get the customer to think favorably about what is being advertised. Technically speaking, however, "advertising" is responsible for "space" or "print"— that is, newspaper and magazine ads, radio and television commercials, and direct mail and other "direct response" activities, plus catalogs and billboards. "Promotion" is responsible for everything else in this area except public relations and publicity. These last two may be assigned to an independent department or to either advertising or promotion, depending on the organization of the company or organization. Since job titles and department designations are quite arbitrary, a detailed job description is highly desirable to avoid turf battles when more than one person or department does any of the above.

Throughout this book, you will find "insights" that are meant to be both aids to memory and actual guidelines to action. Since many of them are applicable to more than one type of project, please browse through these pages and read them all, even if the help and information you need are contained in a single chapter. For example, here are the "Three S's"—the insight that is basic to all of the how-to knowledge you will find in these pages:

INSIGHT 1

Keep it Simple . . . keep it Specific . . . and you're likely to keep Solvent.

You won't go far wrong by sticking to these three!

ADVERTISING, PROMOTION, AND MARKETING, OR "NO, VIRGINIA, THIS IS NOT A 'MARKETING' GUIDE"

Before Professor E. Jerome McCarthy discovered the Four Commandments—or the "Four P's," as they have become known to several generations of students and tens of thousands of marketing professionals—"marketing" was very much in the same state as sex before the Kinsey report. Most people did it sometime, although they weren't sure whether they were doing it right or how it compared with their peers' successes and failures. Marketing, like sex, lacked academic rigor.

Professor McCarthy should probably be credited with codifying the discipline of modern marketing, which focuses on giving customers what they want, rather than limiting their choices to what a supplier wants to produce. It was McCarthy who recognized that marketing consisted of four subdisciplines and categorized them as the "Four P's": Product, Price, Promotion, and Place. The last is really sales, but needing a fourth "P," he decreed that how something got to market and where it was sold—the Place—would be accepted nomenclature. And it was so!

Under this marketing theory, Product is the definition or factual description of the product or service, not its engineering or manufacturing. Thus, Marketing might decide that an automobile would look like a Mercedes, have a top speed of 100 miles per hour, sell for $12,500, and pass a standard crash test in the top 10 percent of its class of cars. How this was to be achieved was a problem not for Marketing, but for Engineering, Manufacturing, and Finance. Marketing also determined basic promotional policies and budgets and decided whether a product would be sold directly, through a wholesaler-retailer chain, door to door, by direct response, or any other way it was to find its Place for the final purchaser.

Probably McCarthy's most important insight was that *profit is not a function of marketing*. Marketing designates the quality of an item and the price needed to sell. Considerations of profit must not be permitted to dilute these attributes. Astonishingly enough from the outsider's view, the system works, with America's telephone and computer corporations and Japan's automotive industry just three of the more obvious examples.

The foregoing is a brief distillation of what $10,000 will purchase at one of the better known business schools. Always remember: You read it here first!

Why This Book Isn't "Marketing"

Do-It-Yourself Advertising confines itself to the third "P," Promotion, with just enough of the others to provide context where required. Literally hundreds of other books exist—many of them quite good—to help with Product, Pricing, and Sales. For the beginner at creating or supervising advertising and promotion, however, the choice in guides is much more limited. I believe this book meets that need better than any of the others.

HOW TO USE THE CHECKLISTS IN THIS BOOK

The checklists in this book are practical for individual do-it-yourselfers, for multi-person staffs, and for working with outside resources. They are suggested models only, however. Modify them to fit your way of working and your needs.

Items on each checklist are numbered for ease of reference. ("Let's look at line 17," rather than "Everyone find the line on production costs.") Items are annotated following each checklist, with the exception of four annotations that would repeat the same thing throughout. To save space and repetition, those annotations are given here:

- **Project title/description.** The *title* is the project name or headline. The *description* is a brief definition of the project, for instance, "32-page, two-color catalog" or "20-foot convention display" or "1/2-page local shopping news ad."
- **Overall supervisor.** The administrator who assigns responsibilities and, where all else fails, resolves conflicts.
- **Budget.** How budgets are set and approved can have a major impact on the time needed for a project. Allow for this in determining the next two items.

- **Start-up date/completion date.** Determine what "completion" means, and note that on the checklist along with the date. Now work backwards to a start-up date that's practical for getting the job done. The start-up to completion is your time frame; what happens within that frame is spelled out in detailed time lines.

Assigning Responsibility

Begin by filling in the checklist with all the known due dates of the project, plus other information available to you. In organizations in which others are involved in a project, try to get the key persons to a single meeting to set the schedule. If that proves impossible, circulate a clearly marked *Preliminary Working Copy* of the checklist, with requests to provide missing data and to keep everyone informed. Due dates assigned to particular persons and departments should be highlighted on those persons' and departments' copies. If any of the assigned dates present a problem to the person to whom they are assigned, *that person must contact the project manager* and negotiate a workable schedule. Give an absolute deadline for when the schedule must be approved or renegotiated by everyone involved, and get the approval of that date in writing! Based on those negotiations and agreements, issue a *Final Checklist*.

INSIGHT 2

In assigning due dates, always assign a specific calendar date. Do not permit completion "ASAP" (as soon as possible). ASAP most often means NEVER.

Make "Final" FINAL!

If at all possible, avoid issuing *revised* "final" checklists; they are an invitation to make all future finals translate to "preliminary." But if you absolutely must do so, be sure that the new checklist is dated and clearly marked as "Revised" and that the original "finals" are equally clearly marked as "See Revised Copy Dated _____ ."
  Remind everyone that getting something perfect is no substitute for getting it done!

NOTE: The checklists in this book are copyrighted. They may, however, be reproduced for personal use. For ease of use on standard $8\frac{1}{2}"$ × $11"$ paper, copy them at 135 percent of their printed size.

| Acknowledgments

I COULDN'T HAVE DONE IT WITHOUT . . .

This book would not be nearly as valuable to the reader if individual chapters and sections had not been read and critiqued by experts in the various fields. For those whose professional resources are available to the reader, I have given company names and locations. I have used them all and recommended them unreservedly.

Chapter by Chapter

Newspaper and magazine advertising design: Susan Jacobs, J-K Art Directions, Milwaukee, WI. *Cooperative advertising:* Walter Dunne, Advertising Checking Bureau, Chicago, IL. *Media research:* Barbara Grahn, Managing Editor, Standard Rate & Data Service, Wilmette, IL. *Direct mail concept and copy:* John Stern, Oak Lawn, IL. *Catalogs:* Morton Levin (my first employer in advertising and, more important, a wonderful friend). *Conventions and trade shows:* Devorah Richards, General Exhibits & Displays, Chicago, IL. *Publicity and public relations* (alphabetically): Carol Dechant, Carol Dechant & Assoc., Chicago, IL; Conroy Erickson, Rand McNally; Robert Willmot, APR, Carus Corporation. *PR photo duplication:* Peter James, President, Quantity Photo, Chicago, IL. *Telemarketing:* Bruce Gollogly, Jr., Britcom Telemarketing, Lombard, IL. *Audio and audiovisual communications:* William Holtane, President, Sound/Video Impressions, Des Plaines, IL. *Video duplication:* Lewis Wilson, Allied Film & Video, Chicago, IL. *Film preparation* (alphabetically): Joseph Erl, President, Chaper I Filmworks, Vernon Hills, IL; John Trip, President, J & J Graphics, Chicago, IL. *Printing:* Donald Ladin, Combined Printing, Northfield, IL. *Lettershop mailing services* (alphabetically): Joseph Cohen (my first and best tutor in this field); Henry Spitz, VP, Lee Enterprises, South Holland, IL.

The Whole Book

(Alphabetically): Alice Hahn, wife, proofreader, literary critic. Kinko's copy service; Paul Baker, Paul Baker Typography, Evanston, IL; Shellie Rounds, administrative assistant and secretary extraordinaire; Harlan Smith, buyer, Kroch's & Brentano's bookstores, Chicago, IL; Nancy Willson, production artist and miracle worker, c/o Hahn, Crane Inc., Evanston, IL.

To all the above, and any I have inadvertently omitted, I give abundant thanks.

FEH

| Contents

| Table of Checklists

DO-IT-YOURSELF
ADVERTISING

1 | Newspaper and Magazine Advertising

The process of preparing newspaper and magazine advertising described in this chapter serves the same function as a blueprint or detailed drawing in the construction of a garden shed. Using identical plans, the professional builder should construct a somewhat sounder and better looking structure than you—but the shed you do produce on your own will be immeasurably improved by following the drawing rather than trying to make things up as you go along.

WHY YOU ADVERTISE

When Thomas Edison was asked the secret of his success, he replied, "Two percent inspiration, 98 percent perspiration." You won't have to work nearly that hard. Think of your task as "10 percent inspiration, 90 percent preparation." That preparation starts with a systematic look at why you advertise and what you expect to get out of advertising.

Put It in Writing

Put into writing your reasons for advertising—*all* the reasons—and the results you expect the advertising to bring. You need this list to give a sharper focus to the ads you are going to create and, probably even more important, to have a method of evaluating results.

How to Set Goals for Your Advertising

In setting goals for your advertising copy, remember at all times that your *results must be quantifiable*. Depending on your competitive situation and specific business goals, list the expected results as a definite number or percentage—not "more sales," but, for instance, "5 percent more sales during the week following the ad." If you have no idea what to expect, put in the number that will justify the cost of the ad *according to your list of goals*, some of which may be long term rather than immediate.

Typical Advertising Goals

Following are some goals a retailer might set. Analogous goals would be set for a manufacturer or a service organization. The sample percentages are arbitrary and are not based on actual case histories.

- **Increase total store traffic** by 5 percent during the week following advertising.
- **Increase the sale of advertised items** by 15 percent over the previous week. (Note that if you are advertising more than one item, you will want to know how each individual item sold, as well as how all the advertised items sold as a whole. This knowledge gives you information for future promotions, even when sales as a whole do not live up to expectations. Be careful, however, to make a special note of purely seasonal successes, such as pumpkins sold just before Halloween.)
- **Increase the sale of nonadvertised merchandise** by 5 percent over the previous week. (Advertising is usually meant to increase traffic, and that should be reflected in increased sales throughout your establishment.)
- **Maintain an increase in store traffic** of 2 percent in the month following the advertising, as against the previous year.

Where to Get Help in Setting Goals

If you are a novice in setting advertising goals, here are some sources of help:

1. **Media.** The publications in which you advertise, the media, have expert representatives who often have information about advertising campaigns such as yours. Whether you plan a single ad or a yearlong series, speak with these "reps" about what you might expect from your ads. But remember that their jobs depend on their convincing you of the effectiveness of their publications, so check their success stories with the people who did the actual advertising—even if they are now your competitors!

2. **Your competitors.** Take your competitors to lunch—one at a time—and ask them what kind of results they get from their advertising. Chances are, they'll tell you. Almost everyone shows off by talking too much.

3. **Trade associations.** Your trade association probably has an entire library of advertising case histories. Call and ask for this and any other help the association might give.

4. **Colleges and universities.** Contact the head of the marketing department. (Advertising is usually taught as part of marketing.) Explain what you are trying to learn, and ask whether that information is available from either staff or research materials. The faculty will help if it can.

5. **Libraries.** Explain your need to the research librarian at your public or professional library. These are extraordinarily knowledgeable professionals with access to networks of information through computer linkups.

6. **Build your own research base.** If no other information is available, run your ads, set "best guess" goals, and begin to build your own records. You'll quickly have

the best data base in town and will be invited to lecture to those whom you previously asked for information. But don't give too much. Remember what we said about your competitors. You be the one who does know how to keep your mouth shut, even when you'd much rather show off. Brag about your bank statement, not your ad results.

SUMMARY

- Know why you advertise. Put the reasons in writing.
- Set goals that can be quantified.
- There's lots of help available. Use it.

HOW MUCH TO PAY FOR ADVERTISING

How much you can, will, or must spend on advertising should be decided as objectively as possible. Take your "why we are advertising" list, and add the following columns:

- Percentage of total ad dollars allocated to your goal.
- The dollar value for achieving the goal.
- The time allowed for achieving the goal.

Using the typical advertising goals given earlier, your list might look like the one in Figure 1.1.

Evaluating Advertising Results

In evaluating the success of your ad, the calculation might seem quite simple, but what if your overall goal is reached but your individual subgoals are not? Does it really make any difference?

The answer depends both on the type of establishment you have and the reasons you set your goals. If you are advertising "loss leaders" to bring new customers to your store, and only regulars show up, you're in a different position from having a sale where your inventory costs have been reduced by a manufacturer, leaving profits the same as at the regular price. These and similar considerations should enter into developing your advertising goals. You want sales, of course, but it requires a different perspective to plan advertising for a funeral home or accounting service than for a hardware store or a farm equipment dealership. In fact, without prohibitively expensive research, how *can* you get a short-term fix on advertising that aims at long-term results? Fortunately, there is a fairly easy, practical, and inexpensive way to do just that.

Krypton Retail Advertising Goals

Media	Size:	Date:	Cost:
Daily Hall	page	10/1	$500.00
Sunday Herald	1/2 page	10/3	600.00
Sunday Choice	page	10/3	400.00
Other out of pocket	photos & type		300.00

Type of ad:
Pre-Christmas clearance special. 14 "sale" items, 21 regular.

Ad Goal:	% Total	$ If Reached:	Time Line:
Increase traffic 5%	20%	4,000.00	10/4–10/9
Sales items 15% over week of 9/27	50%	10,000.00	10/4–10/9
Increase nonsales items 5%	20%	4,000.00	10/4–10/9
Maintain traffic increase 2%	10%	2,000.00	10/11–11/2
Total	100%	$20,000.00	

Note that dollar amounts are increases in sales over the previous time period, not total sales. For new establishments with no sales history, total sales dollars are substituted. For a final record, you will want to add columns for the previous periods's sales, this period's sales, and the increase (or decrease) in sales from the one period to the other.

Figure 1.1 Spending on advertising.

Getting a Preview of Long-Term Results

Although the need you fill may lie months or years in the future, try for *some* immediate response to your advertising *now.* If you establish a good relationship before the need arises, you're much more likely to get the call when it does. So do what the movie moguls do before they spend millions on promoting a film: Check it out with a sneak preview.

How to Sneak a Preview

Purchase or produce a helpful hints flyer along the lines of "10 reasons why you should meet your banker *before* you need a loan" or "10 things to look for when you're ready to buy a house." The hints should be specific rather than general and be directly related to what you do (where to look for dry rot and how to tell it's there rather than "check for dry rot"). The more valuable the advice, the more likely that it will be kept and consulted when a service such as yours is needed. (See Figure 1.2.)

Informational flyers may be available from your trade or professional organization and often are advertised in trade journals. They tend to be inexpensive and may be customized with your name, address, and telephone number at a small additional cost. You can, of course, also produce your own.

If several suitable flyers are available, offer a different one free each time you advertise, to see which one gets the best response. Then use that flyer as long as the level of response continues. If your budget is limited to fewer ads than the number of

PISER WEINSTEIN
Menorah Chapels
Gratch-Mandel · Hartman-Miller

Yes, I would like to receive the Piser Weinstein Medical Emergency Information Card. I understand there is no cost or obligation. Please have Donna Feldman call me for the necessary medical and personal information.

Name _____ Age _____

Address _____

City _____ State _____ Zip _____

Phone _____

Best time to call _____

Figure 1.2 The offer of a free wallet-size medical information card reinforces Weinstein Chapels' image as more than just a funeral home, but a neighborhood friend.

different kinds of flyers available, ask the supplier which one has gotten the most repeat orders. Then use that, providing that it meets your other criteria.

SUMMARY
- Allocate specific dollar amounts to each advertising goal.
- Don't just wait for long-term results to happen. Use a premium to jump-start results.

BUT MICE DON'T BUY MOUSETRAPS: HOW TO FIND THE AUDIENCE YOU NEED

Decide to whom you will be advertising before you write a single word. Often, it's not as obvious as it seems. Suppose you have a baby product. Will you advertise to parents, grandparents, pediatricians, toy store owners, supermarket buyers, etc.? Don't work on what to say until you're absolutely clear about two things:

1. **The audience you're trying to reach.** This may, in fact, be a variety of audiences. The question then becomes one of how many different messages you can

get into one ad. Generally, you are better off to concentrate your advertising on one specific target—the "rifle" rather than the "shotgun" approach.

2. What you want your audience to do. Rush to your shop . . . call for an appointment . . . invite you to their office or home . . . send money . . . send for information . . . authorize a trial subscription . . . Vote! Buy! Try! Call! Write! Drive! Fly! Run! Walk! Taste! Imagine! Sleep! And that's just a sampler to get you started.

How to Pick the Places to Advertise

Pick the "media" (singular, medium)—the places where you will advertise—by how well *they* reach the audience *you* want to reach. The easiest way to do this is to see whether other advertisers trying to reach the same audience are advertising there in a consistent fashion. But don't just look. Telephone advertisers, explain that you're a novice, and ask for anything they might tell you about the success of their ads in specific media. Next, call advertisers who used a medium only once or a few times, and ask the same questions. Ask, too, which media they would recommend that might be more effective. People love to give advice, so be sure to check whether they actually do advertise in the places they recommend.

If You Don't Know Where to Start Looking. If you don't know where to advertise because your experience is in other areas, such as manufacturing or finance, ask your library whether it stocks the Standard Rate and Data Service (SRDS), Inc., directories[1] (Figure 1.3). These huge paper-bound volumes will give you detailed information on practically every medium in your field that accepts advertising. Individual SRDS guides cover the following areas:

- Newspapers
- Community publications
- Business and professional magazines
- Technology markets
- Consumer magazines and agrimedia
- Financial markets
- Spot radio and spot television
- Travel and tourism industries
- Direct mail and card decks
- Manufacturing and processing industries
- Food and food service industries

"Card decks" are packages of postcard-sized advertisements mailed on a cooperative, share-the-cost basis to a specific kind of audience. Their primary use is in business-to-business promotions.

---

[1] SRDS Guides can be purchased from Standard Rate and Data Service, Inc., 3004 Glenview Road, Wilmette, IL 60091. Call them for details at (708)256-6067.

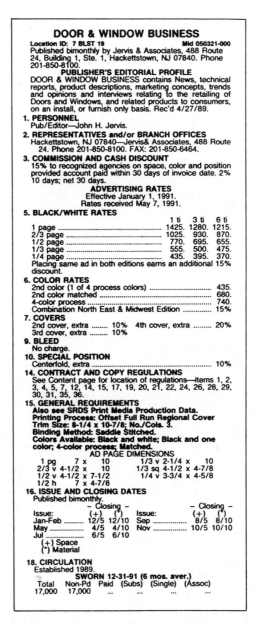

Figure 1.3 Sample SDRD listing. (As published in the March, 1992 edition of *Business Publication Rates and Data*, published by Standard Rate and Data Service.)

An additional volume of the SRDS guides covers production, that is, how to get each kind of ad ready for a specific medium. But you are unlikely to need that unless you are responsible for furnishing the materials for the ads to many advertising media. The same information is available on an individual basis from any of the media you decide to use.

Understanding SRDS Listings. Listings in the SRDS guides follow a consistent format of subject, state, and city, ordered alphabetically within each category. Individual listings (Figure 1.3) begin with brief descriptions of the audience and editorial content of the publication. Then they go through a series of uniformly numbered segments of specific interest to advertisers. Thus, categories 4–7 always explain basic costs, and category 10 covers the availability of premium positions for advertising, such as the page opposite the table of contents. (Many advertisers believe that these locations get exceptionally high readership and are willing to pay a premium to have one of their ads appear there.)

Reliability of Data. Standard Rate and Data Service does not itself research its information, but rather, uses data provided by each publication on an issue-by-issue basis. Many of the publishers supply information on circulation in a standard format that is audited by an agency very much like a CPA firm. *Whether the information is audited is not necessarily an indication of its reliability.* The auditing process is quite expensive and unaffordable by some new publications and publications with a small circulation. Other publications have a long history of satisfied advertisers and feel no need to go through auditing. Auditing is, however, a factor you should consider, especially with publications that have multiple audiences, not all of which are your potential customers.

Category 18 gives the basic statistical information about a publication and tells whether or not the information is based on audited data. Thus, for example, in a December 1992 listing, the audited magazine *Cabinetmaker* tells you that it is "edited for manufacturers of kitchen and bath cabinets . . . ." It also tells you, in category 18, that of its total circulation of 32,000, 2,192 are "Panel Product/ Countertop Manufacturers." If your only interest lies in reaching just those 2,192, find out whether any other publications are available, including some with un-audited listings. Before you decide on any of them, however, ask each publication *why* you should use it to reach your specific audience, and then make your evaluation as you would any other investment—including the possibility that you should switch your promotional effort to direct mail or some other medium. Don't fall into the trap of advertising just to see your name in print.

How to Research a Subject

Although even the SRDS guides can't cover every subject, try them first. Check the classification groupings near the front. If your subject is not there, turn to the index of individual titles and look for a key word. If you still can't find what you need, telephone the SRDS editorial department at (708)256-6067, and ask them where to look. It is possible that no specific medium exists for your product or service. In that case, consider a more general publication that's likely to be read by your audience (the Sunday edition of *The New York Times* by college presidents, for instance, or *The Wall Street Journal* by wealthy retirees).

If, as is likely, you do find your category, contact the appropriate media and ask for an information package: Request several copies of each publication to get an idea of its editorial content as a "home" for your message. Each medium will probably also wish to meet with you. You can arrange that at your convenience.

Making a Final Selection

Once you are ready to make final decisions regarding the media you will use, list all the candidates in order, from most to least favorite, along with their costs, deadlines when materials must be shipped, and "out dates," that is, the dates they actually publish. Then ask yourself the following questions:

- Can you afford to advertise in one of your top-rated publications with an ad size and frequency that are likely to meet your sales plan?
- If not, can you make your ad smaller or run it less frequently and still be effective? The media representatives will have statistical data on both of these points. Ask them for this information if they do not bring it up themselves.
- Can you get your advertisement ready in time for it to be effective? (For instance, retailers may order Christmas merchandise in July. You, as a manufacturer, want your advertisement aimed at them to appear in June. The publication has a 45-day deadline and needs the completed ad in mid-April. So when do *you* really have to begin working on the ad—and will you do it?)

If your answer to all of the above is "Yes!" you are ready to write and design your ad.

SUMMARY

- Define your audience and what you want it to do.
- Find out what your audience is reading, and advertise in those publications.

DESIGNING THE AD

This chapter will guide you in writing a competent advertisement; however, only God can gift you with the talent to be a designer. Therefore, in the hope that we will be forgiven, we do what real designers do. We cheat.

How to Design Your Ad Without Being a "Designer"

Look through the publications in which you expect to advertise, and pick out those ads which you feel are well designed and are aimed at your audience. Equally important, they must be the same size as the ad you wish to produce. Try to find several examples, especially those with different amounts of manuscript—what copywriters call "light," "medium," or "heavy."

Now pick two or three you like best. These will be your models. Everything you do to create your ad will be based on one of them. The reason for choosing several originals is to give you flexibility in how much you say. But whatever the original has—light copy or heavy, large type or small, with a picture or without—plan to do the same. Avoid the temptation to mix and match—to take design elements from several ads and combine them into a new whole. (That is in fact what professional designers often do, but those of us who aren't pros usually botch it up.)

Eventually, you'll give your manuscript, along with your design model, to a typesetter and ask him or her to *approximate* the original. (You want to avoid lawsuits whenever possible.) This aspect of advertising is called *production* and needs a manuscript as well as a design. That's why writing the ad is next. Production follows right after.

SUMMARY

- When it comes to design, don't. Copy, as the real designers do.

WRITING THE AD: THE IMPORTANCE OF BENEFITS

The key to writing successful ads lies in training yourself to turn features into benefits—and then to use benefits to sell the product or service.

A **feature** is anything inherent in your product or service, for instance, punctureproof tires on a bicycle, large type in an insurance policy, nonpolluting soap in a laundry. In essence, a feature is what *you* have put into your product or service.

A **benefit** tells the potential buyers what's in it for them if they use your product or service. For example:

- Are your bicycle tires punctureproof because they're made from uncomfortable solid rubber, or is the benefit that these state-of-the-art tires are so safe that riders won't need to carry patching kits and pumps?
- Large type in an insurance policy seems an obvious benefit for the elderly, but is it necessary if you're trying to sell to newlyweds? How about "No eye-straining tiny type, but a policy designed to be read and understood!" Surely you can develop six additional benefits of even greater value to the person you are trying to pursuade, no matter what you wish to sell.

How to Develop Benefits

Even though you want to end up with benefits, begin with features, since they are what you are likely to know best. List each individual feature at the top of a 5″ × 8″ index card. Start with what *you* know, then enlist the help of anyone who has knowledge you may lack or who might catch an item you've overlooked. Once you're satisfied that you've captured all the features, call an old-fashioned brainstorming session and explain your problem. You have all these great features, but the people you're trying to sell keep saying "So what? What's in it for *me?*" It's the answer to these two questions that are your *benefits*.

Things to Remember in Brainstorming, Whether You Do It by Yourself or in a Group

1. Use a tape recorder so that you can keep note-taking to a minimum—even if you have someone who can take shorthand.
2. There are no dumb suggestions.
3. Do not discuss individual answers now; that will inhibit the free flow of thought and force participants to defend something they may not quite understand themselves.
4. Bring in a new feature the moment the benefit stream dries up. Keep the action lively.
5. If someone suddenly suggests a benefit for a feature that's already been covered . . . great!
6. Don't let *anything* negative get in the way of the process.

Once you and your features are exhausted, type each one, along with its suggested benefits, on individual sheets of paper, and distribute copies to the brainstorming participants. Now is the time for critical scrutiny—and for the addition of those benefits that brought you awake in the middle of the night two days after the original session. Ask everyone to criticize, add to, change, edit, or otherwise modify anyone's suggestions and return the lists to you for a final compilation. Whether you'll have another meeting to discuss this final list will be determined by your working situation, but the end result should be a series of 5" × 8" cards listing features and their benefits, in order of importance *for specific audiences*. Thus, the same benefit may appear more than once but be given different emphasis, as in details of nutritional value in selling puppy food to veterinarians and careful feeding instructions in selling it to the general public.

SUMMARY

*   Features instruct. Benefits sell!

Features Instruct. Benefits Sell!

Practically no one buys anything solely because of its features—it's the benefits that sell. Thus, you do *not* say, "the world's best seeds," but "the world's best lawn!" *Not* "777-horsepower engine," but "from 0–135 m.p.h. in 3 seconds!" And ask yourself where and how anyone is actually going to want to speed up like that and what other uses there can be for a machine with that much power. You'll continue to discover benefits that will surprise even you—and delight you with their pulling and selling power.

Beware of Overkill. Make sure that the benefits you claim are actually those *the buyer* gets. You are legally responsible for any claim made in your promotional materials— for *anything* that appears in print or on electronic media and for which you may be assumed to have given approval. There are some exceptions, such as an innocent mistake in a price that is corrected immediately at the place of purchase—although not a price designed to mislead! In case of doubt, consult your attorney, or better yet, change the benefit to something else. Advertising is not a game to see what you can get away with; it's one of the few ways of communicating what you hope to sell to potential buyers. The end goal is *not* to avoid going to jail. It's to make an honest sale from which the buyer will receive genuine benefits and the seller will earn a profit.

Developing Your Offer

Suppose you've listed every *feature* you can possibly discover in your product or service and overwhelmed the skeptic's "so what" question about each with a flood of irresistible *benefits*. Now it's time to consider the *offer*—the agreement between you and your customers, the promise you make when they buy your product or service.

Planning the Offer. In planning your offer, three different factors need to be considered:

1. **What do you want the reader of the ad to do?** For example, go to your store or shop? Telephone for information? Invite you to make an estimate? Send money? Etc.

2. **What will the customers get if they accept your offer?** Offers range from discounts (10 percent off) to service (oil changed while you wait) to promises (service with a smile) to guarantees (unbreakable, or your money back). Offers can be implied (Swiss quality) or trumpeted (world's best roofing shingles). They can be limited (offer ends Wednesday) or universal (lifetime guarantee). Whatever the offer, try to match it to the needs and interests of your particular audience. If you're not sure and have no other good way to find out, run two versions of the same ad at the same time, changing only the offer, and see what happens. How to do this is covered under advertising production's "A/B Split" a bit later in the chapter.

3. **Can you afford it? Can you afford to offer less?** Obviously, you will make your offer as inexpensive as possible. However, the key is not cost as such, but cost effectiveness or cost per sale. So before deciding on what you can afford, get the best answers possible to four more questions:
    A. Is this a one-time sale, or are you trying to establish an ongoing customer relationship, and how much is each of these worth?

B. How fast must you get your return on the dollars spent for promotion, and will that return come faster if you make the offer more attractive?

C. What do your competitors offer, and should you match that or make your offer even more attractive? And what are the likely consequences to them—and you—of an "offer war"?

D. What are the immediate costs of these options, what are their break-even points, and their payoffs if they succeed?

The chances are that you'll have to make an educated guess at some of the answers to these questions. Do it, but keep your guesses on the conservative side. If there are to be surprises, let them be happy ones.

SUMMARY

- Load up with benefits to hit your target.
- Plan your offer for your customers' wants, not yours.
- When you can't afford the offer, can you afford to offer less?

WRITING THE AD: WHERE TO START

Every ad is made up of four elements:

1. The *headline*, commonly called "the head."
2. *Body copy*, which is everything except the headline and the identifying signature, or "logo."
3. The *offer*, which is part of the body copy, but has to be thought out separately.
4. The *logo*, or signature, which identifies you and is generally the same as or very similar to your letterhead.

My personal way of working is to begin with the offer, go to the body copy, and do the headline last. The offer forces me to understand *exactly* what I am trying to sell and what the buyer gets in return. Chicken at 49¢ a pound, when my competitors are charging 55¢, requires no explanation; but an HMO or the 27th new restaurant to open this month needs a different kind of enticement.

After a "rough" (preliminary) draft of the offer, I do the body copy. My best headlines have generally grown out of a seed planted in the body, which I suddenly realize would make the perfect "head." Of course, once the headline is in place, the entire ad may have to be redone to fit it, but that doesn't matter, as long as we work within the ARM framework, which I will tell you about next.

Where *You* Should Start

Where *you* start really makes no difference. Many writers begin with the headline and work from there. But no matter where you *start*, the headline is of such crucial importance that we'll treat it in detail first.

The Headline (and Illustrations). The headline (and illustrations, if any) are your grabbers. They are the way to catch readers' fleeting attention and get them actually to read what you have to say. To do this, your advertisement, as every other marketing communication, must achieve the three ARM factors.

INSIGHT 3

The Three ARM Factors Every Ad Must Have
A Attract attention.
R Retain interest, so that the reader will become aware of your overall message.
M Motivate the reader to take the action your ad is designed to produce.

Think of these as the ARM portion of "I'd give my arm if only they'd buy." So arm yourself with the best headline you can develop to attract attention.

Two things your headline must do are:

1. Attract the audience that will actually buy the product or at least influence its purchase. Buyers and influencers are not necessarily the end users. Young children neither buy nor influence their parents' purchase of cough syrup, but they are a major factor in deciding on purchases of toys, games, and cereals. Know for whom you write . . . and why!
2. Have carry-over power that will get readers from the headline into the ad itself.

Let's assume that you are writing an ad for a bicycle shop that has added a line for senior citizens. In writing your headline, don't try to be clever or funny. That usually fails, even when attempted by professionals. Rather, begin by stating the most obvious fact, and let your ad develop from there. For instance, you might try

BIKES FOR SENIOR CITIZENS

This approach will keep you out of trouble, but is unlikely to attract very many from the audience you want, unless you spice it up with some *Benefits*. Two of the all-time best benefits are "new" and "free," so let's try to get at least one of those into the ad, perhaps as easily as this:

NEW! BIKES FOR SENIOR CITIZENS

Notice the difference between "NEW BIKES . . . " and "NEW! BIKES. . . . " In this instance, the second version is probably preferable. With a different product—insurance, for instance—"NEW BENEFITS . . . " might well do better than "NEW! BENEFITS . . . ." Always think of what will appeal to your specific audience, and write accordingly.

But there is still nothing in the headline to get very many readers from "A" to "R"—to motivate attention into readership. So let's strengthen the headline with stronger benefits and, if room permits, more of them, like this:

NEW! SPECIAL OFFER
FOR 50-PLUS BIKERS

or

FREE TEST DRIVE OF SENIORS'
NEW RECREATIONAL BIKES
Free Lessons For Nonbikers Who Purchase

Note the change from "SENIOR" to "50-PLUS" in the first headline, and think about how you might make a similar change in the second. In writing headlines, keep refining, with three goals in mind:

1. **Broaden the appeal where possible, but take care not to lose your targeted audience.** "50-plus" may well capture the attention of seniors, plus attract a bonus group in the close-to-senior years. But broaden one step further to "adult," and not only have you lost the focus on your real audience, but you've picked up a number of possible meanings of "adult" that will simply confuse your message. In writing your ad, every single word must be considered for the effect it has on the total message, and nowhere is this more true than in the headline.

2. **Get at least one major benefit into your headline.** "NEW" and "SPECIAL OFFER" show benefits in the first example. The offer might well be the test drive and free lessons spelled out in the second sample, or it might be something entirely different.

3. **Fit the headline into the basic design you've elected as your model.** Count the number of letters and spaces in the headline rather than its words, and work within that limitation. Don't cheat.

A Note on Guarantees, Promises, and Offers

If there is to be *any* limitation or qualification on an offer—such as free lessons only to those who make a purchase—state this immediately in conjunction with the offer. Unless qualified, a "free" offer is legally free to *anyone* who requests it.

SUMMARY

- Start writing your ad wherever in the copy you feel most comfortable; you'll get to the headline soon enough.
- Follow the ARM (attention/retention/motivation) rule for successful copy.
- Stick to the basic design of your models in writing—especially in your headline.

WRITING THE BODY OF THE AD

All your hard work in developing benefits will now pay you back, because this part of the ad should just about write itself.

1. Take the benefits you've put on individual cards or sheets of paper, and arrange them *in order of importance to the person you are trying to sell.*
2. Check your design model, and see how much room you have for copy.
3. Within your space limitations, write the benefits as the body of the ad as either • bulleted or ✔ checked points. Doing this allows you to imply urgency and importance, in the telegraphic style of the ad.
   - ✔ Lets you write incomplete sentences.
   - ✔ Gets the most benefits in the fewest words.

IF YOUR ORIGINAL USES A STANDARD PARAGRAPH FORMAT

If your models use a paragraph format, count the letters in each line, and then use the same space for the telegraphic style. Copy in paragraph format takes a "writer," just as original design takes a "designer." And in most instances, the telegraphic style will be more effective, regardless of writing skill. So stick to what you can do.

---

4. Highlight each benefit with its own bullet or check. You want your readers to know how much they will get. Don't be afraid to pile it on!
5. Separate the benefits from the offer by the use of a "subhead," a smaller headline within the body of the ad.
6. Your offer can be a continuation of the bullet/check format, or it can go to a normal paragraph format. Which it does will depend on the room available and the details of the offer. The goal is to make the offer easy to understand and impossible to resist. Always edit yourself with that in mind.

Features, Too!

What does your audience *have* to know about technical specifications, size, weight, colors, materials, packaging, etc., to anchor the benefits to reality? Consider "Available in blue only" versus "A rainbow of 14 color selections." Or "1/4-hp motor" versus "3/8-horsepower, three-speed motor with reverse option." Or "All standard sizes" versus "20-gallon drums only." Recall how irritated you get when you respond to an advertisement, only to learn that it left out the one key factor that would have told you it wasn't for you (or when you didn't respond and found out too late that it was for you)? Benefits, yes! Pile them on. But don't forget the features. They'll help draw the right customers in and, equally important, keep the wrong audience out.

A Sample

Figure 1.4 shows how the manuscript might look for a small ad for this part of *Do-It-Yourself Advertising*. Instructions for type sizes are given in the margin. (The actual ad, in three different type styles, is shown in Figure 1.5.)

Check out how this sample is loaded with benefits. The headline contains three (new, secrets, success). Every point begins with the benefit of "how to" and then adds one or two more. Even the subhead offers the clear benefits of a 30-day trial and a guarantee; and what could be a clearer benefit than a no-nonsense, no-quibble guarantee? Aim for that if your product or service permits; if not, come as close as you can. The features are there, too, with the number and size of pages, checklists, illustrations, and an index as in Figure 1.5(c), set in the Futura typeface.

INSIGHT 4

Keep a single, clearly marked master copy of any manuscript. Use it to show all changes and corrections, and hold it along with all supporting documents that show when and where the changes originated. On computerized systems, use a printed (hard copy) manuscript for this purpose. Neatly retyped versions will, of course, exist, but the final check is always against the master.

Identifying Yourself: Your Advertising Signature or "Logo"

Somewhere in every advertisement, the advertiser's logo—the particular way you show your name, address, and telephone number—has to appear. No matter how fancy or plain, be sure that your logo does include your address and telephone number. Don't assume that the ad is so appealing that your readers will look them up. They won't. Rather, they'll go to your competitors—the ones who make it easy

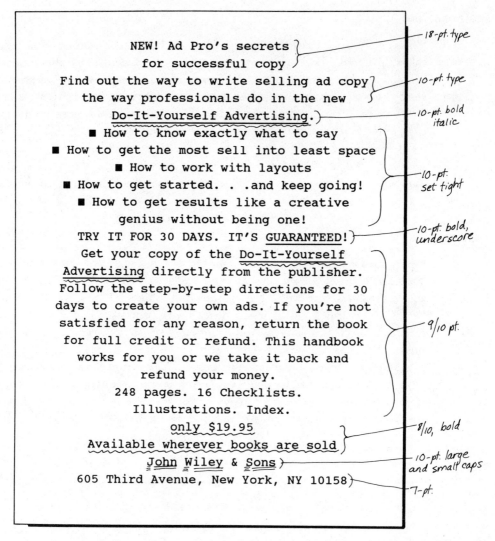

Figure 1.4 Manuscript copy for advertisement for *Do-It-Yourself Advertising* before final price and number of pages is known.

to do business with them. Always remember that no one *has* to buy from you, so . . .

- Make it simple.
- Make it easy.
- Make it a benefit for the buyer.
- Prepare to laugh all the way to the bank.

You've picked a design and written the copy. Now all you have to do is set the type and get it to the media in a form acceptable to them. Fortunately, that's the easiest part, and the next few pages will tell you how.

NEW! Ad Pro's secrets for successful copy

Find out the way to write selling ad copy the way professionals do in the new *Do-It-Yourself Advertising*.

- How to know exactly what to say
- How to get the most sell into least space
- How to work with layouts!
- How to get started...and keep going!
- How to get results like a creative genius without being one!

TRY IT FOR 30 DAYS. IT'S <u>GUARANTEED</u>!

Get your copy of the ***Do-It-Yourself Advertising*** directly from the publisher. Follow the step-by-step directions for 30 days to create your own ads. If you're not satisfied for any reason, return the book for full credit or refund. This handbook works for you or we take it back and refund your money!

only $19.95
Available wherever books are sold

JOHN WILEY & SONS
605 Third Avenue, New York, NY 10158

Figure 1.5(a) Example of the Bookman typeface.

NEW! Ad Pro's secrets for successful copy

Find out the way to write selling ad copy the way professionals do in the new *Do-It-Yourself Advertising*.

- How to know exactly what to say
- How to get the most sell into least space
- How to work with layouts!
- How to get started...and keep going!
- How to get results like a creative genius without being one!

TRY IT FOR 30 DAYS. IT'S <u>GUARANTEED</u>!

Get your copy of the ***Do-It-Yourself Advertising*** directly from the publisher. Follow the step-by-step directions for 30 days to create your own ads. If you're not satisfied for any reason, return the book for full credit or refund. This handbook works for you or we take it back and refund your money!

only $19.95
Available wherever books are sold

JOHN WILEY & SONS
605 Third Avenue, New York, NY, 10158

Figure 1.5(b) Example of the Optima typeface.

NEW! Ad Pro's secrets for successful copy

Find out the way to write selling ad copy the way professionals do in the new *Do-It-Yourself Advertising*.

- How to know exactly what to say
- How to get the most sell into least space
- How to work with layouts!
- How to get started...and keep going!
- How to get results like a creative genius without being one!

TRY IT FOR 30 DAYS. IT'S <u>GUARANTEED</u>!

Get your copy of the ***Do-It-Yourself Advertising*** directly from the publisher. Follow the step-by-step directions for 30 days to create your own ads. If you're not satisfied for any reason, return the book for full credit or refund. This handbook works for you or we take it back and refund your money. 248 pages. 16 Checklists. Illustrations. Index.

only $19.95
Available wherever books are sold

JOHN WILEY & SONS
605 Third Avenue, New York, NY, 10158

Figure 1.5(c) Example of the Futura typeface.

Figure 1.5 The advertisement shown here in three different type faces was produced on desktop publishing equipment. Note the difference between the century-old favorite, Bookman, and a serif face with a modern touch, the popular Optima. Note too the improved legibility of the reverse (white) type, especially in its smaller sizes, when using the Futura sans-serif type. (To see these ads at the sizes indicated in Figure 1.4, enlarge them to 125%.)

The book illustration is a place holder for the actual photograph and shows how well desktop equipment can be used for this purpose. The actual photograph, however, is unlikely to be as emphatic as the placeholder unless you photograph it specifically for that purpose. Discuss with your photographer the differences between shooting for "contrast" and "detail."

SUMMARY

- Use a telegraphic style for the body of the ad.
- Concentrate on benefits, but don't forget the features.
- Let the offer itself determine its writing style.
- Complete your logo with your address and telephone number. Your readers won't do it for you!

ONE FINAL CHECK BEFORE TYPESETTING

You know the audience you need to reach, and you have developed a cornucopia of benefits and offers that should make them buy. Now is the time to analyze your finished copy and layout for its appeal to that particular audience. Answer the following ARM questions:

- Does your headline shout for *Attention* from your specific audience?
- Do your benefits *Retain* and heighten the interest of that same audience?
- Does your offer *Motivate* the audience to the action you want it to take?

If the answers are all "yes," and if the amount of copy matches the model ad you've chosen, you're ready to go to production.

PRODUCTION: FROM MANUSCRIPT AND LAYOUT TO FINISHED AD

Typesetting

Now that you have your manuscript and the ad model you wish to follow, you have four options to use to complete the project:

1. **Outside production service.** Turn over the ad to an outside service and let them do everything else. This is by far the easiest way to go, but it's also the most expensive. And you will still have to supervise and approve everything that's done.

2. **Desktop publishing.** If you are very skillful at using your computer to set type, try to typeset the ad yourself. But unless the end result looks as good as professional typesetting, turn it over to the pros. Professional typesetting should be one of the least expensive parts of the project and will give your ad a polished look.

3. **Typesetting by your medium.** If your advertisement will run in a single magazine or newspaper, find out if the firm you have chosen offers a typesetting service and, if so, at what cost. Often, this is a free or low-cost option, and many publications take pride in doing a fine job as part of their overall service. Some of

these publications will even permit you to run ads they set in other media, so check on that, too.

4. Professional Typesetting. Professional typesetting is generally the best option for the best work. If you don't know any typesetters, just call a few fellow advertisers and ask for their recommendations. (Of course, you'll call the ones whose ads look like the work of a pro.) Here are a few things you should do and know in dealing with typesetters:

Things You Should Do
- Explain that you are using your sample ad as a model only; it must not be copied so exactly that you might get sued.
- Get a cost quotation. Find out if the cost includes any changes and, if not, how changes are charged.

Things You Should Know
- Mistakes by the typesetter, called typos, are corrected without any charge to you.
- Alterations are the changes you make after the manuscript and layout are delivered and the type is set. They are at your expense. There will be a minimum charge for any alteration—even a single comma.
- The best way to avoid charges for alterations is to make sure that your manuscript is "clean," that is, exactly as you want it. But be prepared to make a few changes even so. Typesetting seldom comes out exactly as we'd like. So make whatever changes you must, but try very hard to make them all at once. That minimum charge comes back each time you request another set of alterations!

Before deciding which typesetting option to choose, you may wish to know more about type itself. What's involved in deciding on a particular typeface and why you might pick one over another are covered in the next section.

SUMMARY

- Use professional typesetting. It's the cheapest way to get that professional look.
- Give your typesetter a letter-perfect manuscript. It's the best way to keep your typesetting inexpensive.

Type: Faces, Weight, and Sizes

There are thousands of different styles (faces) of type from which to choose, but there is no need to work with more than a very few. To explore the differences among them, we've taken the sample ad in Figure 1.4 and set it in the three typefaces in Figure

1.5. (The ad shows amateur, rather than professional, design skills and does not reflect the full capabilities of desktop publishing.)

Major Type Families. Every typeface belongs to one of three "families":

- **Cursive** type imitates script or handwriting. It has little use in the body of an ad, but is sometimes used for the logo, as in the name of the publisher in Figure 1.5(b).
- **Serifs** are the small curlicues or fine lines at the tops and bottoms of letters. Bookman and Optima are serif faces.
- **Sans serif** means "without serif" and is any type in that family. Futura is a sans serif face.

The Serif Advantage. Most adults find serif type easier to read than sans serif, with a group of serif designs known as "reader faces" easiest of all. Of the tens of thousands of books, magazines, and newspapers published in the U.S., practically every one uses such a reader-friendly type.

Bookman (Figure 1.5(a)) is a face that has proven its utility for more than a century. Its traditional look is more than compensated for by its legibility, so you should feel comfortable in using it, except when you want a very contemporary tone in your ad.

Optima (Figure 1.5(b)) is a modern reader face and somewhat of a bridge between the serif and sans serif styles. It is adaptable to almost any ad, and its use is more a matter of personal choice than degree of legibility.

Futura (Figure 1.5(c)) is a modern typeface with as much legibility as any sans serif typeface is likely to give. While the serif faces, as a group, are easier to read, you should consider sans serif under certain circumstances.

The Sans Serif Advantage. Sans serif, too, has its advantages, chief among them the following:

- **Compressibility.** Sans serif "condenses," or compresses, type better than serif does. That is, you can get more letters per inch without distorting the type.
- **Contrast.** Often, it pays to be different. If everyone else is using a serif face, at least consider the alternative. Or you may want to draw particular attention to one portion of your ad, such as a special offer.
- **Everyone else is doing it.** If everyone else advertising to your audience is using sans serif faces, try to find out why. Ask the representatives of the media where the ads run and the advertisers themselves. Better yet, run the same ad both ways and track the results. Unlike designers or authors of books, your interest isn't in typography; it's in sales. Do whatever works!
- **Reverse type.** White or light-colored type on a dark background is easier to read in sans serif than serif (although it is generally harder to read in either typeface than standard black on white, such as what you're reading

here). Use reverse type only in headlines, logos, and what ad pros call "violators," those star-burst or other shapes that highlight a very bold statement, such as in the bicycle ad described earlier. *Never use reverse type for an entire ad.*

- **Subheads.** Many designers use sans serif for subheads, with the rest of the ad in serif type. My personal preference for subheads is a bolder (darker) version of the face used in the body of the ad.

About Type Weight. "Weight" refers to the thickness of type. Practically every face ranges from a very thick, "bold" style to a "regular" version considered the most legible for text body, to a thin or "light" design. All of these weights are also available in italic and bold, especially on more sophisticated computerized typesetting machines, which can italicize a term or make it bold at the push of a button. The names given to the degrees of boldness or thinness vary from face to face and are not really comparable. One design's "black" may be darker or lighter than another design's "ultra bold." Your typesetter will have samples with the appropriate names. For desktop setting, your computer can print each version in the styles available to it.

INSIGHT 5

Use a single typeface for your ad. Variations in size and weight are almost always preferable to mixing faces. Do it!

About Type Sizes

Type sizes have a measuring system all their own, called points, with each point being $1/72$ of an inch. This paragraph is set in 9-point ($1/8$-inch) type, but a quick measurement will tell you that none of the letters are actually this size.

Ascenders, Descenders, and Lip. Take a good look at this paragraph. Some letters in it, such as "h" and "l," extend toward the top, while others, such as "p" and "y," extend toward the bottom. Yet despite these ascenders and descenders, none of the lines run into each other. Each letter is confined within a theoretical frame that leaves room at the top and bottom, so no matter how close (or "tight") you fit your copy, there's always space between the lowest descender and the tallest ascender. The exact size of this frame varies with the typeface and may appear larger or smaller than it actually is, according to the design of individual letters. Here are some ways to add legibility:

1. Pick the typeface you find easiest to read.
2. Place additional space between lines. This is often more effective than making the type larger. Spacing instructions to your typesetter are indicated in points. For instance, "9/9" means 9-point type with no extra space, "9/10" means one point of space between each line, "9/11" means two points, etc. The type in this paragraph is 11/13.
3. Reduce the type size, but leave the same point differential. For example, going from 10/11 to 9/11 often increases legibility, while giving a few more letters per line. But don't set copy smaller than 9 points if you can avoid it. The easier your ad is to read, the more likely it is that it actually will be read. Leave tiny type to very personal classifieds.

SUMMARY

*   Serif faces are easier to read than sans serif. Use serifs.
*   The fewer typefaces, the better is the ad. Use a single face of varied weights and sizes.
*   There's no point in running ads nobody will read. Keep the smallest type for the body of your ad at 9/11. *Reduce the amount of copy before you reduce the size of the type.*

Production Considerations for Photography and Art

If your model ad includes photography or art, you have a number of options:

1. Take your own photograph or draw your own illustrations. Let your conscience be your guide.
2. Use a professional photographer or artist. Keep in mind that photographers' and artists' fees are often negotiable and that the quality of their work is seldom affected by their price.
3. Use existing photographs or art, or use graphic materials from one of your suppliers. They may be overly familiar to you, but they'll be entirely new to your audience.
4. Use stock photographs and illustrations—pictures that can be used by anyone for a set fee. There are numerous sources for these, and the suppliers will work with you to find a picture that fits the mood or subject you

specify. Usually, they will also send you a variety of pictures from which to choose.

Where to Find Stock Pictures. Many large cities have local creative arts resource directories. Ask the chamber of commerce, your public library, or the director of your local advertising club. Also, there's always the Yellow Pages and your very helpful media representatives. The production directors of advertising agencies are probably the best source of all. Ask them. They'll be able to do a favor for both you and one of their own suppliers. That's two good deeds with a single telephone call. If you're neither in nor near a large city, ask your fellow advertisers what they do. Obviously, they've solved the problem already and may keep you from much spinning of wheels.

SUMMARY

- Use a professional photographer or illustrator when possible; otherwise get existing or stock art.
- Finding suppliers is the easy part; deciding which one to use is the hardest.

Film for Advertisements

Many publications will accept your ad in typeset form, with a clear indication of where the illustrations, if any, are to go. However, if you need multiple copies of the same ad, or if the publication will accept only film or one-piece art, you will require the services of a color separator film house, even if the ad has no color as such, but is black and white only.

What the Color Separator Does. Color separators take all the elements that make up your advertisement—type, art, and photographs, along with your instructions for making them larger or smaller, into one color or several, and against a tinted or clear background. They then produce a film to the printer's specifications. If the magazine or newspaper requires one-piece art, the film house will use the film to make a photograph called a *print* or *glossy* that is suitable for that medium. This is the same process that is used to provide the "proofs" that accompany the film and that you get to "proof" the fact that the film was properly prepared.

A Record-Keeping Hint. At the bottom of every ad, show the ad number, if any, the media in which it ran, and dates when it appeared. Tell the color separator to leave that information as part of the proof. For ads that do not first go to film, do the same thing and make photocopies for yourself. Keep these record proofs in notebooks that will not be used for any other purpose.

There's much more about film preparation, especially for color printing, in Chapter 10.

ABOUT TESTING

Advertising professionals test everything about their ads when time and budget permit. You do the same, and, like them, rely on your business experience and common sense when you can't. When testing is practical, be sure to structure your ads so that you learn what you want to know.

• **Testing two completely different ads** for the same product or service is fine, provided that your price and offer are the same for both. Otherwise, how will you know whether the result came from the ad, the price, or the offer?

• **In testing one specific item**—a lower or higher price, headline, offer, picture, illustration, typeface, etc.—leave everything else exactly the same and *change the one item being tested only*. If, for instance, you change both the price and the headline, how will you know which produced the result you get. You won't care if you increased the price and sales increased, too, or even stayed the same. But what if sales fall? Was it because of the new price or the new headline? Decide exactly what it is you want to learn, and test that without changing anything else. For example, suppose you wish to test the appeal of the same product to two different audiences. Figure 1.6 shows how this might be done. In each ad, the headline identifies the target audience. In the body of the second ad, the benefit is modified slightly from the first in accordance with the audience's needs. The rest of the copy remains the same. By placing these ads in media that provide cards for reader response, test results are achieved at very low cost.

Testing: The A/B Split

Many newspapers and magazines will run two different ads of the same size in every other copy of an issue, usually at a slight additional charge. Note that this isn't one ad in the first half off the press followed by a different ad in the second half. Rather, it means that, of the copies delivered to houses, apartments, and offices in the same block, or the copies sold at newsstands, every other one will contain ad A, with the rest having ad B. In publishing terms, that's known as a *true A/B split*, and it is just about the easiest, most effective, and least expensive way to test the appeal of different offers, prices, headlines, etc.

Demographic Editions

Many publications offer not only A/B splits, but also *demographic editions*. When you purchase a demographic edition of a publication, you purchase a specific location and/or socioeconomic segment of the total circulation. Large-city newspapers offer neighborhood editions that make it affordable for local retailers to advertise in the "big" paper. National magazines offer everything from over 100 test market locations (*Reader's Digest*) to 1,600,000 top businessmen and women (*Time*). Explore these possibilities with the media representatives, and, *if it makes economic sense for you*, weigh the factor into your final decision regarding your choice of media for your ad.

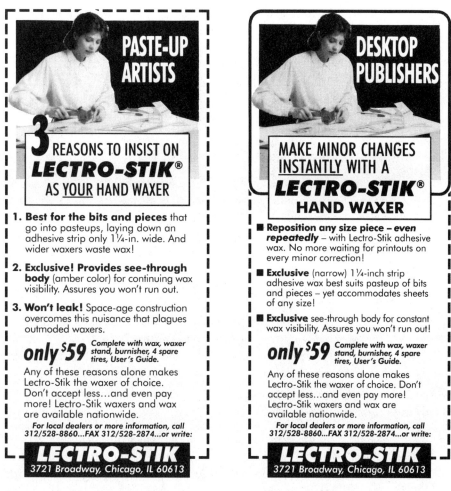

Figure 1.6 One-half-column ads ($2^3/8'' \times 4^7/8''$) testing the appeal of the same product for two different audiences. (Ad design: J-K Art Directions, Milwaukee, WI. Copy by the author.)

WHEN TO CHANGE AN AD

No advertisement retains its selling power forever. Even successful ads are often improved by testing different headlines, benefits, or offers—or sometimes by such a simple thing as changing and advertising new business hours. But never change a successful ad simply because you've seen it so often that you're sure that readers are tired of it. The chances are they're not: in fact, an even better chance is that they're not aware of it at all!

One of the more counterproductive mistakes made by advertisers is to stop running successful advertising because they are bored with it. They've lived with the ad from conception through all the birth pangs, to its final arrival as a fully developed promotion. They want to move on to something new and are convinced their customers feel the same way. But their customers and prospects probably haven't seen the ad at all, and when they do, they won't pay it nearly the attention the advertiser likes to believe they will. There are only two valid business-related reasons for changing an ad:

1. The ad is no longer cost effective.
2. A different ad or a different version of the same ad has proven more effective.

The Only Excuse for a Failed Ad

A second common—and costly—mistake made by advertisers is to invent excuses for advertising that didn't work. Of course, if you are holding a tent sale, and a tornado keeps everyone locked into their cellars, you will certainly take that into account. But very little else, except the ad itself, is an acceptable excuse for a failed promotion. Always go back to the three ARM basics of:

1. **Attention**: Did you get their attention, and how might that have been done better?
2. **Retention**: Did you retain their interest through meaningful benefits, and how might these have been enhanced?
3. **Motivation**: Did your offer motivate the readers to act the way you had expected, and how can you improve the offer?

Learning from Success

Learning from success is much more pleasant than learning from failure, so don't forget to do that, too. Keep detailed records. Analyze them to discover what you did right, and then apply it in the future. Avoid developing new ads without feedback when feedback is available. Celebrating your successes is much more fun than being creative about excuses. And following the directions here should give you lots to celebrate. So go to it!

INSIGHT 6

Beware of the bottom-line success available through drastic reductions in or elimination of advertising. The short-run savings may all seem positive, but the long-term consequences are frequently irreversible. It costs much more to regain than to retain your customers, if it can be done at all.

SUMMARY

•   Test those things most likely to motivate—price, offer, emphasis, choice of media.

- If testing the obvious motivators doesn't point you toward success, think very hard about your product or service.
- Test only one thing at a time, or test totally different promotions. Never change two aspects of the same promotion within the same test; you won't know why you got the results—no matter what they are.
- Continue to use successful ads until something else proves more cost effective.

COOPERATIVE ADVERTISING

Cooperative advertising, generally abbreviated to co-op, is an agreed-upon sharing of specified advertising or other promotional costs among manufacturers and retailers or analogous groups. As Figure 1.7 shows, such co-op can extend far beyond newspapers, radio, and television. Almost anything goes, providing it's within the agreed-upon and specified limitations of the manufacturers' plans.

What to Agree Upon and Specify . . . in Writing

Whether you are the national or local partner in a co-op agreement, spell out the rules under which you participate. Make sure that you agree upon at least the following:

- **Who pays.** How much or what percentage of costs will each of you pay? Specify maximums if any.

- **How co-op accrues.** What goods or services apply to the accrual? How is that amount determined? Over what period of time? By law, the accrual must be proportional for all like outlets or participants, regardless of size or volume. For instance, manufacturers may not give retailers 5 percent of sales for a 100-unit purchase and 10 percent for 200 units, thereby rewarding the larger outlets. Thus, the *degree* of co-op must be the same for every retailer, although it can differ or be absent for wholesalers. Co-op may also be regionalized or otherwise limited, as long as it is equally available to *competing* users.

INSIGHT 7

Co-op accruals are not an additional discount automatically credited to everyone. Co-op is distributed for specified promotional use and is forfeited unless earned in that way.

- **What will be promoted.** This need not parallel how co-op is accrued. Often, all of the co-op earned is targeted on a few promotional leaders.

- **When to promote.** Agree upon dates, seasons, or tie-in events and, above all, the final date on which the co-op accrual may be spent. In specifying dates, consider such possibilities as using unspent Christmas co-op for January sales. Try to be flexible, but remember, accountants live by fiscal years.

- **Where and how to promote.** National organizations tend to favor "name" media. But "shoppers," "penny-savers," and similar free media may be a retailer's best buy. Stay flexible. By law, not only must co-op be proportional, but also, it must be functionally available. That is, it may not be limited to what only the largest accruals can buy.

- **Message approvals.** Both co-op partners are responsible for claims about their products and services. Agree on who creates and who approves advertising. To prevent conflicts, many manufacturers prepare advertisements, commercials, flyers, and mailing pieces that are easy and inexpensive to personalize for cooperating retailers. In fact, most of the advertising that appears in newspapers is prepared in just that way.

- **What's not covered.** Many co-op programs exclude all creative or preparatory charges and cover only the *net* cost of newspaper and magazine ads or radio and television on-air time. But recall Figure 1.7. The purpose of a co-op program is to promote the product or service better and sell more of it. If what will work isn't in the current agreement, add it. Just remember . . . put it in writing!

Auditing Co-Op: How and Why

Most companies with substantial co-op programs audit retailer or other local charge-backs through an advertising checking service. Local advertisers requesting charge-backs submit tear sheets of their ads—the actual pages on which the ads appeared—or some other proof of promotional activity, with invoices substantiating the cost. But if my own experience is any guide, the invoices are sometimes the most creative use of the promotional effort.

While advertising manager for Rand McNally, I was perplexed by how much one of America's leading department stores paid for its newspaper advertising. According to invoices they submitted, ads I assumed would cost around $3,000 were invoiced for over double that amount. By coincidence, the same batch of mail that brought the request for charge-back approval also brought a mailing from ACB, the Advertising Checking Bureau—then, as now, the largest such service in the country. I had not known that such a service existed. Further contact with ACB provided both an answer and a solution to my problems regarding the department store's billings.

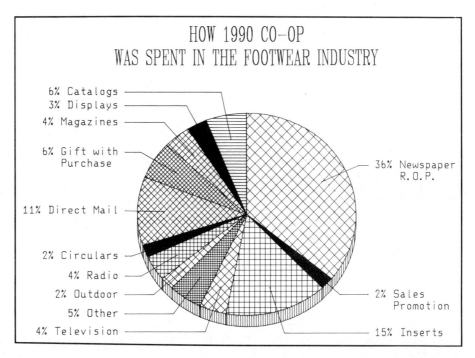

HOW 1990 CO-OP
WAS SPENT IN THE FOOTWEAR INDUSTRY

6% Catalogs
3% Displays
4% Magazines

6% Gift with
   Purchase

11% Direct Mail

2% Circulars

4% Radio

2% Outdoor

5% Other

4% Television

36% Newspaper
    R.O.P.

2% Sales
   Promotion

15% Inserts

Figure 1.7 Cooperative advertising. (Courtesy The Advertising Checking Bureau, Inc.)

The Answer. Billing for almost all publication advertising is based on a projected use of that medium by an advertiser during a calendar year. As distinct from a co-op agreement, substantial discounts are given to those who advertise more—to the "heavier" advertisers. The true rate is calculated at the end of the year, and adjustments are made at that time. The department store that had sent me the invoice had contracted—and was being billed—for a fraction of the space it would actually use. It got an enormous refund at the end of each year. But in the meantime, it had highly inflated invoices to submit for its share of the co-op, and the newspaper had an interest-free loan that it was happy to repay when actual discounts were calculated.

The Solution. For every U.S. newspaper and hundreds of magazines, the Advertising Checking Bureau keeps a running total of the advertisements that appear in it. Other such services track radio and television. All of them can check charge-backs and, where necessary, correct them to their true rate. *In most instances, the corrected charge-back is approved by the retailer.* When the original charge-backs are too high, an audit report specifies actual space or air-time rates and an approved co-op amount. In case of conflict, the service, rather than the manufacturer, becomes a party to the disagreement. Thus, rather than a conflict between a supplier and a customer, you get a debate between accountants. If, as can also happen, charges are too low, notifying retailers about this can hardly be surpassed for creating goodwill. As a

NEWSPAPER/MAGAZINE ADVERTISING CHECKLIST

Project title/description _____ **Date** _____
_____ **Project #** _____
_____ **Checklist #** _____
Overall Supervision by _____ **Deadline** _____
Budget _____ **Start-up Date** _____ **Completion Date** _____

MANAGEMENT DECISIONS	ASSIGNED TO	DUE	IN	MUST APPROVE	BY DATE	IN	INFO COPY ONLY	SEE ATTACHED
1. Quotations			☐			☐		☐
2. Budget approval			☐			☐		☐
3. Project approval			☐			☐		☐

CREATIVE DECISIONS

	ASSIGNED TO	DUE	IN	MUST APPROVE	BY DATE	IN	INFO COPY ONLY	SEE ATTACHED
4. Audience Focus			☐			☐		☐
5. Message of Ad			☐			☐		☐
6. Headline Focus			☐			☐		☐
7. Benefits Focus			☐			☐		☐
8. Offer Focus			☐			☐		☐
9. Writer			☐			☐		☐
10. Designer			☐			☐		☐
11. Colors			☐			☐		☐
12. Typesetter			☐			☐		☐
13. Artist			☐			☐		☐
14. Photography			☐			☐		☐
15. Camera-Ready Art			☐			☐		☐
16. Film for Media			☐			☐		☐
17. Film Shipment			☐			☐		☐

MEDIA DECISIONS

	ASSIGNED TO	DUE	IN	MUST APPROVE	BY DATE	IN	INFO COPY ONLY	SEE ATTACHED
18. Media Focus/Selection			☐			☐		☐
19. Ad Dates			☐			☐		☐
20. Ad Sizes			☐			☐		☐
21. Space Cost			☐			☐		☐
22. Media Notification			☐			☐		☐

MECHANICAL CHECKS

	ASSIGNED TO	DUE	IN	MUST APPROVE	BY DATE	IN	INFO COPY ONLY	SEE ATTACHED
23. Logo OK			☐			☐		☐
24. Address OK			☐			☐		☐
25. Phone(s) OK			☐			☐		☐
26. Editorial OK			☐			☐		☐
27. Legal OK			☐			☐		☐
28. Marketing OK			☐			☐		☐
29. Management OK			☐			☐		☐
30. Copy of Ad as Run			☐			☐		☐

MEDIA LIST ☐ If checked, see back for additional media.

Newspaper or Magazine	Cover Date	Date Issued	Reservation Deadline	Deadline for Film	Size	Colors	Cost

matter of record, the department store never questioned the audited, corrected co-op amount.

Many co-op agreements specify that invoices will be checked by an auditing service. Such services are in every major and most secondary markets and can be found in the Yellow Pages. Most of them specialize in local and regional media. A few, such as ACB, operate nationwide. If you are the co-op provider, balance the cost of the auditing against possible savings in charge-back claims. If your co-op program totals $25,000 or more, auditing is probably worthwhile.

SUMMARY

- Don't limit co-op to the most obvious media; limit it just to those that are likely to work.
- Put co-op agreements into an English both sides can understand . . . and make sure that they do.
- Expect co-op claims to be audited . . . because they probably will be.

NOTES ON THE NEWSPAPER/MAGAZINE ADVERTISING CHECKLIST

These notes are a supplement to the material presented in this chapter. They are not a self-contained substitute for that material.

1. Total of all estimated costs for outside suppliers and internal out-of-pocket charges. This is the figure given for budget approval in #2.
2. Analyses of estimates as fair costs to do the proposed project. Costs may be renegotiated before going to #3.
3. Decision on whether the project is worth the costs, no matter how fair they may be. If approved, this is the figure placed into #2.
4. Determine the key audience at whom the ad is targeted. Everything else about this ad must then be controlled by that focus. How else will you decide on the message, media, and even budget?
5. Not the actual words. That's the job of the writer in #9. What the ad is to say, rather than how it is to be said.
6. The one thing you can say that is most likely to attract your key audience— that will get them to read the message. Not the words, but the thought.
7. Pick the benefits keyed to the audience in #4. If none of the benefits seem particularly suited to that audience, reconsider your choice of benefits or audience.
8. Develop a reason, in addition to its benefits, to use *your* product or service, especially if other competitive options are available. Don't be afraid to echo your competition. If you can't do better, at least stay even.
9. Who will do the writing. If certain things *must* be said in certain ways, let the writer know . . . but be willing to consider alternatives. Even Scripture gets retranslated now and then.

10. Good designers often surprise one. Don't be too hasty to say no to what you may not like at first sight. It's a designer's job to know how to appeal *visually* to your key audience.

11. Color in advertising almost always gains readership. So does size. If dollars are set, ask your media representative for *facts and figures* concerning which works better.

12. Use professional typesetting for advertising that requires design skills. Limit desktop typesetting to straightforward flyers, reports, and other simple-to-set projects.

13–14. Unless you're an expert, discuss art and photography with your film-maker before you order or buy. The human eye and camera often won't see things the same way. (Much more about this in chapter 10.)

15. The last chance to change anything at relatively low cost. Put every instruction to the filmmaker in writing. If someone else does this, go over it with them and make sure you both understand the instructions *the same way*.

16. Film also includes proofs for approval. Check every instruction on the camera-ready art to make sure that it has been followed. Even more important, check the proof itself to make sure that your instructions made sense. Newspaper advertisements seldom are as clear in print as on the proof. If it's hard to read *for any reason* on the proof, it will probably be impossible to read when printed.

17. Let the film shop ship the film and proof to their destination. That's part of its responsibility and know-how.

18. Does the focus of your media match the audience focus in #4? If not, why this selection . . . unless it's the only paper in town? If there's no other medium available, use what is available (and work on building a mailing list).

19. Differentiate between two dates in making magazine selections:
    - The "out dates," that is, when the magazines are actually issued or mailed.
    - The date printed on the cover.

20. Have a reason for the size of the ad you use. Note that it often costs less to create a single large ad and use it everywhere, rather than also pay for the creation of smaller versions for less important media.

21. Dramatic discounts are possible when you advertise fairly frequently in the same medium. Newspapers especially combine "space" with frequency discounts that make it possible to run more advertising at less cost. Ask your media representatives about "rate holders" and any other way to save.

22. Notify each medium in writing. Use a space reservation or media reservation form similar to the one shown in Figure 1.8 at reduced size.

23–29. Someone has been assigned to check each of these items before anything may be printed. Make sure that they do check them and sign off *in writing*. In many organizations, the logo, address, and phone numbers are preprinted in a variety of styles and sizes and *must* be used from that art. It's an excellent safety measure, provided that every such piece is dated and

Hahn, Crane and Associates, Inc., Advertising

2035 Hawthorne Lane, Evanston, IL 60201 • MAIL: P.O. Box 5010, Evanston, IL 60204 • 708/866-9009

SPACE RESERVATION

Date _____

TO THE PUBLISHER OF:

This is authorization to schedule advertising as specified in:

☐ Rate Card # _____
☐ SRDS Dated _____
☐ Other _____
Ad Size/Colors _____
Space Cost _____
Frequency Rate _____

ADVERTISER _____
Address _____
City _____ State _____ Zip _____
Telephone _____
Authorized Signature _____ Title _____

AGENCY _____
Address _____
City _____ State _____ Zip _____
Telephone _____
Authorized Signature _____ Title _____

AD ID # _____
AD HEADLINE _____
_____
_____

☐ Bill to advertiser
☐ Bill to agency
☐ Materials herewith
☐ Materials to follow from:
_____
_____

ADVERTISING SCHEDULE
Date(s) _____
_____
_____
_____
_____
_____

SPECIAL INSTRUCTIONS
Send 2 tear sheets of printed advertisement with billing.
_____
_____
_____

Figure 1.8 Sample media reservation form.

thrown out when there is a change. Experience has shown that practically no one really reads logos. Make yourself the exception.

30. Who is responsible for maintaining a file? Who must see a printed copy before a medium is paid? Normally, only one copy of the printed ad accompanies the invoice. Make copies before you release your only original.

2 | Flyers, Brochures, Bulletins, and Invitations

FLYERS AND BROCHURES: HOW THEY DIFFER

In standard usage, a *flyer* is made from a single sheet of paper. Figure 2.1 shows just eight of the different formats that a flyer may assume. By contrast, a *brochure* is in booklet format. In working with outside sources, find out what distinction *they* make, so that you both speak the same language. Since different suppliers may have different definitions, keep your *internal* nomenclature consistent and "translate" as you go along.

A BRIEF MANUAL OF PROCEDURES

Procedures for creating flyers and brochures should be the same whether you do everything yourself, are part of an internal team, or supervise outside resources. The procedures apply to everything from simple do-it-yourself projects to the most sophisticated agency-produced materials. As with every promotion, creating a flyer or brochure is a five-step process:

1. Learn, or decide upon, the purpose of your promotion.
2. Establish a time frame and remain within it.
3. Establish and remain within a budget.
4. Create the promotion.
5. Produce and distribute the promotion, which is covered as part of Chapter 3, "Direct Mail," and in greatest detail in Chapter 10.

Let's consider each of these points in more detail.

DECIDING UPON A PURPOSE

The Audience

Begin by determining to whom the piece will be addressed. The type and amount of information you include should be guided by its use. For instance, senior management will require a preponderence of financial data, the engineering department will demand production specifications, and an interior designer will be interested only in size and colors. And that's just for the bathrooms!

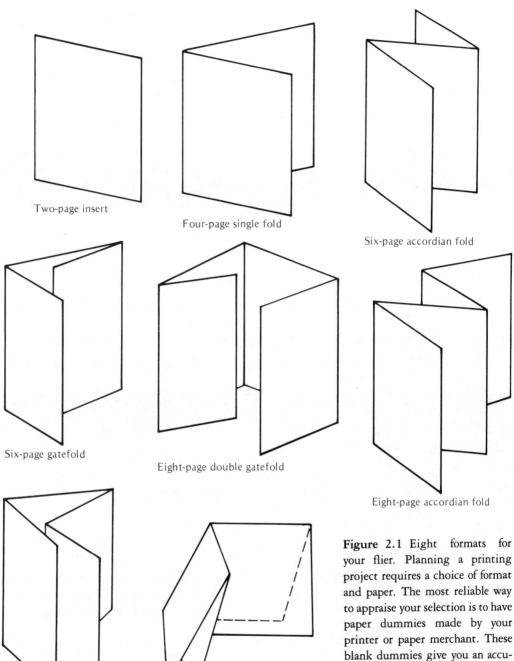

Two-page insert

Four-page single fold

Six-page accordian fold

Six-page gatefold

Eight-page double gatefold

Eight-page accordian fold

Eight-page, two
parallel folds

Eight-page broadside

Figure 2.1 Eight formats for your flier. Planning a printing project requires a choice of format and paper. The most reliable way to appraise your selection is to have paper dummies made by your printer or paper merchant. These blank dummies give you an accurate example of how paper substance, weight and surface qualities look and feel in the format you specify. (Formats shown courtesy of James River Premium Printing Papers. Original art for James River by Hyers/Smith Advertising, South Norwalk, CT.)

If, as is often the case, you must combine information for more than one audience within a single promotion, make it easy for each audience to find and use what it needs. Some simple ways to do this are given later in the section.

How Much to Include

Whether you're a brand new enterprise or long established, don't just guess at how much to tell your audience about who you are and what you have to sell. If you're part of an ongoing organization, accompany several experienced sales representatives as they make their calls. Try to differentiate between sales success based on personality (I like Chuck) and that based on how goods are being sold (I like what I hear and see). If you are a member of an enterprise that is just starting up, you may have to do some or all of the selling yourself!

INSIGHT 8

Always put more detail—whether hard data or a sales pitch—into your printed promotion than into your sales call. There is no way your *readers* can question your flyer or brochure, so give them *everything* they need to make them decide your way.

An extensive guide to what and how much to write begins in a few pages. But don't jump there yet. There's a lot more to do before writing begins.

Using the Promotion

Knowing how and by whom the piece you produce will be used is critical to its creation. Will it be mailed? Distributed by a sales staff? Included in packages? Posted on bulletin boards? Used at trade shows? Or all of these? Let's consider each of these options in turn.

Mailing. Mailings can be self-mailers; that is, mailed without envelopes, or mailed inside of envelopes. They may go by first class or several variations of third class. You may include a coupon or a reply form, or request the recipient to write or call. These and other mailing options and decisions require a chapter all by themselves and are covered in Chapter 3.

Use by the Sales Staff. Your promotion can be a visual aid during a sales call, a leave-behind reminder or both. It can be "Let me walk you through this flyer, which illustrates the important points about our service," or "Let me just leave you this flyer, which highlights the points we've been talking about. You can look it over with engineering, and I'll call you about an order on Tuesday."

Some "political" points must also be considered. For example, in larger organizations, how will the sales staff react if the only address shown on flyers and brochures is the home office? And conversely, how will the home office react if all the responses go to the field? As the advertising or promotion director, you may be the only person involved in the promotion who works for "the company," so resolve any such conflicts before your creative efforts begin.[1]

Enclosures. Make sure that your promotion piece fits into the package. Is your piece the first thing you want seen or the last, and how can you be certain that it will be seen at all? Join the packaging design team first and the packaging crew later. There's no substitute for hands-on experience in this phase of promotional activities.

Distribution at Trade Shows. If you use "help yourself" literature bins at conventions, meetings, or other events, how much of the promotion piece do the bins show: The complete page, the top half, or the top few inches only? The answer will affect the design of the piece, so do let the designer know.

ESTABLISHING A TIME LINE

A time line is the time allowed for the complete project, as well as for each of its subprojects, such as editing copy, typesetting, and doing artwork. For any project involving outside resources, your time line and budget are totally interrelated. Costs are affected by time allocations, and completion dates may not be flexible. The brochure that says "Visit our booth for a special discount" will do you no good whatsoever after the exhibit closes—no matter how creative the excuses are for not getting it done.

Time lines are established by working backwards from a targeted end date and allocating completion dates and responsibility for each of the following benchmarks:

* **End date.** When the project must be completed and what "completed" means: printed, distributed (how?), or received (by whom?).

* **Distribution.** The dates for each aspect of distribution, including mailings and warehousing of extra stock.

* **Printing and bindery work.** The time from the completion of printing film to the delivery by the printer of *usable* printed pieces. For flyers and brochures, a separate bindery may be involved in collating or folding, or the printers may do this themselves. The time line schedules them both.

* **Film and proofing.** Almost all contemporary printing, including newspapers and magazines, begins with a photographed image, *on film*, that will be transferred by the printer onto printing plates. The preparation of this film from the camera-

---

[1] Edward Deming, the U.S. "father" of Japan's industrial miracle, believes that a key error made by the United States is to evaluate individuals only for their immediate, isolated contributions. Everyone is thus forced to be "in business for themselves," and no one works for the long-run good of the corporation or organization.

ready art may be done by the printer or by a filmmaking specialist called a *color separator*. The time needed for preparing and transferring film will depend on both the complexity of your project and the time the filmmaker is available. Advanced scheduling and written confirmation are highly recommended. Just remember that you, too, must keep your part of the scheduling agreement.

• **Proofing** is the checking of a test picture made from the film, before your project is actually printed. A number of different proofing processes are available. They range from the least expensive single-color process producing a picture called a "dylux" to processes generating multicolor "Chromachecks," "Cromalins," and "Match Prints."

(Printing, film preparation, and proofs are so important that they are covered in much more detail in Chapter 10. For scheduling purposes, the thing to know is that the kind of proof you order affects your costs and your ability at quality control rather than completion time. The same original film must be prepared, no matter which process is used.)

• **Camera-ready art** is everything that will be photographed to make the film for printing. Specific considerations must be given not only to the time for typesetting, photography, and art, but also to who must approve any of these steps and their availability when they will be needed. The process of combining the various approved elements into the most practical format for photography is called *key line and paste-up*. Little of either should be needed for simple flyers and brochures, especially those prepared on desktop publishing equipment.

• **Copy, design, and layout.** Who will do copy, design, and layout and who must approve them are often the most flexible elements of the time line, especially if they are done by internal staff. What's sometimes forgotten is that they are also the foundation on which everything else is built. Constructing that foundation is discussed in detail almost immediately in "Creating the Promotion."

ESTABLISHING A BUDGET

There are two types of budgets, and they must not be confused. Both are fixed, but they are based on different conditions:

1. *Administrative budget.* A specific amount is allocated, and costs must not exceed that amount.
2. *Estimate-based budget.* Costs are estimated, and projects are then approved, rejected, or changed based on the estimates.

The budget becomes a time line consideration when it must be approved by someone other than yourself before any work may start. If this is mandated, build in time for getting estimates and quotations, as well as the approval itself.

CREATING THE PROMOTION: AN OUTLINE

The outline that follows is written as if you were the promotional supervisor of a large organization. Exactly the same procedures apply to the one-person shop or any size of organization in between.

I. **Purpose**. The purpose of the piece is the most important reason or reasons for preparing it. Make an absolute limit of three. (How many can be "most" important?) *Put them in writing!*

II. **Sources**. Determine who will provide the information needed to write and design the promotion and when they will be available. Get a backup source, if possible.

III. **Check and approve**. Establish responsibility for the accuracy of information about the product, legal clearance, editorial clearance (spelling, grammar, the house style), and sales input. Determine who will edit—rather than write—review, and have final approval of the project. *Only one person can have final approval!*

IV. **Concepts and presentations**. Depending on how you and your organization work, you may go through a series of concept presentations or go directly to final copy and layout. In either case, the materials must be put through the following steps, whether they be taken mentally while talking to yourself or in formal presentations to others:

A. **Organization**. Organize the information in order of importance to the specific audience that will see the printed piece. Later you can decide how much of the information will actually be used and the style in which it is to be presented.

B. **Emphasis**. Decide which points are to be stressed and which is the most important point of all. Make the latter into your headline.

C. **Illustrations**. Decide on photographs and other illustrations: how many there will be, what kind they should be, and where to get them.

D. **Response**. Determine what you want the reader to do. This is the most frequently understated element in promotional literature. We tell the recipient everything, except why we want them to read the material. (For their good, yes, but for our good, too!).

E. **Policing**. Policing is neither proofreading nor editing, but a final check against our stated purpose in producing the promotional piece. That's why we put that purpose into writing. It's very easy to get so carried away with our creativity, that we forget what we set out to do.

Once the basic concept has been developed, preliminary or "draft" copy and possible designs are produced. In organizations with several layers of management, these are the versions presented for managerial comments or approval. Note that detailed revisions may be required for draft copy and designs, as some managers can't visualize promotional materials until they see them in quite finished form. During my years as an advertising account executive, I've reminded my clients—as gently as

I know how—that they are *paying* for all the changes they order. As an employee reporting to management, I have—equally gently—given notice of impending deadlines. As principal of my own firm, I play both parts simultaneously with schizophrenic delight.

INSIGHT 9

Don't show managers "rough," that is, not professionally finished, design concepts or unedited copy. Despite their insistence that they wish to eliminate the cost of "finished" presentations, no manager in my three decades of presenting things to them, has been happy with anything less.

SUMMARY

- Determine by whom and how your promotional pieces will be used. Make everything fit into purposes consistent with that determination. Put it in writing!
- Time frames control budgets and vice versa. Nothing saves creative and production dollars like adequate time to do the job.
- *Plan* who will be your sources for information, reviews, and approvals. Put it in writing!

A BASIC DESIGN CONCEPT

The One-Third Guide

For a one- or two-page piece (each page is one side of a sheet of paper, not the sheet itself), allow *approximately* one-third of the space for each of the following:

- One-third for headlines and subheads, plus information about ordering or a coupon and your logo—that is, the special way you identify yourself. Frequently, your logo is also the way your name, address, and telephone number appear on your letterhead.
- One-third for illustrations, including charts and their captions.
- One-third for general copy, i.e., the body of the ad.

For three pages or more, use the two-page guide for the first page and the last page, and then divide the remaining space so that you use half for copy and half for illustrations. Of course, these are suggested guidelines only, but they will give you a balanced approach to an inviting presentation.

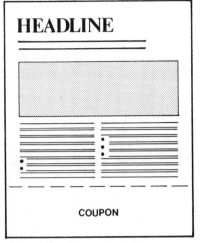

Single-page version
(Use back for mailing)

Front of two pages

Back of two pages

Figure 2.2 Sample layouts for one- or two-page fliers.

Page Size Guideline

Keep your page size $8^{1}/_{2}'' \times 11''$ (letter) or $8^{1}/_{2}'' \times 14''$ (legal size). Either one will fold into a standard No. 10 business envelope and is flexible for multipurpose use.

WRITING THE MANUSCRIPT: THE IMPORTANCE OF FEATURES AND BENEFITS

In flyers and brochures, present features and benefits as nearly equally as you can. Each one needs and supports the other. *What* benefits and features you choose are, of course, determined by your audience and your purpose in communicating with them.

Remember, a **feature** is what is inherent in your product or service. It is what *you* have put in. ("Our lawnmower bag is reinforced with glass threads.")

A **benefit** is what the potential *buyer or user* gets from your product or service. Benefits answer the question of "What's in it for me?" ("The safest grass-catcher bag on any mower. Even loose pebbles and sharp objects can't fly out and harm your loved ones.")

Features are usually easy to find and put on paper. We all tend to be familiar with what we, singly or as an organization, bring to our products and services. But many writers have difficulty finding and articulating equally impressive benefits— especially when the same feature requires different benefits for different audiences.

The Magic Benefit Generator

Whether you're forced to be a true do-it-yourselfer or can bring others into the process, here's a surefire way to generate benefits. Take a sheet of paper. At the top, list the feature and the audience for whom you wish to generate benefits. Now pretend you are speaking to that audience. Read the feature, preferably out loud, and add: "*And you will love it because*"—but don't stop. What follows "because" is the series of benefits. Don't even stop to write. Get a tape recorder (for as little as $20), and use that instead. Do the same for each audience and each feature. *Now* copy the listed benefits from the tape onto paper. When you finish, you'll have not only a complete list of features, but also a practically inexhaustible encyclopedia of benefits. If there are features for which you just can't find benefits, share the problem with the person who created the feature in the first place. (For example, "Why is our grass catcher bag only 8 mm thick when everyone else's is 9?")

Brainstorming

Discovering benefits and gaining a greater insight into features is a brainstorming experience that just about everyone profits from and enjoys. Whenever possible, bring different areas of expertise together and let them help generate answers to your "because" question. Here are some basic rules pertaining to brainstorming:

- There are no dumb suggestions.
- Don't argue about other people's suggestions during brainstorming; just build on them.
- Switch to a new feature the moment answers stop coming.
- "I just thought of something" half an hour later is . . . great! Accept it with thanks.

Steps in Writing

Now you are ready to write! But rather than go at it in a haphazard way, do it like this:

1. Organize the features and benefits by order of importance to the audience to

whom you are writing. This will probably give you different sequences for different audiences.

2. Decide on the number of photographs, graphs, charts, and any other art you want to include, and *make sure you can get them*. Words and illustrations must reinforce each other and work together to get the results you want. You really can't do that unless you know what the illustrations will be.

3. Pick the six most important aspects of the product. Make the first of these the overall headline for the piece. Use the other five as subheads—that is, as secondary headlines for individual sections of the copy or to relate it to a specific audience. If you have fewer than six subjects, work with what you have. Divide one or more subjects into subgroupings if that makes sense. But don't force things! What you are trying to achieve is copy that has a logical flow. Your headline and subheads must give the basic story, even if that is all that is read.

4. Within each section, put all of the points *that will fit* into "bulleted" form as in the "Brainstorming" copy discussed earlier. But don't just leave the copy like this. If only one or two points are to be stressed, rewrite them in regular paragraph style, and then use whichever version seems to look and read better.

State your benefits as factual information, just as you do your features. For ease in understanding the nontechnical terms, keep words to three or fewer syllables and the *average* number of words in a sentence to 12 or fewer. One fairly complicated or run-on sentence can stop your readers in their mental tracks.

Keep your writing as straightforward as possible. The format itself will produce the promotional flair that is needed. The unadorned presentation of benefits and features will strengthen rather than weaken their believability. Limit adjectives and eliminate adverbs; you'll get your chance to use them in the next chapter.

Do not try to force in every single bit of information you have available. If material seems too important to be left out, consider increasing the number of pages, rather than going to a smaller type or having fewer illustrations. But consider also that you ordered your materials in terms of importance. How vital can a seventh or eighth feature or benefit really be?

5. Once you have done all of the preceding things, you still have two more elements to think about and write:
- **The offer.** Tell your readers how to order or to get whatever you have to provide. If there are options, explain them. Make it easy. This is not an IQ test for your customers. Make the information complete. Include toll-free phone numbers and a fax number if available. Give the address to write to. List a specific department for information if there is one. Include *anything* that will expedite a response.[2]

---

[2]Note the telegraphic style in this paragraph. It combines bulleted statements with a paragraph format. It works!

- **Picture captions**. Copy for picture captions must be orchestrated just as carefully as that for any other element. The illustrations are there to help get across the overall message. Like your subheads, pictures and their captions should tell your basic story all by themselves.

INSIGHT 10

Your audience is most likely to read your flyer or brochure in the following order:
1. Headline and subheads.
2. Special offer if emphasized.
3. Illustrations and captions.
4. The body copy in any order that happens to interest them.

Thus, you have three chances to sell or lose the audience, even if your general copy is never read. Use each one!

SUMMARY

- To find out the benefits of your product, base them on what your features do for customers and prospects. What sells is not what *you* put into your product or service; it's what *they* get out of it.
- Organize before you write, and the manuscript will take care of itself. Brilliant copy won't help if your readers can't make out why you are writing. (You want me to do *what? Why?*)

LAYOUT AND DESIGN

With the guidance offered here, you can produce your own manuscript ("copy"). But few of us are given the skill to create our own professional-quality design or layout—that is, the overall visual impression and detailed specifications that make a flyer or brochure work. Unlike newspaper and magazine advertising, for which you can find an existing model to follow, printed pieces tend to be too individualistic for that approach. So use a design studio if you can afford it. If not, you have several other options. All but one are quite inexpensive. However, the somewhat more costly one will also be the easiest for you and give you more time for other things.

- **Use the basic layouts shown in Figure 2.2.** These models were created primarily to guide you in writing, rather than layout, but they can serve both purposes if nothing more sophisticated—or simpler—is required. While they are functional, they make no pretense of being superior designs.

- **Use an existing promotion as a model.** Do this with great care, as you must make certain that the model really fits your needs. Never follow competitors' highly stylized versions. Not only will your product likely be mistaken for theirs, adding to their promotional impact rather than yours, but you'll probably hear from their attorneys as well.

• **Do your own layout.** Let your conscience be your guide.

• **Use a free-lance designer.** No matter where you are located, there are dozens of free-lance designers close by, eager to work with you if only they know of your needs. The easiest way to find them is to place a classified ad in the Help Wanted section of your local newspaper, for example:

> FREE-LANCE DESIGN & LAYOUTS for promotional flyers and brochures. Experience in (whatever you do) is helpful but not required. Call for appointment. (YOUR NAME/NUMBER)

Tell the designers who call what your project is, what your time frame is, and, if possible, your budget for design and camera-ready art. If you have no way of estimating design costs, interview a few of the designers first, and then arrive at a figure based on their quotations. Make sure to *schedule* the interviews. Tell the candidates they will have one hour: 20 minutes to present samples *with their charges for everything they show*; 20 minutes for you to present your project; and 20 minutes to ask any questions. An hour should be adequate with the likely candidates. For simpler projects, allow one week for quotations. For more complicated promotions, allow two weeks.

Cost Factors in Working with Outside Designers

Whether you work with a freelance designer, a design studio, or an advertising agency, the following factors will affect your costs:

1. **Time available to complete the project.** Begin by asking potential suppliers their normal time needs for a project such as yours. What you consider a rush project may be their regular schedule.

2. **Quality of manuscript.** Has your copy been given final approval, or will there be repeated copy changes that will require new layouts? Since *you* pay for each new version, find out how they are charged.

3. **Number of versions required.** Many clients want to see two or three (or more) designs from which to choose. For *major* projects, this is a recommended procedure, but get costs quoted in advance. For routine flyers or brochures, get a single design. It will be the one the designer considered the best of the several he or she attempted before deciding on the one you are shown.

4. **Degree of layout "finish."** This refers to how polished the layout must be. There are three generally accepted variations: "rough," "semicomprehensive," and "comprehensive." What these three terms mean varies with everyone who uses them. Have prospective designers show samples of each kind of finish and explain the difference in their costs.

5. **Preparation of camera-ready art.** Most designers prefer to do the camera-ready art. If your budget permits, let them do it. Not only will you get a better end product, but you will have a happier free-lancer, eager to work with you again in the future.

INSIGHT 11

In giving creative or production work to outside sources, have a budget and time line agreed upon in writing . . . and never change those instructions by "client's alterations" without knowing the time and dollar consequences. Ask your suppliers to recommend alternatives. There may be a better way!

TYPE, TYPOGRAPHY, TYPESETTING, AND DESKTOP PUBLISHING

A discussion of type, typography, typesetting, and desktop publishing, as applied to flyers and brochures, is no different from that applied to advertising beginning on page 20.

SUMMARY

If God did not make you into a designer, even such lesser creatures as co-workers and employers will probably notice. For true design, use a true designer. For routine layouts, use or modify an existing model when it is practical to do so. When it is not, get a professional.

NOTES ON THE FLYER/BROCHURE CHECKLIST

These notes are a supplement to the material presented in this chapter. They are not a self-contained substitute for the material.

1. Total of all estimated costs for outside suppliers and internal out-of-pocket charges. This is the figure given for budget approval in #2.
2. Analyses of estimates as fair costs to do the proposed project. Costs may be renegotiated before going to #3.

FLYER/BROCHURE CHECKLIST

Project title/description _____ Date _____
_____ Project # _____
_____ Checklist # _____
Overall Supervision by _____ Deadline_____
Budget _____ Start-up Date _____ Completion Date _____

	ASSIGNED TO	DUE	IN	MUST APPROVE	BY DATE	IN	INFO COPY ONLY	SEE ATTACHED
MANAGEMENT DECISIONS								
1. Quotations			☐			☐		☐
2. Budget Approval			☐			☐		☐
3. Project Approval			☐			☐		☐
CREATIVE DECISIONS								
4. Purpose			☐			☐		☐
5. Audience			☐			☐		☐
6. Overall Focus			☐			☐		☐
7. Headline Focus			☐			☐		☐
8. Subhead(s) Focus			☐			☐		☐
9. Desired Response			☐			☐		☐
10. Writers			☐			☐		☐
11. Designers			☐			☐		☐
12. Typesetter			☐			☐		☐
13. Artist			☐			☐		☐
14. Photographer			☐			☐		☐
15. Camera-Ready Art			☐			☐		☐
16. Film OK			☐			☐		☐
17. On-Press OK			☐			☐		
MECHANICAL DECISIONS								
18. Page Size			☐			☐		☐
19. Number of Pages			☐			☐		☐
20. Color(s)			☐			☐		☐
21. Paper Stock			☐			☐		☐
22. Film House			☐			☐		☐
23. Printer			☐			☐		☐
24. Distribution			☐			☐		☐
MECHANICAL CHECKS								
25. Logo OK			☐			☐		☐
26. Address(es) OK			☐			☐		☐
27. Phone(s) OK			☐			☐		☐
28. Editorial OK			☐			☐		☐
29. Legal OK			☐			☐		☐
30. Marketing OK			☐			☐		☐
31. Printed Samples			☐			☐		☐

3. Decision on whether the project is worth the costs, no matter how fair they may be. If approved, this is the figure placed into #2.
4. How the item advertised will be used and which use—if there are several—is the most important. Every other item on the checklist must keep the purpose in mind.
5. Are you trying to force different audiences' needs and interests into a single piece? You'll probably lose more in sales than you gain in promotional savings. Do this only if you have no way to reach each group individually.
6. What the message is to achieve as a whole. The general "feel" of the complete piece.
7. The one thing you hope will make the reader stop long enough to learn more about your message. Not the words—leave that to the writer in #10—but the thought!
8. Sell here if you can. But more important, get across the focus message from #6, even if the subheads are all that is read. If #7 and #8 are the 10-second outline that tells your story, you probably have a winner!
9. What you hope the reader will do after reading the piece. If the answer is "Nothing special," why are you producing the flyer or brochure?
10. For the actual words of the promotion. Specify if you want "roughs" or a best effort "finished copy" as first draft. Better yet, ask the writer to produce finished copy, but treat it as a draft. But make sure that you let the writer know you are doing this: Writers tend to get hysterical if it comes as a surprise, after they're done.
11. Will copy be written to fit the design, or will the design be based on the copy? If different persons do #10 and #11, make sure that they can work as a team.
12. For reasonably simple styling, turn to desktop equipment and set your own type. Give your designer samples of your in-house type faces, so the copy can be marked to match.
13–14. Determine who selects, orders, and supervises photography and art. In addition to know-how, it will probably take time.
15. With desktop typesetting, you'll probably create a camera-ready art "paste-up" on your computer. If you are new to desktop typesetting, find out how to make your work practical for your filmmaker to use.
16. You approve the film by checking its proof. Check everything against the instructions on the paste-up, and check the job as a whole. Better yet, if you work in an organization with film and printing specialists, turn to them for help. It's their job. Let them do it.
17. Go to the printer for on-press approval. Printers are more than happy to "hold the presses" and go to you—at hundreds, or thousands, of dollars for press and staff waiting time. But what will you do if you want more on-press changes? Wait in your office again . . . and again. *You* go to the printer!
18. Ask your printer if a small decrease or increase in the page size can make a large difference in savings. If the printer says yes, and the new size is

practical, tell the designers. It's easier for everyone if they create the design with the new size in mind.

19. Does the number of pages in the job precede the creative effort or follow it? Why?

20. While selecting colors is subjective, it's also an art. Accordingly, have it done by an artist if possible. Just make sure that the choices work for sales as well as aesthetics. Not too many of us can read white type inside a light blue background or light blue printed on white.

21. Where only a specific stock will do, use it. Where options are possible, check your printer or paper merchant for what they have on hand. For some projects, the use of two different papers may bring dramatic savings. Ask!

22. If someone other than your printer does the film, be sure that the filmmaker knows that printer's needs. Make certain that they speak *with each other*, not only through you.

23. Selection of a printer and film house is best done by an in-house specialist if one is available. If not, become one by asking your associates in other organizations. Visit their suppliers with them if possible. That's how I learned most of what I know . . . and that's how I continue to learn.

24. Determine what "distribution" means: How many flyers or brochures will be used for mailing, shipping to staff, warehousing, etc.? Requests and orders for your pieces may come from anywhere. But for approving and filling orders a single person must be in charge.

25–30. Someone has been assigned to check each of these items before anything may be printed. Make sure that they do check them and sign off *in writing*. In many organizations, the logo, address, and phone numbers are preprinted in a variety of styles and sizes and *must* be used from that art. It's an excellent safety measure, provided that every such piece is dated and thrown out when there is a change. Experience has shown that practically no one really reads logos. Make yourself the exception.

31. Printed samples generally get wide distribution. Set up a system that won't force you to reinvent the distribution list with every piece produced.

BULLETINS, INVITATIONS, AND INVITATIONAL BULLETINS

Bulletins and invitations are discussed together because, *for advertising and promotional purposes*, their uses are frequently the same. Bulletins are also used for two other purposes with which you may be involved as a creative resource:

1. Bulletins that must be posted, but that no one reads. State and federal offices, personnel and accounting departments, and senior management (among others) issue materials that *must* be placed on bulletin boards. However, unless the information displayed has real and immediate application to the audience for whom it was written, it is simply ignored. And if you ask how that audience knows it can, with impunity, ignore such bulletins, the answer is, They just do.

2. Bulletins that must be posted and that everyone reads. Often issued by the same sources as in item 1, they give information on newly issued or revised mechanical, safety, or material-handling instructions, on public or private requests for assistance, and many other things. The list is endless. In this case, the audience knows what it must *not* ignore.

The preceding two categories, insofar as they require promotional expertise, can be considered flyers and handled as such. Most often, there are models that can be followed and desktop publishing that can be used to produce the camera-ready art.

The Challenge of Optional Posting

A third category of bulletins is of much more concern to advertising and promotion than the foregoing two. This is the bulletin that no one is *required* to post, although everyone who sees it should *want* to . . . and want to read it, too! Usually distributed by mail, it has to jump the initial hurdle of the mail room or secretarial censor, pass its second barrier of managerial scrutiny, and, most difficult of all, crash through the stone wall of passer-by indifference. Since your bulletin competes for posting with all the others received at its destination, the challenge is formidable. Your likelihood of success is directly related to a slight modification of the first insight given in this book, which said, Keep it simple . . . keep it specific . . . and you're likely to keep solvent. Apropos of bulletins, the insight would urge:

INSIGHT 12

Keep it Simple . . . keep it Specific . . . keep it focused on Benefits . . . and you're likely to get posted.

Who Decides What's Posted?

Even if you're sure you know who controls the posting of bulletins at the places to which you mail them, call a dozen of these places at random and check them out. People will tell you almost anything if asked politely, so remember what you want to learn:

- What happens when a bulletin is addressed to an individual by name?
- What happens when a bulletin is addressed to a title (say, vice president of finance) or a job description (e.g., person in charge of posting financial training bulletins)?
- Does the size of the bulletin make any difference to its being posted? Which sizes are actually used?
- Does how the bulletin is received (e.g., in an envelope, as a self-mailer, hand delivered) make any difference?

- About what percent of bulletins received actually get posted?
- Why?

Perhaps the single most important insight this chapter has to offer is this:

INSIGHT 13

Take *nothing* for granted.

The steps in the posting process will tell you how to address and how to send your mailing, as well as what message, if any, to put on it. Usually, a purely informative message, such as that shown in Figure 2.3, is adequate.

The combination of the right name or title, together with an appropriate "teaser"—that is, an interest-focusing outside message—will very likely get your bulletin posted. Now all you have to do is to get it read and acted upon.

How to Get Your Bulletin Read

For posting on a bulletin board, get all the excitement and information on a single page. Don't force your audience to see the other side to understand your message. Create it as if you are producing a kind of billboard, not a brochure!

- **Make the benefit obvious.** In Figure 2.3, "additional training" that is of interest to employers may translate into better pay, job security, a quick chance to advance, or all three for employees. Just don't be too clever or cute. Save that for the section on invitations, which is discussed next.

SENDER'S IDENTIFICATION
ADDRESS

STAMP

*FREE
SEMINAR*

For Employees Needing
Additional Training
in Desktop Publishing

PLEASE POST

Figure 2.3 The same "teaser" copy and design can be used, as here, for an envelope or for a self-mailer.

- **Present the benefit in the largest, boldest, easiest-to-see type.** You want to capture the attention of the casual passerby. So make it easy to read from a reasonable distance.
- **Label everything.** Mention the time, date, place, cost, anything free, what to bring, what the reader will get to take home, how to participate, etc.
- **Sketch a simple map.** Do this for locations away from the home, the neighborhood, or work. Give distances from known locations (e.g., "approx. 3.2 miles west of Exit 89 on State Highway 17").
- **Give a destination phone number.** Do this for people, like myself, who get lost going around the block.

Make the information complete, but keep it as simple as possible. Bulletins often are read in passing. Make it possible to do just that. As a safety factor, place a small "Please post" request in one corner. Always tell people what you'd like them to do. Don't make them guess.

Bulletins for Fun Events

Fun events, from puppy beauty contests to the Fourth of July picnic and the Santa Claus parade, may seem exceptions to the rules for getting your bulletin posted on a bulletin board. They're not! It's the *event* that's the fun. The bulletin must still give every bit of information needed to make the event happen. It's certainly all right to lighten the mood, provided that you don't lose the message.

SUMMARY

- Don't create bulletins no one will post. Learn who decides what's posted and why . . . then make yours fit in.
- If it reads like a billboard, . . . if it looks like a billboard, . . . if it works like a billboard, . . . you've got a great bulletin!

INVITATIONS

All of us have received invitations to events that made us a captive audience for a sales pitch—from the chance to meet the candidate to hearing an ex-president try to sell time-sharing condominiums. Whether it's Tupperware in your living room or executive jets at the Paris Air Show, the party proves an effective sales tool, and the one thing every party has in common is the invitation.

This section focuses on inviting people together for *business* reasons—specifically, to inform them, persuade them, or sell them—and perhaps all three. It is not concerned with purely social or personal functions, although the suggested method of structuring an invitation is practical for both.

A Magical Word

"Invitation" is one of those magical words, like "free," "new," and "now," that many prospective and current customers accept uncritically. You are "invited" in newspaper ads, by radio and television commercials, on bulletin boards, and in the mail. All of these take advantage of the built-in association of "invitation" and "enjoyment." It is this expectation of a pleasant experience that makes invitations such an effective sales tool and one that could be more widely used. Invitations even let you bring together fierce competitors who have nothing but you in common. Think of fitting new golf shoes to shoe retailers at a golf outing, perhaps as a surprise before teeing off. Or what about a wine-tasting session for wine merchants as they sail along on a moonlight cruise. A bit of imaginative soft sell can do wonders.

A Word About Design

Invitations permit even the least creative among us to become designers. When the event itself has a festive feel, almost anything you develop in typography and layout should work, provided that you include the eight pieces of information from the model that follows. For a more formal feel, look through any printer's sample book and pick a model invitation to follow.

Structuring Your Invitation

The basic invitation has an eight-part structure that adapts to just about any occasion. While you may not want to use all eight parts, at least consider each one to make sure that it can be skipped. Let's produce an invitation to a demonstration of a solar-powered car to show how this works:

1	You are invited
2	to the first public presentation
3	of a truly functional
	Solar-Powered Automobile
4	Saturday, June 24,
	10:00 a.m.
5	Zip-Along Racetrack
	Route 13 at Suicide Drive
6	Champagne brunch
7	Free admission and drawing
	For free test drive,
8	R.S.V.P.

1. **You are invited.** . . . Invitations imply an enjoyable event. The very word "invitation" prepares the recipient to be well disposed towards what comes next, so make that word prominent and the very first thing that's seen.

2. **To the first public presentation.** . . . Generally the single most important part of the invitation. Use your utmost inventiveness to make attending the event a *benefit*. Translate attendance into what the attendees will carry away, and then state that as a promise. For instance:
   - The most exciting test drive of your life
   - Your chance to get frank answers from . . . about . . .
   - A full month of free . . .
   - Machine tools you will never have to sharpen
   - Get richer! Get smarter! Get ahead!

3. **Of a truly functional.** . . . Make the description of the event too valuable or appealing to ignore. If a large part of that appeal lies in a guest of honor or a presenter, let your invitation explain who the person is—even if everyone *should* know who he or she is. (For presentations, always use the best presenter rather than the person most knowledgeable on the subject if the two are different. But always have the latter there to help answer questions.)

4. **Saturday, June 24, 10:00 A.M.** . . . Before setting a date and time, make certain that no conflicting activity will keep your most important guests away. Confirm acceptances by phone just before the meeting date.

5. **Zip-Along Racetrack.** . . . Make the location a benefit if possible. Glamorize it (e.g., historic, beautiful, unique), and make it a place that is easy to get to. As with bulletins, provide a map for people who drive and a telephone number for those who may get lost.

6. **Champagne brunch.** . . . Mention food only if it's free or, for longer meetings and events, how it will be made available. Make it sound good, but don't overpromise. Let your surprises be pleasant ones.

7. **Free admission and drawing.** . . . State the charges if there are any. For professional meetings that have a fee, be specific about what is covered and what will be provided. Be generous with the things that cost little (e.g., writing materials and note pads, outlines of presentations, tote bags, door prizes). Be equally specific about what attendees will pay for themselves (e.g., travel and lodging, specific meals, gratuities). Be mindful of possible legal problems with overly generous benefits. For example, a $500 luxury weekend for a $50 fee may raise questions later. Be prepared to document legitimate business necessities and off-season rates, or have advance approval from the appropriate attorney.

8. **R.S.V.P.** Make accepting the invitation easy. Include a reply card (and envelope for privacy). Encourage responses and questions by phone. Have your reply form restate the major benefits, as well as any conditions of acceptance—especially those that favor the respondent. For example, a dieting program might read:

> ☐ YES! I want to get ready for fat-free gourmet cooking by attending a FREE Oil-No-More hands-on demonstration on Monday, November 9, from 2:00 to 4:00 P.M. at the Ritzy Hotel, Suite 1000. I understand that all cooking materials will be provided without charge and that I must respond before November 1 to attend.

That's one I wouldn't miss for the world, and I'm skinny as a rail!

SUMMARY

- An invitation promises something special. Keep that promise!
- In business invitations, tell those who are invited more than enough to get them to come. Your competitors, especially at conventions and trade shows, may be trying to get them, too.
- Follow up on acceptances. Confirm them by phone just before the event to let people know you *really* want them there. *Expect* about 20% fewer than accept, . . . but *prepare* for 10% more.
- The how-to of actually giving a professional party is covered in Chapter 5. Don't miss it!

NOTES ON THE INVITATION/INVITATIONAL BULLETIN CHECKLIST

These notes are a supplement to the material presented in this chapter. They are not a self-contained substitute for that material. This checklist covers the creation, printing, and mailing of invitations. It does not concern itself with who is invited or why, except insofar as that information (#6–7) must be reflected in the invitation.

1. Invitations generally take up only a small portion of an event's total cost. Has that complete budget been approved, and does it include the number of invitations you plan to use (#14)? If either answer is "no," get written approval (#3) before you continue.
2. Allow a week to get cost quotations and whatever time is required for their approval. On budgeted projects, these quotations should not have to go back to management for another round.
3. If the budget as a whole has not been approved, can you get approval on the invitation portion? Give the decision makers absolute deadlines beyond which invitations are useless.
4. Arrangements for speakers or other attractions or entertainment must

INVITATION/INVITATIONAL BULLETIN CHECKLIST

Project title/description _____   Date _____

_____   Project # _____

_____   Checklist # _____

Overall Supervision by _____   Deadline _____

Budget _____ Start-up Date _____   Completion Date _____

MANAGEMENT DECISIONS	ASSIGNED TO	DUE	IN	MUST APPROVE	BY DATE	IN	INFO COPY ONLY	SEE ATTACHED
1. Invitation Event OK	____	__	☐	____	__	☐	____	☐
2. Quotation	____	__	☐	____	__	☐	____	☐
3. Budget	____	__	☐	____	__	☐	____	☐
4. Speaker(s)	____	__	☐	____	__	☐	____	☐
5. Free/Charge	____	__	☐	____	__	☐	____	☐

CREATIVE DECISIONS

	ASSIGNED TO	DUE	IN	MUST APPROVE	BY DATE	IN	INFO COPY ONLY	SEE ATTACHED
6. Audience	____	__	☐	____	__	☐	____	☐
7. Focus	____	__	☐	____	__	☐	____	☐
8. Copy	____	__	☐	____	__	☐	____	☐
9. Design	____	__	☐	____	__	☐	____	☐
10. Key Line	____	__	☐	____	__	☐	____	☐
11. Key Line OK	____	__	☐	____	__	☐	____	☐
12. Film OK	____	__	☐	____	__	☐	____	☐
13. Printing OK	____	__	☐	____	__	☐	____	☐

MECHANICAL DECISIONS

	ASSIGNED TO	DUE	IN	MUST APPROVE	BY DATE	IN	INFO COPY ONLY	SEE ATTACHED
14. Quantity	____	__	☐	____	__	☐	____	☐
15. Mailing List	____	__	☐	____	__	☐	____	☐
16. Telephone List	____	__	☐	____	__	☐	____	☐
17. Self Mailer	____	__	☐	____	__	☐	____	☐
18. Envelope Mailer	____	__	☐	____	__	☐	____	☐
19. Components	____	__	☐	____	__	☐	____	☐
20. Size(s)	____	__	☐	____	__	☐	____	☐
21. Stock	____	__	☐	____	__	☐	____	☐
22. Stock Colors	____	__	☐	____	__	☐	____	☐
23. Printing Colors	____	__	☐	____	__	☐	____	☐
24. Mail Destination Date	____	__	☐	____	__	☐	____	☐
25. Mail Replies Due	____	__	☐	____	__	☐	____	☐
26. Phone Replies Due	____	__	☐	____	__	☐	____	☐
27. Class of Mail	____	__	☐	____	__	☐	____	☐
28. Film House	____	__	☐	____	__	☐	____	☐
29. Printer	____	__	☐	____	__	☐	____	☐
30. Mailing Service	____	__	☐	____	__	☐	____	☐
31. Records/Reports	____	__	☐	____	__	☐	____	☐
_____	____	__	☐	____	__	☐	____	☐

generally be made far in advance of an event. Who decides? Who follows up? What's the last possible moment for including changes in plans.

5. What's free, and what costs, if any, will be charged to the participants?

6–7. Identify the audience to whom you are mailing the invitation and the specific focus of the invitation—the benefits, to the audience, of attending.

8–9. Identify the writer and designer of the invitation. Who follows whom? Who must approve the copy? When must both be done?

10. Will there be a paste-up or simply a keyline produced by the typesetter or desktop publishing system?

11. Keyline approval is the last chance to make changes before the production of film. Give those who must see the actual keyline an additional copy for their notes and comments. Don't let them write on the original art!

12. Approval of film proofs is a combined design and advertising function, even when both are carried out by the same person. Design makes sure that the work has the quality specified on the original art. Advertising makes sure that *everything* that was on the original is on the proof and that the designer's instructions still make sense when seen in print. Wear one hat at a time, but be sure that both do get worn.

13. For routine jobs, most printers can be left to their own devices. For large, complicated, or otherwise critical projects, be at the printer to give on-press approval. You'll be so bored that it will be the perfect time to read the entire copy one more time . . . and actually call all the telephone numbers and check on the addresses. About 10% of the time, you'll be very glad you did!

14. The quantity is frequently more than the mailing list. Ask about nonmail distribution to staff and field workers and for last-minute follow-up.

15. Who supplies the list, contacts the sources on the list, and checks to make sure that it is reasonably accurate? When using outside lists, responses only, not the list as a whole, become your property for future use.

16. Will you phone to issue invitations or as a reminder to those who accept? For initial invitations, what is involved in getting the phone numbers and in getting through to those you call? Test by actually trying to call a dozen potential guests before you commit yourself to getting results.

17–18. If you are using a self-mailer, skip #18 and #19. If you are using an envelope, check with suppliers of envelopes regarding standard sizes and costs. It's seldom economical to customize envelopes for fewer than 10,000. Before you get *too* creative, check with the post office to make sure they'll accept the mail as designed. They almost always say yes, but check.

19. Components include the invitation plus any other elements, such as RSVPs and reply envelope. Don't be afraid to load up the invitation. If travel is involved, add a map. If the speaker is special, tell why. If the event is extraordinary, tell how. Use an invitation-size sheet for each of those items, and watch attendance soar!

20. Invitation sizes are determined by the envelope. If the quantity is large

enough that you can use a mailing service or letter shop, check about the practicality of inserting the invitations into the envelopes by machine. Do this before *anything*, including the mailing list and how it will be addressed, is ordered.

21–22. Not every paper stock comes in every color, especially when you want to match or contrast an envelope. But you can often print the stock into the color you want. It costs practically nothing extra when that color is a tint of a darker ink used on the same page. Ask your film house and printer. You may be pleasantly surprised.

23. Use any color paper and ink you wish—as long as the message can be read. Printed in light pink and blue, your project may well die before the very eyes of those too nearsighted to see it.

24. The mail destination date should be determined by considering the audience to whom you are mailing the invitations. How booked up do they get for the time involved? How willing are they to commit their time far in advance? If you're not sure and can't easily find out, telephone a few invitees and ask. They will thank you for your concern!

25–26. When *must* you have replies to permit final planning for the event? Telephone (#16) key prospects a few days before the deadline to invite them or to confirm their acceptance. There's nothing like an actual human voice to generate response.

27. Most invitations are sent by first-class mail. Use a stamp or a printed permit that looks like a meter. For larger mailings, don't prestamp the RSVP envelope. But just to play safe, test your level of response by adding a stamp to every tenth reply envelope. Let results guide future invitations.

28. For routine mailing pieces, your printer may wish to supply the film. Whether you agree or use a separate film house, the proofing process (#12) is the same and is a production responsibility rather than an advertising decision. Where the two jobs are handled separately, thank those involved, and let them do their job.

29. Printing is also a production function. For major projects, insist on being kept informed. For others, let those doing the job do it without your help. If you are a printing novice, ask them to help you learn. Don't pretend to expertise you don't have: You do not have to know how to fix something to insist on its being done right.

30. Letter Shops work on schedules, too. Don't surprise them with projects out of the blue, or you may be blue indeed when you get the bill. Usually, anything can be done if you are willing to spend the money. Just remember . . . it is *your* money. Plan, stay on schedule, and save.

31. What records must be kept? By whom? What analyses of results done? What reports made and to whom?

3 | Direct Mail and Data-Based Direct Marketing

DIRECT MAIL

This chapter has three goals:

1. To help you create your own direct response mailings.
2. To guide you in the supervision of mailings done by staff or outside experts.
3. To give you the basic rules and cautions for doing both.

Because of its frequent denunciation as "junk mail," this chapter begins with a brief history and defense of direct mail selling. It then continues with some basic rules and cautions about what's likely to work—and what isn't—in selling by mail. The chapter concludes with specific guidance on how to create a direct mail promotion—always keeping in mind those basic rules and cautions. Four of these will be absolutely critical to your success:

1. The single most important factor in selling by mail is the list.
2. Test whenever possible.
3. Believe the numbers.
4. Know the value of a customer, not just of the order.

Help Abounds

Practically every major city in the United States has a direct marketing association that is able and eager to help you. Check the Yellow Pages. If you are unable to locate the association by this means, contact the Direct Marketing Association, Inc., Dept. DM Clubs, *Association Networks*, 11 West 42nd Street, New York, NY 10036-8096. Ask for the nearest club, and enclose a stamped, self-addressed envelope. Easier yet, call them at 212-768-7277. Then join your local association. They will help you, even if you're not a member, but the continuing contacts alone are worth the price of admission.

In addition, there is one indispensable magazine you must read: *Direct Marketing*, published by Hoke Communications. Call the company toll free at 800-229-6700. In New York, call 516-746-6700. Subscribe. Lots of additional magazines exist. All are good and some are even free.

How the Term "Junk Mail" Came About

In the 1930s and 1940s, a number of syndicated newspaper columnists had a readership and following matched in devotion only by a later generation's rock stars and anchor persons. One of those columnists—I believe it was Westbrook Pegler—became infuriated when his very young daughter somehow was placed on a mailing list of purveyors of suggestive undergarments and nightwear. In his rage, he wrote several columns damning what he called "junk mail."

The story might have ended right there, except for Pegler's syndication. The publishers of several of the newspapers that carried his column greeted the term with absolute delight. They recognized it as the ammunition they had prayed for in battling an opponent that had just become a meaningful competitor for advertising revenue—the growing direct mail industry. Editorials denouncing junk mail appeared with increasing frequency, shedding tears for an overworked postal staff—which they forgot to mention also carried their own publications at an even lower rate.

Their attack continues to this day and has gone largely unchallenged in public. Of the perhaps 10 letters to the Editor I write each year answering print media and talk show attacks upon direct mail, not one has ever been published. And my experience is typical of the industry as a whole. The only thing direct response has going for it in this battle is a history of success. Somehow, calling it "junk" has not been able to erase that fact from its users' business plans.

TO CREATE OR SUPERVISE: WHEN TO DO EACH

Of course, *any* project may be supervised rather than self-produced, depending on the time, budget, and talent available for it. Since I have no skill for doing layouts and designs, I have always employed others for those tasks, no matter how "simple" the project or how much time was available. Along the way, I've learned some basic rules any design should follow:

- Show and tell the readers what you are selling. If what you say and picture isn't absolutely clear, they won't guess. They won't buy!
- Use type that's easy to read. The less sans serif the easier it will be to read.
- Keep it simple. The fancier the design, the more costly it will be to print it well.

These and other such "rules" are found throughout this chapter. Use them when you do the job yourself. But even more important, insist upon them when you turn work over to others. Do this *before they begin*, as part of your directions, not as expensive, time-consuming "client's alterations" after they've completed initial copy and design. Make them part of your own checklist if they're not already included in the ones presented here.

What You *Must Not* Do Yourself

Two kinds of mailings must be created by direct mail professionals and should never be attempted as do-it-yourself "gifted amateur" projects:

1. A project, no matter how seemingly simple, that determines the survival of your business. (Of course you'll go to a specialist for a heart transplant, but will you try your own simple appendectomy?)
2. True direct mail "packages," such as the annual multi-component *Reader's Digest* sweepstakes, giant "bedsheet" folded and refolded self-mailers, pop-up or other multidimensional projects. On anything that will cost over $15,000, allow 20% for a good free-lancer, and you'll probably be ahead in dollars and results. Good management includes learning to recognize the difference between getting something done exactly as you would do it yourself and having it done competently in some other way.

Doing Your Own Mailings

Help with creating your own mailings begins on page 71, but don't go there yet. The basics of lists, testing, and numbers that you must know for success hold true, no matter who does the mailing or what it costs. The next few pages explain them and how to apply them to what you write, design, and mail.

SUMMARY

- Selling by mail is sales, not advertising. Budget accordingly.
- If you can't average at least $20 per response, you probably can't do mailings and stay in business.
- If you can't charge *four times* the cost of manufacturing or service time, don't sell by mail.
- When *everything* hinges on a successful mailing, use a professional. If everything hinges on a single, untested mailing, reconsider your options. What if the mailing doesn't work?

MAILING LISTS

The single most important factor in selling by mail is the mailing list. The art and science of selecting lists lie in our ability to match the recipient with the offer—to mail only to those most likely to buy. No matter what we are selling—no matter how appealing the offer—if the recipient is not in the market for our products, nothing else matters. We're not going to sell dog food to cat fanciers; we're not going to sell chain saws to apartment-dwelling couch potatoes.

There's no better prospect than a satisfied customer. The most responsive mailing list is almost always made up of your present customers and clients, provided that such a list exists and that they have been well served in the past. That is why so many businesses use such ingenuity to gain your name and address when you pay by cash. You're their best prospect for mail order, too.

People with like life-styles tend to purchase alike. The key to selling is to determine which life-styles match what you are offering. There are thousands of mailing lists available through list companies and brokers. (Chicago's business-to-business Yellow Pages give 96 such companies.) The more we know about the meaningful characteristics of our current customers or clients, the easier it will be to find likely prospects by matching their customer profiles to ours. What's "meaningful" may not be a matter of common sense, so discuss it with a mailing list professional. Then check the advice you get in a test mailing. When, however, even your customer list *seems* to contain little useful information, some basic research is probably in order:

- For consumer lists, services exist that can match addresses with socioeconomic census data. Use the *n*th-name system of every 20th, 50th, or 500th name, depending on the size of your list, for a test mailing. You'll get a wealth of information on these people's life-styles.
- For business and professional lists, existing directories can tell you everything you need to know—from an individual's specialization, age, income, family, and automobiles owned to a corporation's history, profits, officers, and credit rating. If a certain piece of information seems pertinent, it's there for the matching.
- A mailing list specialist can help you analyze your lists. *Before* you request such help, get firm, written cost quotations and current references, and check them out.

For New Businesses

When your business is new, without customers or clients, there are four possibilities regarding mailing lists:

1. Lists exist to fill your needs. Your market is so well defined that available lists are all you need to get started.
2. Your market is hidden within a larger audience for which there are lists.
3. Lists exist, but they are not available to you.
4. No known list exists that will fill your needs.

Let's consider each of these in more detail.

Lists That Fit. With lists that fit, your most important decision may seem to be whether to use the list as a whole or to start in with a test. But before you do either of these, check on the percentage of previous *mail order buyers* in that list, no matter what they have bought or what you are selling. The propaganda about junk mail has worked, and millions of consumers *who are on lists* will not buy by mail! Have the sources of the list give you those proven direct mail buyers only. (Forced subscriptions to association magazines and newsletters don't count.) It's almost always easier to sell such buyers a second time than to sell nonbuyers the first. If no list of previous buyers exists—and you feel that you must sell by mail—test!

Lists That Hide. Let's assume that you have a special racket for overweight, left-handed tennis players, but no mailing list exists for such individuals. A broader "umbrella" list of all tennis players, however, is available. Should you try to sell your submarket within it?

The answer involves the same analysis you should do before any other mailing. Do as little blind guessing as possible. Work with what you know or can learn—for instance, the percentage of left-handers in the general population and the degree of overweight seen at local tennis courts and clubs. While this type of "knowing" is far from certain, it's better than sheer guesswork, and it lets you go to the next step: the calculation of testing costs and the application of test results as a predictor of complete mailings. A number of easy-to-use formulas exist for this purpose (see page 88.)

Lists That Remain Private. Many mailing lists are so valuable to their owners that they are never made available to anyone else. This is especially true of business customers and prospects. General consumer lists tend to be less jealously guarded, for two reasons:

1. Increased use of a mailing list tends to build a larger universe of frequent buyers. As different kinds of products and services are offered, more recipients get into the habit of ordering by mail, making the list increasingly valuable as a source of proven mail order buyers.
2. For many owners of a list, the income from renting the list is a major factor in their profitability. Suppose a list of 200,000 names generates rental revenues of $25 per thousand 15 times a year. How much of the product would have to be sold to produce the same number of dollars in net income!

The fact that some lists are not generally available tells you that some people have been able to build them for themselves. Perhaps you can do it too.

When No List Exists. Even when no list exists for a particular market, it's probable that the names are there if only you can find a way to get at them. It is possible that no one else has previously wanted just those names badly enough to create a list. But it's more likely that gathering the list would have been too difficult or costly. When no list exists, think very hard about making direct mail the key to your selling effort.

Things to Know About Using Lists

Eliminate Duplicate Mailings Where Practical. When using more than one list, the possibility of duplicate mailings becomes increasingly likely. Through a computerized system called Merge/Purge, most of this duplication can be eliminated. But before deciding to use this program, discuss the *process and costs* with both a mailing list expert and a mailing service. Cost alone may not be the key factor: Recipients may become so annoyed at receiving multiple copies of the same thing that they will consider it junk mail and pay no attention to it. Testing here, as elsewhere, will be the best way to discover what, if any, increase in response is achieved—at what cost—by Merge/Purge.

Some Legal Limitations on the Use of Mailing Lists. When using a list other than your own, the rental agreement almost always calls for *one-time mailing use only*. You may *not* copy the list or any part of it, or use it for any other purpose, unless agreed to, in writing, by the owner of the list. Rental lists are "seeded," that is, they include a few names specifically added to discover such unauthorized use.

Any response to your mailing, however, whether it is an order, an inquiry, the acceptance of a premium, or anything else, makes the respondent's name yours to use in the future. With many mailings, you justify their cost by gaining repeat customers, rather than selling a product or service one time.

Customer or One-Time Buyer. Know what you need to gain from mailing—one-time sales or long-term customers—and evaluate the results accordingly. But beware of paying for customers and then giving them a product or service that reduces them to one-time buyers, or budgeting for customers while having nothing more to sell. Direct response may be the one way of doing business where you *can* sometimes lose a little bit on each sale and then make it up in volume—but only if you also know how to play *that* tune.

SUMMARY

- Nothing else is as important as your mailing list.
- Your best prospect is a satisfied customer.
- Your best noncustomer prospects are selected from previous mail order buyers, no matter what they bought.
- Predetermine what *you* are buying—customers or one-time sales, or both—and what each is worth.
- Lists abound. They are often very price competitive. Check them out.

THE ABSOLUTE NECESSITY FOR TESTING

In direct mail, or any other kind of direct response advertising, the likelihood of getting things just right and most cost effective on the very first try is quite small. We can, of course, and often do produce profitable mailings on just one try. But *most* cost effective is most often the result of testing, a process that never stops in many direct mail organizations.

INSIGHT 14

Before performing any test, decide which category will determine the outcome. Will it be percentage of response? Average order? Number of orders?[1] Cost per response? Quality of response? Something else? Be sure to record and analyze each of these. Just because we don't get the answer we want doesn't mean that another answer isn't better.

In testing, the version ("package") that does best is called the control. Everything thereafter is controlled by (evaluated against) this package. Most of us tend to use "control" synonymously with "success." Its actual meaning is "the best results *thus far*," which are subject to change with every mailing.

A Word of Caution: When a test shows an extraordinary improvement over the existing control, do a retest with a larger portion of your list if possible. Don't hesitate to change to a package that works better. Believe the numbers; just make sure that they aren't a one time fluke.

Test One Thing Only

Changing one or more factors in our mailings may give us a better response, but it may also have no effect or decrease returns. Even an increased response may have to be balanced against higher mailing costs, and lower costs may have to be balanced against fewer sales. It is quite common to test totally different mailing packages against each other—one or more quite expensive and the others somewhat plainer and less costly. But when testing to see whether *a specific package* can be made more effective, *change only one thing if you wish to understand the results*.

Structuring a Test

Suppose that you have a reasonably successful package printed in full color (four colors) and offering a specific product at a specified price. You wish to find out if any of the following will be more cost effective:

- Changing the offer.
- Changing the price.
- Changing to a less costly mailing package.

Since it takes a mailing of $5,000^2$ pieces to generate fairly predictable results, you will need 12 different mailings totaling 60,000 pieces for your test. The reason we

---

[1] One of my mailings once produced just a single order from 6,000 prospects. It totalled $500,000, from the A&P supermarket chain. Our client did not object to the paucity of responses.

[2] Many direct mail experts are convinced that it takes at least 10,000 names, especially for business mailings, when using more than one list and when duplicates are eliminated by merge/purge. It is the net quantity that counts—what comes out, not what goes in!

need so many, as Table 3.1 shows, is that we are testing one specific factor in each mailing, yet testing that one factor against all the other 11:

- Each of the prices is tested against all combinations of offers and colors.
- Each of the color arrangements is tested against all combinations of offers and prices.
- Each offer is tested against all combinations of colors and prices.

Should one of the offers be tested at random—for instance, the four-color offer A at $15.95 against the two-color offer B at $22.50, one will probably sell better than the other. But you have no way of knowing why—whether it was the offer or the price or the color that was responsible for the increased sales. Nor will you know which factor(s) you might change for even better results. You seem to need to perform all 12 tests to get your answer! But don't give up on testing as being too complicated and costly. Help is on the way immediately after the next paragraph.

When to Stop Testing

If you go back to Table 3.1, you'll see that adding one more price will add 20,000 units for four more packages. Testing envelopes against self-mailers, or first-class postage against third-class postage, however, will double the number of units needed—from 60,000 to 120,000. We'll soon run out of names or money or both before we run out of tests, so let's take another look at testing.

Five Ways to Approach Testing

1. **Test everything.** Test your product or service in exactly the way that was described in the last few pages. It's what the largest, most successful mailers do.

2. **Decide what might really make a difference, and test just that.** For instance, of the 12 options in Table 3.1, test only the four-color offers A and B at $15.95. If one is successful, or close to successful, test the other two prices for the same package.

Table 3.1   Why a Three-Factor Test Requires 12 Mailings

Type of Offer	Test Package	Test Price and Number of Pieces		
		$12.95	$15.95	$22.50
Offer A	4-color	5,000	5,000	5,000
Offer A	2-color	5,000	5,000	5,000
Offer B	4-color	5,000	5,000	5,000
Offer B	2-color	5,000	5,000	5,000

Now test what has become your control against that same package in two colors. The result is that you've mailed 5 sets rather than 12. In other words you've mailed 35,000 fewer pieces and saved about $6,000 just in postage. For mailings where four colors might be perceived as an extravagance—to nonprofit organizations, charities, hospitals, etc.—test two colors or one color first. But do try four colors also. Don't assume; test the product.

3. Test fewer than 5,000 names. When you *really* need to test how a large number of changes will influence results, and restrictions on budget, time, or names make testing 5,000 names impossible, test 2,000 names instead. Then take the top two or three results, and do a "real" test of 5,000 each. If you can possibly avoid it, don't go from a 2,000-name test to a "rollout"—a mailing of a much larger portion of your list or a complete mailing of the entire list. If you do not have time for a real test and results are important, either don't mail, or use a professional—and pray!

4. Use telemarketing to test before you mail. If your primary concern is your offer or price, give serious consideration to a telemarketing premailing test. Properly structured, it's fast, accurate, and the way to find out why someone doesn't buy, as well as why they do. (See Chapter 8 for a more detailed discussion of telemarketing for premail testing.)

5. Use print media to test before you mail. Find print media—magazines, newspapers, and newsletters—that go to the audience you want to reach. Check with each one to learn whether it accepts preprinted advertisements on postcard-weight stock. You want the best results from your test, and a reply card almost always increases response. That card, in combination with a toll-free number, should give you the best results. If card stock is not acceptable, but regular paper inserts are, consider an order form similar to what is used in most catalogs, preaddressed and, *if publication policy permits*, postage free.

How to Prepare Your Print Media Test. Let's use the 12 variables shown in Table 3.1. Do the following:

- Prepare each test as an $8\frac{1}{2}'' \times 11''$ insert with all of the four-color or all of the two-color offers printed together. If you are printing on postcard-weight stock, for easy removal, have the card edges perforated.
- After printing, have the 12 versions separated by your printer or bindery and collated sequentially, that is, into the order 1, 2, 3, 4, . . . ,12. This gives you random, valid testing. What you must not permit is using all the #1's first, then all the #2's, etc.

Testing Just Two Variables. If only two variables are to be tested, discuss, with each publication, the practicality and cost of running an "A/B split" advertisement with a reply card. (See page 26.) This format gives statistically valid results.

INSIGHT 15

Do not expect the percentage of response from a print media test that you would get from direct mail. If print gives you a clear winner and time and budget permit, test the winner in the mail against the two runners-up. Otherwise, use only the winner for the complete mailing. The least that you want to learn is the reliability of your print media testing.

A word of warning: Many professional publications build their circulation by sending multiple copies to the same destination, although not often to the same person. Persons within the same organization will thus get different versions of your offer! If they compare and contact you about the differences, *tell them you are running a test*. They'll understand.

INSIGHT 16

Various laws permit you to test different offers in the same mailing or advertisement. Check with the post office concerning current restrictions—if there are any—before testing. *It is good business practice to fill all test responses at the lowest price being tested, no matter what the final price turns out to be.* If that should be one of the higher prices, write the respondents who purchased with the lower prices in mind a thank-you note, and mention the price at which you will fill their orders in the future. If a lower price wins, congratulate those who purchased with the higher prices in mind on recognizing value, explaining that the large volume of orders now permits a cost saving . . . *and would they like to order some more at the unexpected saving!*

Code Everything!

Create a letter or number code for every variation in response. You want to know where, when, and in what quantity it was used. Change the code for *every* variation, including tests and "rollouts," to check on the influence of mailing dates. It is a critical part of evaluating direct response success. Analyze all results (professionals call this *back-end analysis*), and get professional guidance if you are not sure how to do this.

SUMMARY

- Rented lists permit one-time use only, but responses are yours . . . forever.
- Test! Wouldn't you rather be 98% sure *before* you mail?
- Tests are expensive. Use them for what's really likely to make a difference.

- For responses to have predictive power, limit each test to one thing only.
- Believe the numbers, but have an adequate statistical universe on which to base your faith.

CREATING YOUR OWN MAILINGS: THE LETTER

Chapter 2 covered the creation of the flyers or brochures we might include in our mailings. In Chapter 3 we will concentrate on letters. Just as the list is the most important external factor in determining whether direct mail will be successful, the letter is almost always the most important internal element within the mailing itself. In my experience, which ranges from self-mailers to catalogs to elaborate multi-component mail "packages," *every* test has shown the cost effectiveness of including a letter. Most of the letter/nonletter tests I've been involved in were used to convince clients who were new to direct response selling. But the most convincing test of all was caused by an accident. It involved a simple, one-paragraph memorandum something like that shown in Figure 3.1.

A mailing prepared for Rand McNally offered, in the largest type that would fit on the envelope and cover of our brochure, the biggest discount that company had ever offered on its children's books. The mailing, to those on the publisher's regular customer and prospective customer list, was a resounding flop. Practically no one ordered. Then the mailing service called. Its staff had just discovered the 5,000 letters that were supposed to be mailed and realized that the mailing had gone out without them! Would we permit them to duplicate the mailing at their expense, but this time including the memo? Rand McNally agreed. The result was as dramatic a success as the incomplete predecessor had been a failure.

SUMMARY

- Letters work!
- Practically everyone likes to get mail.
- Practically everyone looks at the letter first. Take advantage of that fact.

Writing the Direct Mail Letter

Practically anyone can write a good sales letter, provided that they follow the same two-step approach used by most professionals:

1. Decide what you want the recipient to do.
2. Decide what's most likely to get the recipient to do it.

The writing itself is often the easiest part. Where most of us go wrong is that we try so hard to make our letters sound businesslike and professional, that they seem

From the Desk of Bennet B. Harvey

Dear Buyer:

The enclosed brochure offers the biggest single discounts we have ever been able to give you on our children's books. Don't pass up this extraordinary profit opportunity. It expires on September 1st and may never come again.

Bennet B. Harvey
Vice President

Figure 3.1 Testing has repeatedly shown the effectiveness of including a letter in mailings. Above is a simple one-paragraph model letter.

forced and no longer believable. So if you're not yet a direct mail pro, don't write to the person who will actually get the letter. Rather, write to a friend, real or imaginary, who knows *just a little bit less* about the subject than your real audience. The friendship will provide the warmth in tone. The little bit less will keep you from leaving out anything important. Often, we're so afraid of insulting our recipients' intelligence that we leave out those "obvious" facts which show that we know what we're talking about!

The Two-List Approach to Letters

I *always* start out with two short lists that I keep pinned on the wall, in front of my eyes.

List One

- What, exactly, I want the recipient to do.
- How, exactly, the recipient is to do it.
- How, exactly, I will fulfill my end of the deal, especially if the mailing is more of a success than I expect.

Based on a consideration of these three points, you may need to restructure your response to the mailing, especially as telemarketing becomes more important to the sales effort. And in case you can't believe that success can be more of a problem than failure, be warned by the following "success story."

My own worst direct mail "disaster" involved a letter that promised to "give you the world for 14 minutes of your time." It also promised to deliver the world—a handsome desk-size globe—through a personal visit from a sales representative. The sales manager, who had no faith in premium-induced response, agreed to the mailing only to humor me. There were 14 company reps and 28,000 names on the mailing list. There was a 31% response. That meant more than 8,600 visits from reps and a like number of globes to be given away! It was our first mailing for that client and the last one where we had to plead for permission to test for results.

List Two

- The benefits and features used to create the brochure to be used in the mailing. If no such list exists, because there is no brochure or because you don't plan to use one, see page 43 and create that list now.
- The three most important benefits from the list. For each of them, find at least three reasons why that specific benefit is more important than the other two.
- A comparison of the benefits, with their supporting reasons, together with a statement of the combination that offers the most *for the audience to whom you are writing the letter*. If you can't decide which combination is best, it may not make any difference, but more likely, you need to learn more about your audience and how *it* benefits from what you are trying to sell.

You now have *the* benefit about which you tell the recipients and at least three reasons they should act to get that benefit *now*. With both of the aforementioned lists at hand, you are ready to write (or supervise the writing of) your letter.

The Three "Tells"

In writing your letter, do not try to emulate the pros, with their cascading cornucopias of compelling reasons for complying with your offer. Keep it simple. Use the "what, why, how" technique:

> What: *Tell* your audience *what* you want it to do, but translated into a benefit *for each one of them*, not for you.
> Why: *Tell* them *why* they should do it, using the reasons you found to be the strongest *for them*.
> How: *Tell* them *how* to do it—*How* easy, *how* fast, *how* safe, and *how* resounding the benefit is if they act *now*.

The sample letters shown in Figures 3.2 and 3.4 can serve as models for applying this technique. They were written not for this book, but to help solve a very real business problem faced by one of my clients. Some background information is needed to understand the approach.

Background. For two decades, the Lectro-Stik hand waxer grew in annual unit sales. Throughout this time, the manufacturer had sold through retail outlets only. Now, for the first time, unit sales did not exceed the previous year's sales for the same period. The decline could not be attributed to competition, because, although a number of competitors had recently appeared on the scene, their much higher retail price and less sophisticated electronics were felt to keep them out of contention.

Assignment. My assignment was to discover the reason for the decline in sales, and return Lectro-Stik to its previous growth pattern.

Approach. It took me four weeks to come up with the plan you have probably already formed just from reading the background. It took another month to convince Lectro-Stik to act on the suggested approach—to *increase* the price, thereby giving retailers the same high profit they were getting from selling the competitors' models. At the old price, there was no *economic* advantage to the retailer in recommending Lectro-Stik over the other brands and every economic interest in switching the customer to someone else. My plan was as follows:

- **The strategy.** Give retailers and wholesalers an economic reason to push aside the competition and recommend Lectro-Stik.
- **The tactic.** Let them stock up at the current lower $45 cost and then sell at the new $59 price, which basically matches the competition. The $14 difference between the old and the new price is theirs . . . an unexpected profit bonanza—if they act *now!*

3721 BROADWAY • CHICAGO, ILLINOIS 60613
PHONE: (312) 528-8860   FAX: (312) 528-2874

(Date)

SPECIAL "EARLY BIRD" NOTICE[1]

Make $14 more on every Lectro-Stik Waxer[1]
—$1 more on every box of wax—[1]
you order now to sell after September 1st![2]

Dear Lectro-Stik Dealer:[3]

• The list price of the Lectro-Stik Hand Waxer will increase from $45
to $59 on September 1[4]..our first price increase in eight years.

• The price of our 10 oz. box of wax will go up proportionately, from
$3.50 to $4.50.[4]

• Your generous discount percentage will remain the same with slight
rounding of prices.[5]

HOW TO MAKE A MINT![6]
ORDER WAXER AND WAX NOW, AT THEIR OLD PRICE,
FOR DELIVERY BEFORE SEPTEMBER 1. THEN, AFTER
THE 1st, SELL THEM FOR $59 AND $4.50. **YOU KEEP THE
DIFFERENCE** OF $14 PER WAXER AND $1 FOR WAX!

Call, write, or FAX your order now as part of your long-range planning.
We will continue to sell through our dealer network[7]..so STOCK UP
FOR PROFITS and order soon!

Cordially yours,

Bill Fisher

Figure 3.2 Letter to customers and prospects already familiar with the waxer.

- **The test.** Since the total mailing was less than 5,000, Lectro-Stik tested 5 percent of the list with a simple "early bird notice" letter. The purpose was not to test the actual mailing, which had not yet been completed, but to test the appeal of the offer *to potential buyers who were familiar with the waxer.* The final mailing was designed to go to a much broader list requiring a lengthier explanation of the product.

The test was a success, as was the mailing two months later. The following notes explain why the letters were written as they were. Figure 3.3 shows the envelope in which both letters were mailed.

Notes on the "Early Bird" Notice (Figure 3.2)

1. Echoes the message on the envelope.
2. Another echo and the first explanation of "long-range planning."
3. The test went to current dealers only.
4. The first explanation of the new profits.
5. Reassurance that profits will continue into the future.
6. A restatement, for the third time, of windfall profit possibilities . . . explicitly on the envelope and in points 1 and 6, implicitly in point 4.

INSIGHT 17

In a direct response, make your main point at least three times in *each* major part of the promotion—in the letter *and* in the brochure, as well as in other pieces that might be included. The *words* don't have to be the same; the *meaning* does.

LECTRO-STIK CORPORATION
3721 BROADWAY
CHICAGO, ILLINOIS 60613

STAMP

NOW...
MAKE $14 MORE
ON HAND WAXERS—

$1 MORE ON WAX REFILLS

Special Early-Bird Notice for Long-Range Planners

Figure 3.3 The same envelope was used for both early bird mailings.

7. Additional reassurance to the dealer, because the "early bird" was asked to order so far in advance of the price change. This letter was mailed in May, the full mailing in July.

Notes on the Letter for the Second Mailing (Figure 3.4)

1. Use this box device in one of two ways: (a) When you have a single point you wish to emphasize—in this case, the extraordinary profit opportunity—but you want more than just a few words with which to do it. The box focuses your readers' attention and tells them instantly whether or not the rest of the letter must be read. (b) When you wish to cite a brief statement from someone other than the person signing the letter as a testimonial—for example, a note from the CEO of your company telling how important this letter is to the reader, or a plea from a local relief worker hoping we'll listen to the national appeal.

2. All three of your "tell them" reasons are in these three lines:
   * *What* you want is that dealers recommend the Lectro-Stik product rather than the competition's. In this case, that can be implied rather than stated. Retailers and wholesalers aren't stupid; they know their profit on the waxer won't increase unless they do just that.
   * *Why* they should do it—in addition to profits—is detailed later on. Here, we concentrate on the single most important reason: profits!
   * *How* to gain the benefit is made simple and easy: Order *now!*

3. Personalize the letter—that is, address the dealers individually by name if that is practical. If it is not, note the welcome variation from "Dear dealer."

4. One of the oldest rules in direct mail selling is to make your most important point(s) at least three times. The theme is profits, but while raising prices and profits to match the competition has to be announced, that alone gives dealers no particular reason to favor Lectro-Stik. It removes the lower profit negative, but what's needed now is a jump-start to the positive.

5. That jump is here, a reiteration and amplification of point 2. In writing direct mail letters, all the rules are working at the same time—especially the ones that say to keep it simple, . . . make it easy, . . . and make one point at a time; but, where possible, make it in multibenefit fashion. In three short paragraphs, readers have learned (in points 2, 4, and 5) what you want them to do, what's in it for them (especially in 2 and 5), and how to gain this benefit (also in 2 and 5). Everything else in the letter will reinforce what you have already said.

6. When possible, use a key word loaded with benefits to add even more value to your message. Dozens of words might have substituted for *profit*, such as "benefit" and "value." But if profit is the theme, be as generous with the term as clearly

Lectro-Stik
CORPORATION

3721 BROADWAY ● CHICAGO, ILLINOIS 60613 ● PHONE (312) 528-8860

FAX 312/528-2874

(Date)

(1)

MAKE $14 MORE on every Lectro-Stik Waxer, **PLUS**
MAKE $1 MORE on every box of Lectro-Stik Wax
. . .you order now and sell after September 1! (2)

---

(3)

To Our Valued Dealers:

For the first time in over eight years, inflation has forced us to increase the price of the Lectro-Stik Waxer and Wax. Effective September 1, 1991, the nationally advertised price of the Waxer will be $59 and the 10-oz. box of wax will be $4.50. (4)

Order now for shipment *before* September 1st and we will fill your order at the price of $45 per Waxer and $3.50 per box of wax. That's a mammoth increase in your profits now. . .and a huge on-going larger profit from now on. (5)

YOUR CUSTOMERS WILL PROFIT TOO (6)
By featuring Lectro-Stik, you give your customers much the best on the market—by far! No other hand waxer gives them more than 2 of these 6 state-of-the-art features. . . *All standard on Lectro-Stik!* (7)

1. **LEAKPROOF**

2. **TRULY HANDY.** Rolls on an economical strip 1-1/4" wide vs. bulky waxers that lay down strips up to 3" wide.

3. **NEW TIRES** These should last the life of the waxer.

4. **SEE-THROUGH BODY** for instant wax visibility. A Lectro-Stik exclusive!

5. **ELECTRONIC HEATING** for precise control and long life. Won't burn out or fluctuate. . .as do some competitors' thermostats.

6. **"TACKIFIER"** is **NOT NEEDED** and **NOT USED** in Lectro-Stik Wax. Sticky tackifiers make it harder to position the bits and pieces that go into pasteups. . . negating the very advantage wax is designed to give!

(8) Write, FAX, or phone your order *before* September 1st and let us know when you want delivery (before September 1). It's the profit bonanza of the decade! Do it now. (9)

Cordially yours,

Bill Taylor

P.S. **TO HELP YOU SELL EVEN MORE, WE'LL BE RUNNING ADS — AS ENCLOSED.** Get FREE reprints with room to overprint or rubber stamp *your name.* Just write or call with quantity and whether to fold. (10)

Figure 3.4 Letter to prospects not familiar with the waxer.

78

understood meaning permits. *Don't become cute*, however: Very few businesses find what they do funny.

7. The six features that follow grew out of a feature-benefit analysis like the one explained on page 43. Notice how they let dealers justify—to themselves and their customers—their recommendation of Lectro-Stik without any mention of price. Note, too, that every point gives both the feature (presenting the dealer as expert) and the benefit (presenting the dealer as the customer's friend), in language that does not demand great technical expertise. When—as sometimes does happen—a feature and benefit are exactly the same, leave them that way. We seldom gain from making things more complicated than need be!

8. A repetition of the "how to take advantage" information. Always put it just before the signature, no matter how often it's mentioned elsewhere. That's where your readers will look for it. Don't disappoint them.

9. In the final version of this letter, one sentence was added immediately before this call to action. It said, "A preaddressed order form is enclosed." And don't think you are insulting your readers by statements like "Do it now." Repeated tests have shown that they will; or worse yet, if the exhortation is left out, . . . that they won't!

10. P.S.s tend to be the best read portions of letters, so they are often used to give one more repetition of the writer's single most important point. In this instance, the news of a national advertising campaign was felt to be even more important. The additional offer of free reprints is well understood by the industry and needed no further explanation.

Post Office Clearance

For your mailings, get *written* clearance from the post office as a first step, not as the last. Show those in charge at the post office a layout of the envelope or self-mailer with the key words in place, and request approval for mailing the items. They will date, indicate "ok," and sign that layout. If they refuse, find out why. The reason may be an easily changed technical detail, not the mailing itself. When they approve, ask whether there is any way to make postal charges less costly—from changing the size of the self-mailer or envelope to changing the way it is addressed. Legal clearance is next. But keep in mind that there's little point in asking—and paying for—legal guidance before you've taken advantage of the *free* and generally very able assistance from your postal staff.

Always remember you are *legally bound* to any commitment promised by your mailing. Make certain that you know the implications of what you are offering and what you must do to make good on the promise. Don't guess. Know!

When planning a look-alike simulation, such as a window envelope's see-through "check" or a seeming legal or governmental notice, consider both the percent you anticipate will respond and the percent you anticipate will have a negative reaction because they have been "fooled." John Dewey's warning that we are responsible for the foreseeable consequences of our actions applies to business as well as morals. Fortunately, in direct mail, it's easier to foresee the consequences. Test!

SUMMARY

- Include a letter in any mailing you do. It's what transforms mass mail into personal communication.
- Be absolutely clear about what you want the recipients to do . . . and that you can handle the response if they agree to do it.
- Translate your self-interest into benefits for your prospective customers. Don't tell them about your wonderful seeds; tell them about *their* glorious garden.

ENVELOPES AND TEASERS

The "teaser" is the message—actual or implied—by which the sender gets us to open an envelope or to look through a self-mailer. Like the headline in our ads, its job is to capture our attention—to separate a particular piece of mail from all the others and get us to explore it a bit further. The majority of teasers, especially in business-to-business mailings, can be do-it-yourself projects. Others should be attempted only by professionals, although you may, of course, be charged with overall supervision.

For Professional Pens Only

Some mailings tease us with offers we cannot refuse, in giant type right on the envelope or the front of the self-mailer. Figure 3.5 is of this variety.

Other mailings tease with the look of important documents, legal forms, or checks, and the simple request:

POSTMASTER: Dated material. Please expedite.

The Other 90 Percent

Set aside the mailings you'll assign to the pros: anything to do with insurance, finance, and banking; contests, games, and sweepstakes; clubs (for books, foods, or records), continuity programs, and negative options; fund raising and politics, and almost all consumer direct response. That still leaves 90% to get done. Most are business-to-business mailings, and you *can* do those yourself by applying some businesslike techniques.

SENDER'S IDENTIFICATION
ADDRESS

STAMP

YOU
MAY HAVE
ALREADY
WON
$10,000,000!

Check Your Personal Entry Number and Other Details Inside

Figure 3.5 Sample of an envelope "teaser." Note how much stronger the message is without the "00" after the decimal point. Try it and see.

If you are writing the mailing yourself and are not a direct mail professional, leave the envelope blank. No teaser is almost always better than *any* teaser that is poorly done. Would *you* throw away a plain envelope without any teaser—without even looking inside? Well, neither will your recipients.

If you do decide to use a teaser, here are some guidelines:

• **Make your message instantly compelling.** In larger companies, it's likely that it will be screened by a mail clerk, secretary, and administrative assistant. (As a counterpoint to this statement, however, I have never been able to get any of my secretaries to open any of my mail marked "personal." Not even my telling them, "If it's truly personal, I'd want you to be the first to know," convinced them. Neither did the fact that not a single piece of that mail was really personal. All of it was direct mail advertising.)

• **Relate the teaser to what comes next.** Or relate what comes next to the teaser. When your readers open the envelope or self-mailer, continue the message of the teaser. Expand on, expound on, and solidify the benefit hinted at or promised in the teaser, before you go on to anything else. The fastest way to lose your audience is to remove the reason you gave them for paying attention.

• **Make it easy to read.** Be as creative as your imagination and skills permit, but relate the message to your audience. Be aware that art directors and interstate trucking firms *may* require a different approach, but don't take that for granted. Prepare several versions, make copies, and ask a dozen members of the group to whom you are mailing your promotion which version they like best. Then, after they have told you, ask them why they like it best. There is no *statistical* validity in the responses, but you should at least learn whether you are totally off base. You're not trying to eliminate the test; you just want to zero in on *what* to test.

The Response: More Than Just a B.R.C.

Busy readers, especially in the business community, often go directly from the teaser to the "b.r.c."—the business reply card. They like to discover what the offer is going to cost them—in dollars, time, effort, or some other commitment. So many of us now do this from force of habit, that mailers load the b.r.c. with the key benefits. Usually, it echoes the offer, the guarantee, and the conditions, as in Figure 3.6.

To Card . . . or Not to Card

The format you choose for your customer's reply, whether a card, an order form, a formal contract, or something else, will depend on what you can get your readers to do and the impression you want them to have about you. For many business mailings, practically no one uses the response form you enclose, they use their own purchase orders instead. But don't eliminate the b.r.c.! It's what gets sent to the purchasing department with instructions to "order this." The more complicated the offer, the more important it is that there's a fully spelled-out agreement for your recipients to copy or to return.

•   **Use a reply card** when the offer is simple and there's no need for privacy or confidential information, such as credit card or personal telephone numbers.

I have been both astonished and shocked at the increasing number of businesses that ask me to give my credit card numbers and my signature on the back of a reply card. You have an obligation to protect a customer who might not know better, so *don't do this* in mailings you prepare.

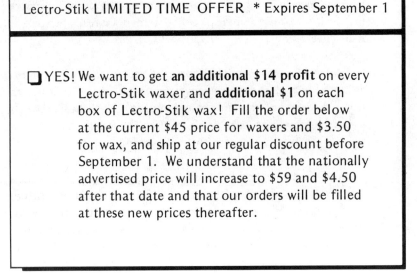

Lectro-Stik LIMITED TIME OFFER * Expires September 1

◻ YES! We want to get **an additional $14 profit** on every Lectro-Stik waxer and **additional $1** on each box of Lectro-Stik wax! Fill the order below at the current $45 price for waxers and $3.50 for wax, and ship at our regular discount before September 1. We understand that the nationally advertised price will increase to $59 and $4.50 after that date and that our orders will be filled at these new prices thereafter.

Figure 3.6 Sample business reply card.

• **Use an order form** when the offer is complicated, there is a need for privacy, or confidential information is requested.

• **Include an envelope** when asking for payment by check or money order or when multiple pieces need to be returned.

• **With multiple product mailings**, especially if the items being sold are similar, illustrate them on the order form when possible. (As advertising manager for Rand McNally, I once dramatically increased sales of a premium atlas by picturing similar-sounding atlases on the order form. Being new to the company, I could not immediately connect product names with the stock numbers then used to identify them on reply forms. Pictures made the connection instantly obvious. My assumption that some of our busy customers might have the same difficulty, especially when a sales representative was not present to assist in ordering, proved correct.)

• **As a multiple-product (or service) supplier doing a single-product mailing**, list your other products on the order form. Doing so can have astonishingly positive results. Feature the subject of the mailing by framing it within a box such as the one used in the letter shown in Figure 3.4, and then list as many other items as you wish. Use very short descriptions if names are not self-explanatory. Thus, if you are a manufacturer of bicycles introducing a new model, you might also list other models and peripheral equipment such as helmets, pumps, and tool kits. If you have not done this before, . . . test! In my experience with a variety of companies, the results have been positive, but each universe of mail recipients is different. Always remember that with direct mail, you do not have to take anything for granted. Test!

Telephone, Toll-Free, FAX

Give *all* the options you have available. If you do not yet have toll-free or FAX capability, use a local service bureau for a test. FAX will be easy to find at most secretarial services. For handling of toll-free 800 numbers check the Yellow Pages. Suppliers of both options are becoming increasingly competitive in price and service. Shop before you buy. Put your agreement in writing.

SELF-MAILERS AND REPLY CARDS

Think of your self-mailer as a large sheet of paper on which you are going to print and then cut out an envelope, a letter, a brochure, and a coupon or reply form. But instead of cutting them apart, you fold the sheet in such a way that, when unfolded, they present your message in a logical fashion. Figures 3.7 through 3.11 show a few examples.

Figure 3.7 uses a basic page size of $8\frac{1}{2}'' \times 11''$ or $9'' \times 12''$. Almost any printer can run and fold the double gate fold format economically. Use this as a self-mailer or as the flyer in a multipiece envelope mailing.

Figure 3.7 Double gate fold format. Use this as a self-mailer or as the flyer in a multipiece envelope mailing.

Figure 3.8 shows the single fold with return flap. It can be a self-mailer, a newspaper or magazine insert, or enclosed in an envelope as part of a multi-unit mailing. The flap is removed and folded for mailing. The front cover can be folded as shown (it can even fold down to business letter size) or be used in its full $8^{1}/_{2}'' \times 11''$. The advantage of this format is that the first opening goes to a letter and the second opening to two facing pages—what printers call a spread.

The third opening is a 4-inch flap that can be used as a reply form when folded in the middle. Be sure to get the latest postal specifications on the size and weight of the paper used for the flap.

Self-Mailer Advantages and Disadvantages

The advantages of the self-mailer are its lower cost, the immediacy of its message, and its ability to "stand out in the crowd" of recipients' business mail. *The disadvantages* are that it may be less response efficient than a "standard" mailing and that it is often perceived as junk mail. Do not take any of these for granted, however. Test if possible!

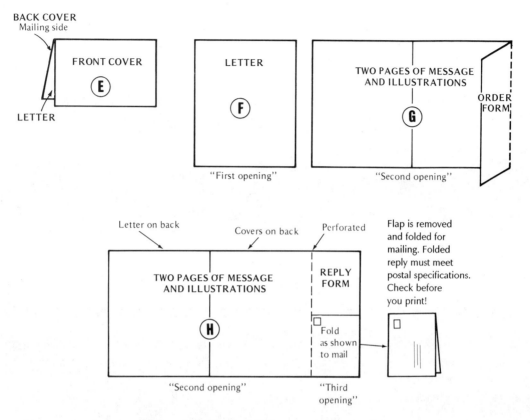

Figure 3.8 Single-fold format with return flap.

The Triple Postcard

An interesting variation of the single fold with flap is the triple postcard, consistently one of those formats with "the most bang for the buck," in my experience. To make a "dummy," or sample (see Figure 3.9), take an 8½″ × 11″ sheet of paper, fold it horizontally into thirds, and cut along the fold. Tape the shorter ends together to make a single strip. Cut 1/8″ from one end. Then fold as shown in the figure.

A teaser or brief note can go on the front cover addressing side (A). Currently, postal regulations do not require that this card be sealed, but check for the latest rulings before every mailing.

The back cover (B) may be used for your letter or other supporting materials—professional evaluations, testimonials, or any favorable printed comments. Many recipients look at the back before they check the inside, so use benefit-laden headlines or subheads to create and hold interest.

For easy folding, the reply card (C) is slightly shorter than the other two sections. Note that you do not have to use the entire panel for the reply. Postal regulations give you the option of creating a smaller card (check the latest regulations for exact sizes) with the remaining space—section BB—available for other purposes.

Figure 3.9 "Dummy" of triple postcard, front and back. (A) Front cover, addressing side. (B) Back cover. (C) Reply card. For easy folding, the reply card is slightly shorter than the other two sections.

When using the "postage-free" reply format, note that there are severe restrictions on what, other than the address, may appear on a postage prepaid return address side (C). With the smaller format for the reply card, area BB can emphasize telephone and/or FAX service, deadlines, savings, guarantees, and so forth.

Figure 3.10 shows the second opening of the triple postcard. The messages on all three cards are now visible. Note that area EE may be used for optional messages even if the ordering side is extended to its full size *and* you use a prepaid return format (C, Figure 3.11).

Use the space in portions D, E, and EE in any way you wish. It does not have to divide neatly into thirds. Let your message create the format!

In designing the triple postcard, it is generally preferable to use panel C for the return address and panel F for ordering or other response information. As the card is opened, the recipient has all the necessary information in one straight-line commu-nication, following our very first insight: "Make it simple."

Figure 3.10 Second opening of triple postcard.

Figure 3.11 Triple postcard with return address (C) on outside.

Additional Triple Postcard Suggestions

Your triple card does not have to have a removable reply card. Design it to be returned with section C on the outside (Figure 3.11), and two, or all three, of the sections are returned to you. Make certain that the card will refold easily. *No optional message* may appear on the return address side. Check with the post office regarding regulations on such self mailers. Two advantages of the triple card format are as follows:

• **Questionnaire and other research answers seem less formidable in the triple card format.** For ease of processing, limit answers to the D-E-F interior only. This has proven a particularly successful device when accompanied by a short explanatory letter and sent in an envelope. It has, however, also worked as a self-mailer. As always . . . test.

• **Lower-cost paper, rather that card-weight stock, can be used for the two- or three-section reply.** Consider allocating the same dollars as for card stock, but purchasing a finer paper for first impression impact. Before you decide, test. Get paper samples from your printer, make dummy copies to size, and send them to yourself. Better yet, send a dozen to people you know across the country and have them returned.

THE MAILING COST/BUDGETING FORMULA

All calculations for the formula shown on the next page must be based on firm quotations. The cumulative cost of all test mailings or other premail tests is included as part of the total cost when estimating profitability. Some companies and organizations charge mailing tests to advertising and final mailings to sales. The formula will let you do it either way.

MAILING COST/TESTING & BUDGETING FORMULA

Project title/description _____   Date _____

_____   Project # _____

_____   Checklist # _____

Overall Supervision by _____   Deadline_____

Test Quantity _____ Rollout Quantity _____ Completion Date _____

Budget _____ Start-up Date _____

		TEST	ROLLOUT
A.	**CAMERA-READY ART**	$_____	$
	• Creative Supervision		
	• Concept	_____	
	• Design/Layout	_____	
	• Copy	_____	
	• Editorial	_____	
	• Type	_____	
	• Photography	_____	
	• Art	_____	
	• Key Line/Paste-up	_____	
B.	**FILM**	_____	_____
C.	**ENVELOPES/CONTAINERS**	_____	_____
D.	**PRINTING**		
	• All Printing	_____	_____
	• Special Folds/Die Cuts	_____	_____
	• Other _____	_____	_____
E.	**BINDERY/MAILING SERVICE**		
	• Inserting all elements into		
	envelope or container; seal	_____	_____
	• Merge/Purge, if used	_____	_____
	• Lettershop, in addition to the above	_____	_____
	• Postage	_____	_____
F.	**MAILING LIST(S)**	_____	_____
	TOTAL	$_____	$_____

✔ *These calculations are required for EACH test or rollout with differences in out-of-pocket costs. Note that camera-ready art is prepared for the test (A) and has no charges for rollout. New film may be needed. Multiple suppliers are less likely for a letter shop, but check it out!*

> **VALUE OF THE NEW CUSTOMER!**
>
> In evaluating returns, do not neglect the dollar value of gaining a new customer. It is a vital part of any evaluation in which getting customers as well as one-time buyers is your goal.

		TEST	ROLLOUT
G.	**COST OF GOODS PER UNIT**	$_____	$_____
H.	**MINIMUM ACCEPTABLE PROFIT**	_____	_____
I.	**SALES PRICE PER UNIT**	_____	_____

THE 3-STEP CALCULATION

STEP 1. $\dfrac{A + B + C + D + E + F}{\text{Quantity Mailed}} \times 100 =$ Cost per 100 mailed $ _____ (Eliminate "A" for Rollout)

STEP 2. $\dfrac{\text{Cost per 100}}{I - G - H} =$ Percentage of return needed for minimum acceptable profit.

STEP 3. Based on the percentage of return needed to justify mailing, modify and/or test various options before deciding on any rollout.

INSIGHT 18

Your pretesting estimates are used to calculate the likely profit from a complete mailing—tests plus roll-out. But once that testing is completed, only the profits it predicts from the roll-out—*without including the cost of the tests*—should control further action. The money spent on testing is gone, no matter what its results! That is why some firms budget testing as "Advertising" and roll-outs as "Sales." The dollars are the same, but management tends to feel better.

The $20 Rule Applied

Earlier in this chapter, it was suggested that profitable selling by mail required a $20 minimum order. To see why, let's apply the formula given in Step 2 of the three-step calculation shown and assume a $20 price with $4 cost of goods including overhead, a $2 (10%) profit requirement, and a 50¢ per unit mailing cost. The formula now looks like this: $50 \div (20 - 4 - 2) = 3.57$ orders per 100 mailed to break even. Increase the price to $25 and break-even becomes 2.63%; lower mailing costs to 40¢ or increase the price to $30 and break-even is reduced to 2% +. Many mailings produce the 2% return; few achieve 3.57. Calculate as you plan. Adjust your costs where possible. Test!

NOTES ON THE DIRECT MAIL *CREATIVE* CHECKLIST

These notes are a supplement to the material presented in this chapter. They are not a self-contained substitute for that material.

1. What the mailing is to achieve. This can include immediate sales, finding long-term customers, building a base on which to sell through personal, telephone, or additional mail follow-up, information gathering, etc. If more than a single purpose is selected, pick one as key. Where else in life would you devote exactly the same effort to every objective?
2. Budget for direct mail *creative* stops with camera-ready art (#13) and possible outside charges for #14 on. How the total project is budgeted and what must be approved before creative design may begin are decided here.
3. What, if anything, is to be tested. The time allocated not only for the tests themselves, but for analyzing and following up on them. #4 must have this information to build a workable time frame.
4. The specific time frame for the creative process and how it relates to testing, plus the time required to satisfy all the other checklists noted at the bottom of this page.
5. Specific supervision for the creative processes if there is such supervision different from the overall supervision. If several supervisors are involved, decide here who may and who may not override whom.

6. All we can learn about our obvious audience(s) and, possibly, new prospects we had not realized were there. (In regard to the latter, body odor (B.O.) was once invented to find a need for a strong-smelling soap practically no one had known they wanted.)

7. The specific focus (approach) of each test in attempting to achieve #1. Most often, this is done by giving the copywriters broad guidelines on which to use their personal creativity.

8. If research is wanted or needed, what will it cost? How long will it take? Who will do it? Who must approve? And, most important, what actions will you take on the basis of the research results? Start with the last point first. If the answer is "none," go directly from #7 to #9.

9. If new to writing, do just one approach before going on to the next. Then base the second approach on the first, the third on the second, etc. Now go back and redo the first. You'll be astonished by how much you've learned and how fast you've learned it. This chapter gives you a step-by-step approach. Use it *every time*.

10. Direct mail design is a specialized art, so find and use a specialist, especially if you are a beginner.

11. For simpler projects, try desktop publishing—but only if your in-house printer meets professional standards. Professional typesetting tends to be the least expensive of outside costs.

12–13. Not just a nice illustration, but a picture that does something—that moves the viewer to share your objective. Would the Sistine Chapel be nearly as much of an attraction if the finger of God were closed into His fist? Generally, use art for emotion and photography for fact . . . but always be ready to be pleasantly surprised.

14. Who prepares it? Who approves it? Who reviews it with the filmmaker? Who, if anyone, may change it, based on the filmmaker's suggestions?

15. If this is not the only approval required, the designers (#10) should at least be consulted . . . and listened to. They'll be the only ones to catch the "obvious" *design* mistakes no one else sees.

16. This is often a quite time-consuming process, but it is absolutely essential. If possible, send two persons—one who knows how to give on-press ok's and one to learn how to do it. There's much more to this part of the job than meets the eye.

17. Testing and analysis affect everything the creative people will do if given the opportunity to learn about it. Accordingly, share the results, no matter what they are. And be specific: It's hard to do better next time if all we're told is "It failed." It's even hard to do as well if all we know is "It's great!"

18. The final authority on the mechanics of language, the house style, and the technical accuracy of the text, the editorial person or department sees the *final manuscript* and checks the *final type* against it, whenever that is ready. Make no changes in either one without editorial approval. Also, how many "final" versions may there be?!

DIRECT MAIL <u>CREATIVE</u> CHECKLIST

Project title/description _____   Date _____

_____   Project # _____

_____   Checklist # _____

Overall Supervision by _____   Deadline _____

Budget _____   Start-up Date _____   Completion Date _____

MANAGEMENT DECISIONS	ASSIGNED TO	DUE	IN	MUST APPROVE	BY DATE	IN	INFO COPY ONLY	SEE ATTACHED
1. Purpose	_____	___	☐	_____	___	☐	_____	☐
2. Budget	_____	___	☐	_____	___	☐	_____	☐
3. Test(s)	_____	___	☐	_____	___	☐	_____	☐
4. Time Line	_____	___	☐	_____	___	☐	_____	☐
5. Supervision	_____	___	☐	_____	___	☐	_____	☐
CREATIVE DECISIONS								
6. Audience(s)	_____	___	☐	_____	___	☐	_____	☐
7. Focus	_____	___	☐	_____	___	☐	_____	☐
8. Research	_____	___	☐	_____	___	☐	_____	☐
9. Writer(s)	_____	___	☐	_____	___	☐	_____	☐
10. Designer(s)	_____	___	☐	_____	___	☐	_____	☐
11. Typesetter(s)	_____	___	☐	_____	___	☐	_____	☐
12. Photography	_____	___	☐	_____	___	☐	_____	☐
13. Art	_____	___	☐	_____	___	☐	_____	☐
14. Camera-Ready Art	_____	___	☐	_____	___	☐	_____	☐
15. Film/Proofs OK	_____	___	☐	_____	___	☐	_____	☐
16. On-Press OK	_____	___	☐	_____	___	☐	_____	☐
17. Test Analysis	_____	___	☐	_____	___	☐	_____	☐
MECHANICAL CHECKS								
18. Editorial OK	_____	___	☐	_____	___	☐	_____	☐
19. Legal OK	_____	___	☐	_____	___	☐	_____	☐
20. Postal OK	_____	___	☐	_____	___	☐	_____	☐
21. Letter Shop OK	_____	___	☐	_____	___	☐	_____	☐
22. Logo	_____	___	☐	_____	___	☐	_____	☐
_____	_____	___	☐	_____	___	☐	_____	☐
_____	_____	___	☐	_____	___	☐	_____	☐
_____	_____	___	☐	_____	___	☐	_____	☐
_____	_____	___	☐	_____	___	☐	_____	☐
_____	_____	___	☐	_____	___	☐	_____	☐

Separate checklists cover testing & budgeting, film & proofing, printing & bindery, and letter shop mailing.

© 1993, Fred Hahn

19. Direct mail and other direct response advertising are regulated by federal, state, and, by the time you read this, possibly even local, laws. (Sales tax collection is just one of the legal issues.) Make yourself knowledgeable, and if in-house legal expertise is not available, use your direct marketing association to lead you to where it is.

20. Your post office approved your design in writing, including any message you plan to put on the outside of your package. Right?

21. Your letter shop mailing service saw dummy samples of your package, told you they could do it, and quoted a price in writing. And the mailing package hasn't changed without their knowing it. Right?

22. Someone has actually looked at every logo, every address, and every telephone number on the mailings. And so have you. Right?

MAIL ORDER, DIRECT MARKETING, AND DATA-BASED DIRECT MARKETING

Data-based marketing is based on two criteria: (1) the existence, availability, and use of pertinent information on which you can base your marketing decisions and (2) the modification of that marketing effort as new data become available.

Data-based *direct* marketing involves exactly the same things. Its only difference is in the way it sells—directly rather than through others. For example, a mailing that urges you to buy by mail and makes it practical to do so is a basic part of mail order direct marketing. Exactly the same mailing that urges you to make the purchase in a retail outlet is mail advertising. Quite a bit more than nomenclature is involved in this difference.

As the introduction to this book noted, marketing concerns itself with "the four p's,"—product, price, place (sales), and promotion. In direct response, what we normally think of as promotion is actually sales—our advertisement and method of selling are one and the same. Promotion, therefore, is best budgeted and utilized for research to find better ways to make sales work. The distinction is arbitrary, but of value in (1) selling the absolute need for advertising to management and (2) keeping the research budget from skewing ultimate sales costs.

Establishing Your Data Base

Imagine that you are a sales representative with 25 key accounts. In your customer data notebook, you keep the names of your clients with, as far as you can learn, their business reasons for dealing with you—price, delivery, quality, etc.—as well as such things as their birthdays and favorite places to eat. You'll note others on the staff who are important to the purchasing decision, and you'll note the "politics" involved in the decision. You'll try to discover the key compitors' approach to luring your business away and how you might react to it. This notebook is for clients or customers. You have an analogous file for prospects. Both of these information-laden resources are your data base. The data base is invaluable, but only as long as you continually *both* update your information *and* act upon it.

Now, expand this example to thousands or millions of names. The process still holds. But now your data are on a computer, and a whole new set of considerations is required:

• Which department "owns" the computer? Accounting? Order processing? Estimating? Direct marketing? What is the pecking order? Most systems generate data through order entry. Access to that information and to computer time for its analysis is critical to data-based marketing.

• What can the computer do? That is, what is its capacity for receiving, analyzing, and acting upon each piece of information? If your sales efforts involve 1,000 different items, how much time and capacity are involved if you want access to everyone who ordered any single item? Any one of 100 different categories? 25 categories? Can the computer do the same for prices? Frequency of orders? Any combination of these? Can it add, remove, and correct data quickly and easily? Can it protect data? What are its limitations, and how does it fit into today's state of the art? Note that *your* computer is not involved with lists you purchase for mailing, but only with supplying in-house lists and handling responses. Purchased lists go directly to a mailing service.

A Note on Style: Go back and reread the preceding two paragraphs—not for content, but for style. Note the many short sentences and sentence fragments. See how question marks emphasize the need for answers and action. Mentally remove those question marks, and substitute commas. You'll have an instant demonstration of the need to *keep it simple*.

What You Really Have to Know

Determine what you must know, store, and be able to manipulate by computer to improve sales. What would you do with different kinds of information if you had it? Differentiate between "nice to know" and "vital for improved performance." In his autobiography, Sloane Willson, a president of General Motors, tells of seeing a "severely handicapped" person working in one of the plants. In a casual comment to his companions, he wondered how many such employees were at GM. Six months and tens of thousands of dollars later, he got a research report giving him the answer he didn't need to a question he'd long since forgotten he'd asked. Your computer will, if instructed, do the same thing—endlessly store expensively gathered information you thought you wanted, but didn't know what to do with once it arrived. *Before* you ask for it . . .

1. Determine what will be done with *any* information once you have it.
2. Be open to and welcome unasked-for information, unwelcome informa-

tion, and inconclusive information. They can be as important to your marketing as actual sales. Believe the numbers . . . but in addition to getting just the facts, consider whether it makes any difference to know why also.

Data-Based Direct Marketing and the "Four P's"

1. *About the Product (or service)*.
   - Research for customer needs before anything is produced. Research further when you get conflicting answers. (Yes we want the lowest price. No, we don't have time for comparison shopping.)
   - Research for satisfaction after the product or service has been delivered. (Is it what you expected? Are you satisfied? How might it be better?)
   - Modify the product or service based on what you learn, providing it is practical, cost effective, and in your long-term interest to do so. And remember . . .
   - Your concern as a marketer is *not* with profit, but with customer satisfaction.

2. *About Price*.
   - Data-based analysis lets you produce a "best" price before more than your test is put into print, on the air, or is used in telemarketing.
   - You determine that price based on *your audience's criteria*. It is the audience that makes the buy/no buy decisions.

3. *About Place (Sales)*. Determine how the order will be solicited, how it will be received, and how it will be filled.
   - Will you use only mail? Newspaper or magazine print advertising? Radio and TV? Telemarketing? Package inserts? Or some combination of these?
   - Will orders be received by mail only? By telephone (including a toll-free number)? By FAX (including a toll-free number)? Or by some combination of these?
   - Will everything be shipped from a single location or from regional centers? Which will be faster? Which will produce lower shipping costs?
   - How will you control drop shipments sent directly from manufacturers or wholesalers rather than by you?
   - Should you do direct response only? Establish your own retail outlets? Sell through others? Use your promotions to help you answer these questions!

4. *About Promotion*
   - Test your product, price, and sales approaches as requested by those in charge of each. Note that this testing is *not* limited to mail, but may—and often does—include telemarketing, focus groups, and other types of research.

- Assist the people in charge of the product, price, and sales in evaluating test results.
- Apply specified results in test promotions to validate research.
- Test direct mail or other direct response media continually, from minor revisions to totally new approaches.
- Believe the numbers.

INSIGHT 19

Analyze every direct response effort as if it were a test.

---

4 | Catalogs: A Project for Creative Nitpickers

Producing a catalog is different from any other promotional project you are likely to undertake. It permits, but does not demand, copious creative flair, combined with meticulous mastery of mountains of minutiae, expertise in a half-dozen technical specializations, financial acumen to match that of a dedicated auditor, the human relations rapport of a soother of egos, and the management skills of a mover of mountains. Even I do not claim to be able to juggle all of those at the same time during the actual production of a catalog. If you can possibly avoid trying, neither should you.

This chapter guides you, step by step, through the creation, production, and distribution of a catalog. Unlike some of the other chapters, it concentrates less on creativity and more on procedures that let your creativity have maximum impact. It tells you *how* to achieve superior copy and design, not *what* to write or draw. It assumes that *you* are the soother of egos and mover of mountains. If, in addition to that, you could take on additional roles, ask yourself whether you really should. In any major catalog with which I have been involved, just those two functions alone have been a full-time job. Where staff is available, assign what you can and do only what you must. And what you must do is assume responsibility for the job as a whole. Management is unlikely to accept as an excuse or explanation that you were too swamped with detail to supervise. No matter how much better you could do it than the person assigned to the details . . . don't! Your function is to manage. Do it!

INSIGHT 20

If you are new to management, it will be hard not to insist that everything be done exactly as if you had done it yourself. But few of us do our best as clones. Force yourself to recognize when proposed solutions, although different from your own, will work. That's what makes you a good manager—and a great soother of egos, too.

DECIDING ON GOALS AND CONSTRAINTS

Management

In most organizations that use a catalog, its budget and over-all purpose must have management approval. Automobile dealers and department stores, as well as other retail outlets that have a sales force, are in a different position from vitamin manufacturers, food-of-the-month clubs, and giftware importers that sell *only* by mail. And what is the purpose of the gift catalog issued by your local art museum? The "mission" of each of these catalogs must be defined at the highest level and then produced with that goal in mind.

Marketing

Marketing is the overall activity that encompasses the creation and production of your company's product or service, its pricing, its sale, and its promotion. Advertising, including the production of catalogs, is only one—albeit important—part of the total marketing mission, which, like the management mission, must be incorporated into your decisions relating to the catalog. The function of the catalog in the sales plan is of vital importance. It must be defined *in writing*, to avoid later "retroactive omniscience."

Editorial Matters

Someone must have final approval over the *technical accuracy* of the features and benefits presented in the catalog—i.e., over *what* is said rather than *how* it is said. The exact authority of this person and who, if anyone, can override it, must be defined in writing.

Legal Matters

The law is quite clear. You are responsible for anything you claim, promise, and generally say in your promotion. Get legal clearance while the catalog is still in its manuscript stage, not when it is printed and ready to mail!

Copy

Copy is the preparation of *every word* of the manuscript, no matter who writes it. Assign specific responsibilities for information on ordering and your policy on returns, as well as for product descriptions—for the nuts and bolts as well as for the glamour.

Design

Design is a rendering of the visual impression given by the catalog. The design concept may be presented for approval in rough form or with as much detail and finish as the designer wishes. In either case, it must be finished enough to show how the major elements that make up the catalog merge into a synergetic whole. Among those elements are the catalog's covers, type, descriptions, illustrations, ordering information, and mailing envelope, if one is used.

Layout

Layout is a detailed rendering of how each page of the catalog and every other element of the "catalog package" reflect the design concept. The layout may be prepared by the designer, but is frequently done by a specialist in turning design into a practical blueprint for writers, typesetters, artists, and photographers. Approval of the layout—not the design—is the signal for the start of the physical production of the catalog.

Production

Everything begins with agreement on a production schedule. This schedule is controlled by the approval process, which follows in the next section, and how that process fits into the catalog checklist. The process and checklist may differ from what is suggested here, but both are needed and best put into writing.

A SYSTEM FOR INTERNAL APPROVALS

The approval process is unique to each organization. Fight, if you must, to organize and limit the number of approvals required. Nothing is as frustrating as waiting for approvals from managers who assign deadlines and then do not find time to meet them themselves.

The approval steps in creating and producing the catalog constitute a process rather than a specific number of persons. Whether you do it all yourself or have a staff, the procedure is the same. No matter how large the staff, the project manager should be the person with the most advertising expertise. Assign this function first, to let that person play a key role in filling the other slots.

Figure 4.1 shows the steps involved in the approval process, from creation to printing of the catalog:

PRODUCING YOUR CATALOG

The production of a catalog involves three sets of activities:

1. Preproduction activities
2. Physical production of the catalog
3. Postproduction activities.

Preproduction Activities

Probably the single most important preproduction decision is agreement on the date when the catalog must be ready to mail or otherwise be distributed. Every other decision will be driven by that date and the inflexibility of the printing and distribution schedules.

STEP	ASSIGNED TO:	APPROVALS BY:	CONFLICT RESOLUTION BY:
1. Initial discussion/ assignments	————	————	————
2. Creative suppliers: design, copy, photo, art	————	————	————
3. Production suppliers: type, key line, film, printing, die cutting, etc.	————	————	————
4. Design presentation	————	————	————
5. Copy: concept presentation	————	————	————
6. Complete layouts	————	————	————
7. Complete draft manuscript	————	————	————
8. Editorial oversight, proofing	————	————	————
9. Art/photography approval	————	————	————
10. Key line approval	————	————	————
11. Film (proof) approval	————	————	————
12. On-press (printing) approval	————	————	————

Figure 4.1 Approval process for printed materials—creation to printing.

Meetings. The number of meetings required for producing a catalog—or for any other promotional project—depends on the degree of independence assigned to advertising by management and sales. In most organizations, this is management's decision to make. It reflects the importance of the project, the specifics of the sales message, the amount of time available for their supervision, and probably most important, the degree of autonomy earned by the promotion department through its own performance.

Approvals. A number of signed approvals are almost always required to start production of the catalog. These include the approvals of management, finance (the budget OK), marketing, sales, and advertising. Other departmental OK's may be involved later on and are designated when the catalog is first discussed.

First General Meeting

Call an initial meeting of all interested parties, including the in-house design, print production, and editorial departments if they exist in your organization.

INSIGHT 21

For meetings at which senior managers are to be present, ask them to call the meeting. Attendance will jump.

In the memorandum calling for the meeting, specify what is to be discussed and the decisions required, together with a *brief* outline of data that will help in making the decisions. The meeting should cover at least the following subjects:

- **Budget.** Give the cost of the entire project. Show costs for the most recent similar catalog. Outline reasons why the cost of the new one may be higher, lower, or the same.
- **Theme.** Get agreement on any overall sales or marketing theme the catalog must reflect. This is *not* an attempt to coin a slogan, but to get direction.
- **Physical specifications.** Specify any general or special considerations that must be followed. Among the possibilities are fewer or more products to be shown, modification of the physical size of the catalog to permit its broader use and the inclusion of more or fewer order forms or enclosures.
- **Due date.** Set the date of the first use of the catalog. Answer the following questions: What use? Where? When? How many?
- **Mail date.** Set the date when catalog is to be *received* (rather than sent out).
- **Special instructions.** Give specific instructions from management, marketing, and sales for items not already covered. Make sure to differentiate between instructions and suggestions. Get the instructions in writing.
- **Approval process.** Determine who must see and approve the items covered on the checklist if this is not already established procedure. In what order? Who has *final* sign-off?

Let us consider four of these subjects in a bit more detail.

Budgeting. You will be starting on either a new creative effort or a revision of an existing catalog. Where only minor revisions are needed, such as updating prices and getting a new cover design, a budget is easy to specify. Even when a major new creative effort is called for, a budget can be estimated. Where similar work was done during the past three years, use that figure, adding 5 percent per year for inflation, except for postage. Get exact current postal rates and use that amount. Where no comparable recent costs are available, ask likely suppliers to give you "ball park" estimates. Add 5 percent to those, too. Present both options at the first meeting. Management appreciates—and rewards—that kind of foresight!

Theme. One of the major purposes of the initial meeting is to come to agreement on a theme for the catalog though *not* on how the theme is to be implemented. The latter is the responsibility of the advertising people.

Every catalog has a theme—that is, it conveys a message to its recipients, whether or not its sender intended to put that message into its pages. The theme can range from "We are better at what we do than anyone else" to "We don't know what we're doing" . . . from "Nobody beats our service!" to "Service? Beat it!" Obviously, some of these themes are implicit rather than explicit and not what the producer deliberately planned. *Some* theme is going to be there, so be sure it conveys what you *want* to say. Do not permit its accidental creation by inattention to *any* detail!

Physical Specifications. The concerns of senior management with the details of physical specification are likely to reflect the importance of the catalog in the marketing plan. The more critical the catalog is to sales, the more intense will be the pressure for direct involvement from the sales department. Unlike some of my colleagues in advertising, I do not find that frustrating. As I point out to my associates: "If Sales doesn't sell, . . . *nobody* gets paid." The sales people may actually *know* something that can help. Ask them, and see how quickly they change from interdepartmental adversaries to cooperative friends!

Other Considerations. The other four subjects—due date, mail date, special instructions, and the approval process—are likely to be routine. They are covered at the initial meeting to make certain that the advertising people can proceed without getting caught in unforeseen booby traps, e.g., an earlier than expected due date, special instructions you didn't get because you didn't ask, or a new link in the approval chain that you "should" have known about.

The Approval Ladder. Only one person (or a committee) can have *final* authority for any aspect of the production of a catalog. If your organizational meeting does nothing else, have it create an approval ladder to determine who must approve each step and who must resolve or dictate solutions to conflicts. In multilevel organizations, keep senior managers out of these conflicts. That's why the rest of us are around. Do, however, keep senior managers informed—not about the problems, but about their solutions!

SUMMARY

- Begin planning for the catalog with a proposed schedule and budget estimates. Conclude all meetings with a review of the decisions made.
- Issue your own meeting report. Spell out every decision as *you* understand it.
- Have everyone who must approve anything sign off on it.
- Do not begin the catalog until approval is granted or your report is officially corrected in writing.

PHYSICAL PRODUCTION OF THE CATALOG

"Producing" a catalog and catalog "production" have somewhat different meanings. *Producing* is all inclusive. It goes from the first discussion of the project to "back-end" analyses of results and what they mean for future efforts. *Production*, on the other hand, refers specifically to the period from the initial copy and design through printing and distribution.

Assignment and Scheduling

Catalog production involves eight major areas:

- Writing copy
- Design and layout
- Art and photography
- Typesetting and desktop publishing
- Key line and paste-up
- Film preparation and proofing
- Printing and binding
- Distribution and mailing

Some or all of these will be assigned to outside suppliers. The first order of business will be to find and approve these suppliers and to agree on a schedule for the work to be supplied. In working with either an inside or an outside supplier, the following insight should be your guide:

INSIGHT 22

The Laws of Outside Services
LAW I: Everything takes longer than it takes.
LAW II: Everything costs more than it costs.

Writing Copy

If your products or services require specialized understanding, at least the first draft should be written in-house. Outside writers can and do add their own special touch. Let them provide the sell that dramatizes your data.

The Function of Copy. The function of catalog copy will be one or more of the following:

1. To sell the reader who is unfamiliar with your product or service (the new order).

2. To sell the reader who is familiar with your product or service (the reorder).
3. To persuade the reader to ask for samples or an in-person presentation (major industrial purchases, computer or telephone systems, educational programs, etc.).
4. To reinforce the sales message the reader has gained from a presentation or examination of the product (the auto dealership, trade shows, etc.).

For 1 and 2, the function of catalog copy is, at a minimum, to give enough information to let the purchaser order. This information probably includes an order number, price, and basic "hard" data such as sizes, colors, and materials. In addition, guided by space and policy, there will be descriptions, illustrations, and, sometimes, special inducements to get the reader to buy.

Keep in mind that audiences remember less from presentations than the sales force likes to believe. They also remember less of the written message than writers like to acknowledge. Therefore, for catalogs that reinforce a presentation, let the written message echo the spoken one, in emphasis if not in exact wording. By reinforcing each other, the messages make the whole become greater than the sum of the parts.

For all four functions of catalog copy, show, rather than tell, the reader if at all possible. Today's audience is more likely to be visual and oral, instead of literary. This does *not* mean that the copy must be exceptionally brief; rather, it must be as succinct as you can make it and still do its job.

Train yourself to read your own copy with the mind-set of your most likely audience. Pretend that you have never heard of the product. Would you understand the message? Would you want to learn more about the product? Is there a practical way to give that information—in text or picture—right in the catalog? Your readers are busy and frequently impatient. Make their lives as easy as you can. Efficiency and consideration always reflect well on your company.

Now read the copy with the mind-set of an audience that has been to a presentation. Have you attended such a presentation yourself within the past six months? Have you videotaped several of them—especially the audiences' positive reactions to the points being made? They may not be at all the points you would assume just from *reading* the presentation back at your office. Nonetheless, they are the high points your catalog should echo.

Finally, review your checklist of catalog imperatives—stock numbers, prices, quantities, colors, sizes, materials, special offers, conditions of sale, etc. Now look at your copy as a whole, and ask yourself the following questions:

- Does your copy sell the uninformed reader?
- Does your copy confirm the partially committed reader?
- Does your copy make it easy and practical to order?

If the answers to these questions are "Yes," you've done your job. If the answer is "no" to even one of them, continue to work on your manuscript until all the answers *are* "yes." When it comes to copy, don't settle until you have it in writing!

An Approach to Getting Manuscripts Approved. Throughout the production of printed materials, getting manuscripts approved offers endless opportunities for confusion, delay, and ill will. If more than a single person is involved, the following suggestions will help alleviate all three problems.

1. **Appoint a single *final* approver.** A final authority is needed for each different aspect of the catalog—the factual accuracy of descriptions, numbers and prices, the promotional approach, grammar and spelling, the house style, and legal clearance. Determine who will comment and who will rule. Designate a final authority for resolution of conflicts.

2. **Initial suggested Draft copy.** Circulate the draft copy of the catalog to all designated parties, *except those in charge of grammar and spelling.* Their time-intensive editorial expertise should not be requested until all other revisions have been agreed upon.

3. **Negotiate . . . and settle.** Where conflicting suggestions or instructions are given about the same subject (for instance, differences in promotional approach), have the suggesters negotiate a resolution among themselves. But don't let the process drag on. That's why there's an authority in charge of resolving conflicts.

4. **Create a single master manuscript.** After, and only after, it is agreed upon, clearly marked, and dated, send it to the editorial people. There are likely to be conflicts between what they know is correct and what the promotion people consider necessary. Here, too, negotiation should be attempted, but in most instances, promotion will win. Of course, you do not wish to appear illiterate, but your copy must sell. Editors are not blind to this need; they often have excellent suggestions for resolving promotion and editorial problems. Ask them. Then thank them!

INSIGHT 23

A single master manuscript, as ultimately corrected and approved, becomes the original against which everything else is checked. Only one master may exist, though clearly marked copies may be circulated. Subsequent changes must be added to the master, with appropriate authorization noted. While "clean" (retyped or computer-corrected) copies of the master may be used, proofing is done against the original master, no matter how messy it may become with changes and corrections.

Design and Layout

Design and layout are not the same thing. The *design* of the catalog is the overall visual and aesthetic concept underlying the material presented. The design gives your catalog sales impact just from its appearance and "feel." The *layout* is the arrangement of words and illustrations within the overall design. The design is analogous to an architect's sketch for a building, with the layout the later detailed blueprints for the construction crew.

Design Sources and Costs. The creation of design concepts is often assigned to an outside source. For important projects, such as producing a catalog, several sources may be commissioned, with the understanding that just one will be selected to complete the project. *Each of these designers is paid an agreed-upon amount for its work!*

When assigning this or any other project to a designer, be clear about what the designer is to achieve. Get agreement *in advance* from concerned in-house managers about the goals for the catalog. Since debate inevitably occurs on questions of design, agree on a final arbiter for both the design goals and the results achieved.

When there is more than a single designer, give *exactly* the same guidelines to each. If, as often happens in discussing a project with a designer, you modify your instructions or add to them, inform your other designers of these changes. Keep the playing field level, but remember who could help you think, as well as do.

Whatever the final instructions, you will want to see at least the following:

- The front cover, or the cover "wraparound" where the front and back are one.
- The inside front cover and page 1—the first thing the recipient is likely to turn to.
- The typical treatment of a single item on a page or spread.
- The typical treatment of multiple items on a page or spread.
- A one-of-a-kind page, such as the page containing the ordering information, an index, or a table of contents.
- The order form or other reply device.

These items should be presented in fairly detailed renderings, with major headlines shown in their suggested typefaces and colors clearly indicated. The other pages may be presented in rough "thumbnail" sketches, usually one-quarter of the final page size, to show that the designer has resolved the major visual problems without any obvious oversights. To return to the analogy with an architect, you want to be sure that there are windows and bathrooms in your house, as well as a stairway to the second floor.

Bidding the complete job. Most designers will want to bid on the complete job. Let them do so, but get their bid to specify each of the following, even when the "package" is bid as a whole. *You* want the cost of each component for your own information and for future comparative shopping.

Costs included in the designer's bid

1. Original designs.
2. Page-by-page layouts, including type specifications and necessary instructions to artists and photographers.
3. Art and photography.

4. Supervision of art and photography.
5. Typesetting.
6. Key line and paste-up, including all instructions for film preparation.
7. Supervision of film and proofing.
8. Hourly or a full project rate for revisions and client meetings.

A note about profits. Outside sources cannot work for you, unless they earn a profit on your projects. It is important for them to know that you understand this. If their billing structure is such that they make a small profit on each aspect of the total job—from initial concept through printing supervision—and you want less than this from them, be certain that they know this *before* they accept the job. They can then adjust their cost structure to permit a profit. Otherwise, they will adjust their level of commitment to give you "what you paid for."

INSIGHT 24

Once a catalog or other promotion project is well under way with an outside source, there is little opportunity to change suppliers. Think of yourself as a marriage broker who has to make both parties happy with each other for a long time.

SUMMARY

* Differentiate between design and layout before deciding on the same supplier for both.
* Before assigning multiple components to a single source, find out how much the supplier will charge for *each* component if, *for any reason*, you pull (remove) the job. Get the costs in writing.
* Remember the supplier's pledge: "My clients are my friends, and I'll do *anything* for my friends—except work for nothing."

Art and Photography

WARNING! Artists and photographers frequently have different charges for outright purchase of their work, versus a one-time or specified limited use. Decide whether you will need more than a single use of their work. It is the least expensive of their charges. Whichever you order, get written agreement about *further use of works by artists or photographers themselves*, except as examples of their own work for presentation. Exceptions *must* have your written approval. Get *everything* in writing!

The conventional wisdom states that for catalogs, photography is better than art. There are some exceptions, however:

* Use art for highly styled treatment when impression is more important than reality.

- Use art where it's better at showing necessary detail, e.g., for certain hardware, colorless products, or the interior workings of closed systems such as pumps and people.
- Use art for dreams that have not yet been realized. Unbuilt homes are a typical example.

Unless you are an advertiser who uses art as a personalized signature, use photography for everything else. It gives a psychological as well as a visual perception of a "real" product.

What to Specify on Your Purchase Order for Art

- **The cost of the initial concepts.** If, for *any* reason, the project is cancelled or the final art is not assigned to a certain artist, you still have to pay the artist for his or her work. Not liking the concept does not release you from payment; after all, that's why a "concept" is ordered.
- **The cost of final art.** Specify an outright purchase. If that price seems too high, check on the cost of one-time or limited use—if that is practical. Negotiate!
- **The time allowed for delivery** of the concept and for final art after approval of the concept.
- **Any penalties for late delivery.**
- **Any penalties for delivery of final art that does not meet the agreed-upon concept.** (A personal experience may make this clear. An artist was commissioned to illustrate the Robert Frost poem, "Stopping by Woods on a Snowy Evening." Despite the poem's line that "My little horse must think it queer/To stop without a farm house near," the art showed a farmhouse—lighting the woods Frost saw as "dark and deep." The artist explained that he did understand the poem; he just liked his art better and would not change it. He did not get paid for it either. Note that this had nothing to do with the quality of the drawing, which was excellent, but everything to do with following an agreed-upon concept.)
- **Put everything in writing** and have the agreement signed by the supplier. Your verbal instructions alone are not proof that they were received . . . and very little else focuses attention like writing one's name upon a contract.

The Photographer. While there is an astonishingly large number of excellent photographers, not all of them are equally good at the same thing. Check their samples for the *type* of photography you hope to achieve, rather than expecting to find an exact sample. Selecting a photographer is very much like selecting an artist, except that you will want to work with someone whose studio is fairly close to where you work or live. It's common practice for the client to be present while the photographer works. No one else is as likely to know the products and to keep the photographer from making "obvious" mistakes in what is combined for each scene or shot.

Finding your photographer. If you have not already established a source of photographers, ask your corporate art director, your designer, or other advertising people to make a recommendation. Visit photographers' studios to get a feel for how you might work together. Ask those with whom you might wish to work to give you their costs on a daily rate, a half-day rate, and a minimum per-shot rate for repetitive photography needing little setup time. Get references and check them, especially for meeting deadlines.

How to order. Give the catalog layout to each photographer you have selected as probably qualified. Have each quote a price for the total job, including an estimate for the additional cost of film and processing. This quotation is for *complete ownership by you* of all photography, with the exception of any pictures the photographer may wish to use in a personal portfolio of samples.

If several photographers meet your criteria, have each one do the same picture for the catalog. Keep the picture simple, however; you'll be able to tell the difference among them. After reviewing their work with your art director and production director, make a decision on whom to use.

What to specify on your purchase order for photography

- *The cost of the entire project*, including photography, film, and processing.
- *The cost of a photographer-supplied art director or stylist.* You may wish to supply such a person yourself or have one supplied by your design studio. If the latter, get the studio's cost of the charges before giving the assignment.
- *The cost of any props or outside purchases made by the photographer.*
- *The time required to complete the job.* Specify the start-up time and the finishing time, not just the number of workdays. Specify what happens if *you* are not able to start on time or supply materials, as well as if the photographer causes delays.
- *Specify whether photos are to be shot for contrast or detail.* But first, discuss this with your filmmaker and printer.
- *Specify your outright ownership of all photography.*
- *Put everything in writing.* Have everyone sign before you buy.

Getting Your Production Manager and Art Director Involved. On any project that will involve the purchase of design, art, photography, film separation, and/or printing, go over the project with your organization's art director and production director before it is assigned to the outside sources. Also, go over it with them before the completed art is actually approved. Their contributions can save you much frustration and, frequently, much money. Have the art and production directors:

- Review your *instructions* to suppliers. They will recognize when you've asked for too much . . . as well as when you've requested too little.
- Review quotations from suppliers, as well as their concepts and production layouts. They will know which prices are negotiable without losing quality. They will also alert you to problems a design may cause in the

production of film or in printing or binding. You may elect not to follow their suggestions, but you will be wise to obtain them!

- Review the art and photography for their *reproduction* quality, as well as purely aesthetic considerations. Listen to their warnings!
- Accompany you to the print shop when major jobs are produced. They will be much more demanding—and get better results at the same cost and within the promised time!

Finally, recognize the contribution of the art and production directors publicly. They will have earned it!

SUMMARY

- To show products, use photography rather than art, unless you have a special reason to do otherwise.
- Artists and photographers get paid whether you like their work or not, so specify what you need . . . in writing.
- Get your experts involved before work is assigned. It's easier and cheaper to avoid problems than to fix them.

Typesetting and Desktop Publishing

Desktop publishing, the ability to produce both layouts and high-quality typesetting from a personal computer, has revolutionized much of the production of catalogs. It is now *possible* to do a great deal of typesetting in-house. But before deciding to do it yourself, the following points must be considered:

Reproduction Quality. How good is your typesetting as camera-ready art, compared with type from a commercial supplier? How well will it photograph? In all probability, in-house typesetting *will* be of high quality.

Design Quality. When in-house typesetting fails to meet promotional needs, it is most often because it lacks the qualities a trained typographer adds to typesetting. Some of this lack results from the use of less sophisticated equipment; some is caused by a lack of training. Likely problem areas include the following:

- **Line spacing.** How much room should you leave between each line and between paragraphs? This will vary, depending on the size, density (a lighter or darker version of the same type), style (sans serif or with serifs), and characteristics of each typeface.
- **Letter and word spacing.** How much room should you leave between each letter in a word and between words in a sentence. This will vary for the

same reasons mentioned in regard to line spacing, as well as because one has to make a subjective judgment about legibility. Contemporary typography tends to leave little such room; that is, it is "set tight." Your older, 50-plus reader will find a "looser" setting easier to read. Know your audience and act accordingly.

- **Flexibility.** Find the style you want within a given typeface—ultralight to ultrabold, regular, italics, small and large capitals, etc. With true computer-generated typesetting, this is unlikely to be a problem: most so-called desktop systems, on the other hand, are quite limited. Figure 4.2 shows eight professionally set typefaces used by leading designers for catalogs and other advertising projects.

- **Staffing.** Who can take over when trained personnel are on vacation, ill, absent for some other reason, get fired, or quit in the middle of a rush project?

Some Typesetting Considerations. The more important the project, the more critical is the first impression of its product. Therefore, lean towards outside, professional typesetting.

Today's technology permits almost anyone to proclaim themselves a typesetter/typographer. Before using an unfamiliar outside source, ask about their employees' training and ask for references and samples. You want a *typographer*, the typesetting equivalent of an art director or designer. Typesetting without typography can now be done in-house.

A *word of warning*: Your less important projects have a cumulative impact that is just as great and just as profit or result sensitive as your most important ones. *Everything* that bears your name represents *you* and is the only messenger of that moment.

- ✔ Less important? Yes.
- ✔ Unimportant? Never!

Typefaces. Try to limit the number of typefaces used *in the body* of the catalog to one or two. There are so many variations available *within* each face, that creativity won't suffer. In addition to the obvious changes in the size of the type and the use of standard italics or boldface, computer typesetting systems give you practically unlimited degrees of boldness and styles that can have dramatic impact. Changing the amount of space between lines and between paragraphs, indenting or not indenting paragraphs, making all lines of uniform length ("justified") or letting the margins fall where they may (ragged right; very seldom, ragged left), and the use of capitals for *short* headlines are useful devices.

Serif vs. Sans Serif Type. Sans serif (square) type is harder for most adults to read than type with serifs (the little flourishes at the ends of each letter, as in the type in this book). The more sans serif type there is in a document, the more the difficulty in reading increases. Hundreds of studies on the legibility of type verify this rule, and—to my knowledge—not a single study contradicts it. Many *designers* suggest

This is 10 point Bembo Roman, often chosen for its suggestion of tradition. First designed in Italy in 1495, it was revived in 1929. *As you can see, Bembo Italic projects an image of grace and refinement.* Bembo is often used with Small Caps and Oldstyle Figures, such as 1234567890. It is frequently employed in annual reports and publications of non-profit organizations.

This is 10 point Garamond 3 Roman, preferred for its classic feel. It was designed in France during the sixteenth century and bears its creator's name. *Garamond 3 Italic, like Bembo Italic, is graceful and refined.* It also enjoys a complement of Small Caps and Oldstyle Figures, such as 1234567890, in addition to the normal 1234567890. It is frequently used in university and hospital publications that solicit contributions from alumni or philanthropists.

This is 10 point Sabon Roman, which was designed in the 1920's, but is based on Garamond, with much of the same charm. *Sabon Italic differs only slightly, yet perceptibly, from Bembo Italic.* Designers often use Sabon as a substitute for Bembo or Garamond for a change of pace.

This is 10 point Bodoni Roman, classified as "modern," with its distinctive slab serifs and sharp contrasts. ***Bodoni Italic is dignified and not at all flowery.*** **First designed during the Italian Renaissance, Bodoni was all the rage in the earlier part of this century and is now making a comeback in annual reports and high-quality newsletters.**

This is 10 point ITC Berkeley Oldstyle Book, based on a 1938 design, and often selected for its elegant details. *ITC Berkeley Oldstyle Book Italic is even more detailed, as evident on the Q, & and z.* The face is sometimes used in advertising for a less subdued traditional look, and sometimes in brochures and other shorter publications.

This is 10 point Palatino Roman, a more modern serif face. Its contemporary feel comes from the taller x-height on its lower-case letters and the wider feel of its upper case. *Palatino Italic lends a touch of elegance when needed for emphasis or titles.* Palatino can be used for anything from newsletters to fine art books.

This is 10 point Futura Extra Black Condensed, often chosen for its excessive boldness. Previously thought suitable for headlines only, it is now sometimes used in text to achieve a radically modern feel. At this size, it requires additional letterspace to be readable. The face has been used in invitations to art gallery openings and nightclubs, for example.

This is 10 point Univers 55, often chosen for its sans serif simplicity and its subtle character. That subtle character differentiates it from Helvetica (not shown), whose ubiquity from train platforms to instruction manuals renders it undistinguished. Univers is less blocky than Helvetica, yet just as consistent.

Figure 4.2 Eight currently popular typefaces used by leading designers for catalogs and other advertising projects. (The examples and explanations are from the author's favorite typographer, Paul Baker Typography, Inc., Evanston, IL.)

sans serif because of its designlike, chiseled look. Get the opinion of a typographer before you agree.

Costs. To give quotations on typesetting, your typographer/typesetter must have from you a reasonable estimate of both the length of the manuscript and its degree of difficulty. For catalogs, it is best to wait until you have a completed layout that shows both of these. If you must estimate in advance, find the cost of a similar project and add 10 percent (last year's catalog price, plus 10 percent), plus an estimate for any additional length or difficulty.

Typesetters estimate original setting costs based on the number of lines and the number of changes in typeface and style within a copy block (another reason for keeping it simple!). After the type has been set, they charge for client-ordered changes on either an hourly rate or a rate reflecting the number of lines corrected. There is always a minimum cost just to put the job into production—to take it from storage, set up hardware and software to work on the specified project, make the changes or corrections, and return the job to storage. That cost is there whether you change just one comma to a semicolon or whether you change every other word on the page. Typesetters do not charge for their own mistakes, called typos or PEs (printer's errors), but only for *client* changes and alterations.

In getting quotations for lengthy typesetting jobs, get the costs for setting with no client changes and the formulas for changes in 5 percent and 10 percent of the lines (i.e., 32 pages times 35 lines per page, or 1,120 lines, with 56 lines corrected for 5%), and so forth. Since you will probably have two or three sets of corrections, estimate those costs also. Get the agreed-upon pricing structure in writing before you assign the work.

Chapter 1 also presented a discussion of typesetting beginning on page 20.

SUMMARY

- Typeset in-house only if you have the right equipment and personnel. Either one alone is not enough.
- Find and use a typographer you trust, whether you set in-house or out. (It's OK to battle with your typographers, but usually they should win.)
- Get estimates that include more changes than you know you're going to make. You'll still be too low.

Key Line and Paste-Up

In almost all printing, what is to be printed must first be photographed. In its simplest form, this photographing is an automatic process such as the one used on a Xerox™ copy machine. The Xeroxed copies are the final printed pieces. In more complicated printing, right up to multicolor catalogs, elements from a variety of sources may have to be brought together on a single page. For instance, you may wish to combine drawings, photographs, type, tints, and reverses on a page. The different elements that appear on each page and the instructions that tell the filmmaker *exactly* how to put all the pieces together are given on a *paste-up*, which, in turn, is produced on a *key line*.

The Key Line. A key line is an outline of the size and shape of the printed page. For multipage projects such as catalogs, key lines are usually prepared as "double-page spreads" or "facing-page spreads." (The two terms mean the same thing and are interchangeable. They are also redundant, since a "spread" is defined as two facing pages. Verbal habits die hard—if ever.) The most important requirement of the key line is that it have a system for defining the exact outer limits of each page and that this system be consistent throughout the project. A common way of doing this is through *crosshatches* at the four corners. They look like this:

┐   ┌

┘   └

There are two reasons for using such a system:

1. When more than a single color of ink is put onto a page, each color is prepared as a separate piece of film and is later transferred to its own printing plate. The crosshatches are the printer's guide for superimposing the colors on top of each other during the actual printing—a task called "keeping the job in register."
2. While the key line for most projects is *prepared* as facing pages (pages 2–3 together, 4–5 together, etc.), no project of five or more pages can *print* that way. Instead, the filmmaker cuts apart the filmed pages and rearranges them in the order they will be printed, so that a simple eight-page film may look like Figure 4.3.

In the rearranged sequence for printing, the sum of the page numbers of any two facing pages is always one more than the total number of pages being printed. Thus, the page numbers of each of the facing 8-page spreads totals 9. In a 16-page unit it will total 17, and in a 32-page unit—the largest most printers can produce—it will total 33. That your film agrees with this rule is one more check you can make without having to be an expert . . . and should make, even if you are.

INSIGHT 25

For 64 pages or more, consider preprinting key lines using a "nonreproduction blue" ink that can be seen by the paste-up artist but not by the camera. It's common trade practice, and your artist can explain how it works.

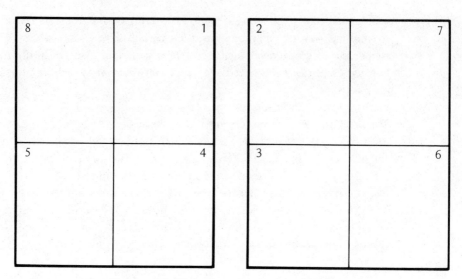

Figure 4.3 Eight-page film may look like this.

The Paste-Up. The keyline may be prepared on a variety of backgrounds, with special, inexpensive "boards" available for that purpose from commercial art suppliers. Think of these as the base upon which the paste-up artist creates a montage that will be photographed for printing. Until the 1970s, practically all such montages were fastened to the key line with paste or glue—hence the term "paste-up." Today, many paste-ups are actually prepared with a wax adhesive.

The number and variety of pieces affixed to the key line should determine the material from which it is made. The more "pasting," the heavier will be the base paper or board. Usually, all the type is pasted directly onto the key line. Artwork and photography are generally represented by a photostat or other inexpensive reproduction marked "COPY" or "SIZE & POSITION ONLY." The original art or photography is seldom of the exact size needed and is usually considered too valuable to "paste up," even if it does fit.

Where elements will overlap or butt directly against each other, they can be placed onto one or more clear plastic overlay sheets that make them easier to position. When using such overlays, make sure the cross-hatches match throughout. Each overlay is photographed separately, and the hatch marks are used for subsequent alignment.

Instructions for the paste-up are put on a sheet of transparent paper that is fastened *securely* to the edge of the paste-up and that covers the work to be photographed. Use this sheet to give detailed instructions about colors, the placement or treatment of art and photography, items that need special handling, or problems you wish to call to the attention of the filmmaker with pleas for help or requests to "use your best judgment." *Do not* write directly on top of anything that is to be photographed, except with a very soft pencil or felt-tipped pen. Any impression made by the pressure of your writing will be reproduced on the film! Where possible, place an X in the spot to be noted, circle the X, and draw a line—very lightly—from the circled X into the margin. That's where you write your instructions.

Approving the paste-up. The paste-up is the last chance you'll have to make changes without adding very expensive film costs. Be prepared for the possibility that a number of your colleagues will want to make changes *now*, so give them *copies* clearly marked "FINAL CHECK BEFORE PRINTING." (No one touches the originals except you!) You may need a final FINAL check from the editorial people, with a separate final check on all pricing. If not, at least make certain that no prices have changed since the previous approval. Final legal, managerial, and departmental readings will have been set by policy, as will the need for a statement about "pricing subject to change without notice."

As always, get approvals and requests for changes in writing. This is the time to differentiate between the changes people would like and what they really need!

SUMMARY

- Preprint key lines where practical. Your smaller printer is probably your best supplier.
- Treat the paste-up as if it were valuable original art. It is!
- Write all instructions on the paste-up overlay, and then go over *each one* with the filmmaker. It's a great review and a revelation about nomenclature.

Film Separation and Proofing

The following explanation, though somewhat simplified, is essentially accurate. Additional information on film separation and proofing, including a checklist, is given in Chapter 10.

Modern printing is a process in which various colors can be placed on paper in one of two ways:

1. Special colors can be printed one at a time or in combination using inks made up just for the project at hand. Thousands of such colors exist, and others can be created at will.
2. More commonly—especially for the reproduction of materials that were in color as originals—colors are reproduced by combining just four inks that are specific tones of red, blue, black, and yellow. These are the "process colors" used in "full-color" process printing. Almost all full-color catalogs and other promotional materials are printed this way.

From Paste-Up to Film. For multicolor printing, film is prepared by special cameras (more commonly today by laser scanners) that, through a series of filters, "see" the original work as shades of red, yellow, blue, and black. The recombining of those four colors is the printing process. However, depending on the original, some of what the human eye sees may not be captured by this color separation camera.

INSIGHT 26

Discuss the capabilities—and limitations—of a separation camera with your film supplier before art or photography is assigned. It's a lot easier and cheaper than trying to "fix" the material after it's delivered!

Stripping. In "stripping," the filmmaker takes two or more pieces of film and tapes them together. We can think of this as a "film paste-up." Stripping can also be used to move elements closer together or place them farther apart after they have been transferred to film.

Contacting. "Contacting" means that a film—original or itself a copy—is copied. The "original" for that project is its "first-generation" film. The copy is "second generation." This process is used when first-generation film may not be cut for repositioning or is not available, although a copy is. This frequently happens when the original film is part of another project and must be maintained in its current form. Fortunately, a copy can usually be made through contacting. If that copy is then used, it becomes second-generation film. If the copy must be transferred once again by contacting, the contacted film becomes third generation. Knowing the film generation is important. Each copy made by contacting will lose some of the quality of its original. Think of it as making a copy of a copy of a copy. Thus, the more generations, the less fidelity there is to the original. However, the more careful and talented the film separator, the less loss there is overall. Expect a 2- to 4-percent loss per film generation, which is hardly noticeable until the third or fourth generation. After that, it is definitely a factor in loss of reproduction quality.

INSIGHT 27

Accidents can happen anytime anyone works with film. So don't just check your own corrections—check *everything*. But don't change anything unless *absolutely* necessary. Correcting film is costly and requires equally careful rechecking every time.

The Printer's Guide. The proof that is marked "OK for printing" or "OK as corrected" (Note the difference!) is signed and dated. It becomes the printer's guide against which the printed piece is checked. In reviewing the proof, be mindful that "what you see is what you get." Do not give your approval until you are satisfied with what you do see!

Of course, you will let your print production and art departments take the lead in checking and approving proofs. If such departments are not available, use your designer. It is *these people's* area of *expertise*; it is *your* area of *responsibility*.

Single-color proofs. Where only one color will be used in printing, the color chosen and the sophistication of the design will determine how closely the proofs must match the printed piece. An exact match of a specific color is more costly than a routine monotone, but as with multicolor proofs, it is the only way to know what you will see when you get the printed piece.

Folding dummy. The folding dummy is produced in one color on paper that is light enough to fold easily. This proof is folded or formed by the printer into the exact shape and format of the final printed product. It is the folding dummy that lets you see how facing pages actually look when all the elements are present and that lets you know that all the elements are the way they were specified. The following is a list of things to check in using the folding dummy.

☐ Are all the pages present and in consecutive order?
☐ Do elements that run across the center of facing pages (across the *"gutter"*) line up?
☐ Do the index and table of contents reflect where the elements are placed? If not, which one is wrong? Do all cross-references check out?
☐ Do all the elements fit together? Do the materials fit into the envelope? Are items that bind together the proper shape and size? Etc.
☐ Are comparable elements positioned properly? For instance, are all the page numbers (called *folios*) in the same location on the page? Is the use of section or page headings consistent. If not, is the inconsistency deliberate?
☐ Is all mailing information present and accurate? Telephone numbers? Direct dial? Are all legal and self-protective requirements met? For example, is such information as "Printed in USA," "Prices subject to change," etc., present?

This is the final chance to see the job as a whole before printing. Take the opportunity—and time—to check *everything*.

SUMMARY

- The filmmaker's camera does not see the way you do. Learn its capabilities and limitations before a multicolor project is begun.
- Expect the worst; check *everything* each time you proof.
- The OK'd proof becomes your printer's guide. Don't settle for less than you want or need on the assurance that the printer can fix it. The chances are, they can't!
- Encourage creativity, but check with the post office before you approve anything new and different in size, shape, or format. Post office staff are there to help. Let them!

Printing and Binding

Printing is a process in which original materials—the paste-up or computer-generated camera-ready art—are photographed and separated onto film. Each film holds one of the colors used in printing. The photographic image is transferred from film onto a printing plate and then printed.

The best advice that can be given about working with printers and binderies is to know what you want to achieve, but never to tell them how to do it. A personal anecdote is illustrative.

My introduction to advertising ("Why don't you try it for three months and see how you like it?") was with a modest retail chain that paid for an exceptional promotional department by syndicating its stores' catalog. The three months turned into three years, during which I wrote every word of every catalog, as well as the syndication promotions that put our only two competitors out of business. I obviously had a gift for copy. Fortunately for me, my boss, Mort Levin, had a gift for instruction and became the first of my many great advertising coaches.

The Christmas catalog was by far our biggest annual effort. Over a hundred stores used it nationwide, and Levin decided to reward me for my efforts by letting me supervise its printing. Actually, what he really wanted was to go to Minnesota, and the printing schedule conflicted with the short duck-hunting season in that state.

I didn't care. I was in charge!

One week later, I found myself at one of the very first commercial printers to use the then revolutionary new high-speed "web" presses. It was 3:30 A.M., and the printing staff had spent eight hours trying to produce a printed sheet that matched the proof, continually asking my advice on how to make it better. Foolishly, and out of sheer frustration at not getting what I wanted, I told them. Nothing worked. Actually, I was fairly sure that the problem was not fixable that way. The printed catalogs looked dirty. There was a light layer of ink on areas that should have been pure white. We had lost contrast and sharpness. The real problem, as I later learned, was in the printing plates. The presses should have been stopped and new plates made. But this is exactly what the printer did not want to do. He'd spent hours getting his new press "in register," with colors correctly positioned on top of each other. New plates would mean that he'd have to do it all over again—not to mention the time the press would be "down" while the plates were made.

Somehow—though I really knew better—he convinced me that the printing was as good as the press could make it. I approved the printing "as is," knowing that I had done something wrong, but not sure what. One thing I was sure about: I was going to get fired!

This story has an ending with two parts. In part number 1, I did not get fired. When Levin returned, he took one look at the catalog and—rather than blaming me—totally blamed the printer for taking advantage of my inexperience. Fortunately for me, he didn't equate my ignorance with stupidity. We never did business with that printer again. Part number 2 is one of the few technically correct examples of irony in my experience. Despite its apparent drabness, that catalog proved to be the most successful in our firm's, and our hundred-plus customers', history. I assume that the products—and my copy—overcame all else.

Things You Can Do

1. Get a firm quotation, as well as samples of paper to be used, based on actual layouts and specifications. An excellent safety measure is to show the potential printer a copy of the designer's concept and ask whether printing it will present difficulties. Then act accordingly.

2. Any unusual folds or combinations of materials or sizes may cause difficulties and increase costs. Check these aspects for possible problems as early as possible— certainly, early enough to change them to something more practical if need be.

3. Anything unusual in shape or size must be checked with the post office for mailing approval, as well as for special handling charges. Make an exact sample (called a *dummy*), and have someone in the post office permits section *approve it and sign the approval*.

4. If the catalog, or any other mailing, will be sent by third-class bulk rate, and you mail fewer than 100,000 pieces, a fractional ounce of additional weight should not create budgeting problems, but check for the latest postal rates to make sure. If, however, you will be mailing any materials first class, have your printer give you an exact dummy made from all of the different papers that you expect to use (Figure 4.4). If you are close to any whole ounce in weight, do something to make the project lighter. *The chances are that adding ink to the paper will be enough to put you into the next ounce and a higher postage rate.* Consider making your project 1/32″ smaller on one side. That's generally enough to compensate for the weight of the ink. But check with your printer and your mailing service to make sure.

5. Deal with printers and binderies through your print production department. Its staff are the experts in these areas. Ask them to explain what they are doing and why they are doing it. Your job is to *know*, not necessarily to *do*. So join them at the printer and bindery when your projects are being produced. Ask about anything you do not know or understand . . . but remember to insist on what you want to achieve. Questions about "more red" or "less blue" or "heavier black" are turned over to the production or art staff. If you are the only one at the printer or bindery, point to the proof and repeat the magic words:

> That's what we want. I wouldn't begin to try to tell *you* how to get it.

Resist the temptation to claim more expertise than you have.

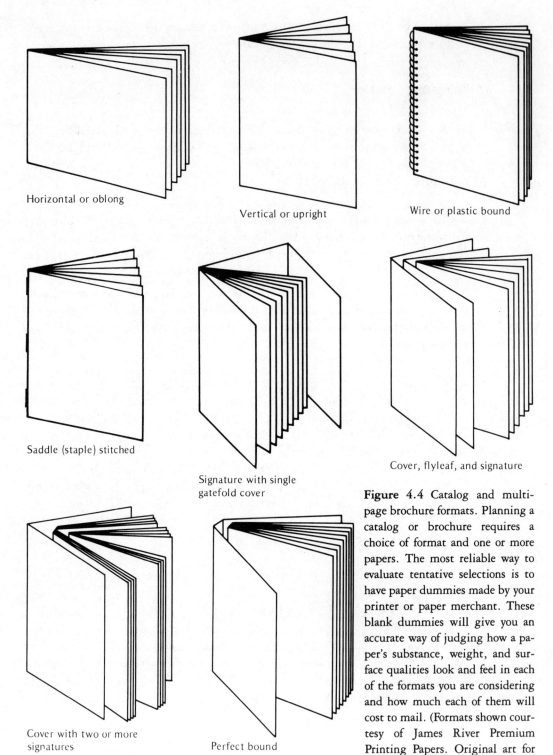

Horizontal or oblong

Vertical or upright

Wire or plastic bound

Saddle (staple) stitched

Signature with single gatefold cover

Cover, flyleaf, and signature

Cover with two or more signatures

Perfect bound

Figure 4.4 Catalog and multipage brochure formats. Planning a catalog or brochure requires a choice of format and one or more papers. The most reliable way to evaluate tentative selections is to have paper dummies made by your printer or paper merchant. These blank dummies will give you an accurate way of judging how a paper's substance, weight, and surface qualities look and feel in each of the formats you are considering and how much each of them will cost to mail. (Formats shown courtesy of James River Premium Printing Papers. Original art for James River by Hyers/Smith Advertising, South Norwalk, CT.)

SUMMARY

- Printers know how to print. Don't try to help, even when they ask.
- The proof is your bible. Remain a printing fundamentalist.
- The press run won't get better after you leave. Stay until you are satisfied with what you see.

Additional information on printing, including a Printing Checklist, is given in Chapter 10.

Distribution and Mailing

Distribution refers to catalogs sent in bulk to outlets and sales staff, to company offices and departments, to the warehouse for bulk storage, and to the mailing facility for handling.

Mailing refers specifically to those catalogs mailed to customers, prospects, and any other groups and individuals specified by management.

Determining Who Handles the Mailing. Postage costs will be exactly the same and the delivery time will be approximately the same, no matter who handles the mailing. Your mailing service should therefore be chosen for the following reasons:

- **Distance from bindery.** What will it cost to ship the bound catalogs to the mailing service? A bindery that has its own mailing department is preferred over one that does not, *other factors being equal*.
- **Cost of service.** Cost is based on the size and weight of the catalogs. Get a written quotation. Be sure the potential mailing service staff sees a layout of the mailing side of the catalog—usually the back cover—while there is still time to make changes. Their equipment may make it impossible to put the address where your layout indicates. That's generally an "easy fix" for you, given adequate time; it may be an impossible fix for them.
- **Reliability of service.** If you are planning to use a supplier for the first time, get references *and check them*.

Seeding the Mailing List. When using mailing lists, give the mailing service the names and addresses of some of your fellow employees (in different parts of the country if possible), as well as the names and addresses of some in-house staff. Then ask these people to let you know *exactly* when they receive the catalog. This will give you a record of when catalogs are received in various parts of the country and whether there are any likely problems in the mail handling. Do this with *every* mailing, whether you use an outside list or your own.

Paying for Postage. Postage must be received by the post office before mailing. For bulk rate mailing, postage is paid into a special account established by the post office in your or your supplier's name. Find out from your mailing service what bulk rate information has to be printed onto the catalog, to whom the check for postage is to be issued, and when that check must be received. As this is written, the post office does *not* require that such a check be certified.

INSIGHT 28

Do *not* let your printer rush a sample *of anything* to your employer, the chairman of the board, or anyone else. Invariably, it will be one with a glaring mistake, such as a page printed upside down that they later corrected but were saving to show how alert they were to your oversights. *You* deliver the sample, checking it very carefully first. It's *your* project. You do the showing off!

SUMMARY

- Get *exact*, complete dummy samples from the printer as soon as designs are approved. You'll need them to learn the cost of postage and to make final postage-related adjustments. Your post office will help.
- Seed the mailing lists with the names of some people who'll tell you when the catalog arrives. Add your name, too.

Much more detailed information on Lettershop Mailing Services, including a Lettershop/Mailing Checklist, is given in Chapter 10.

IT ISN'T OVER TILL . . .

Postproduction Activities

Here's a way to close out the current catalog before the next one comes due: Use the items applicable to your situation, modify where necessary, . . . and Celebrate when done!

- **What to return.** Get all products used for photography and return them to stock. Make sure that your department is credited with their return, because you were surely charged when they went out. Gather any other materials (such as original art or photo props) that were borrowed for the project, and return them as promised. Anything of value must be insured and return delivery signed for.
- **What to store.** Store the complete catalog paste-up after checking for any missing pieces. Determine who will follow up on missing elements and when they are to report on what they have found.

Remove photos and transparencies, and file them in the advertising/promotion department. You will want instant access to them for other projects. These photos should be noted "best" and filed with any backup shots.

Save all price quotations, purchase orders, and advisory or instructional memoranda in a permanent project file.

- **What to throw away.** Thirty days after the catalog has been distributed, notify management and departments that you will dispose of "all manuscripts, proofs, and incidental paperwork" concerning the project, unless they instruct you to the contrary by a certain date (say, 7 days hence). Unless you are ordered to save any of these materials, throw them out!

Recordkeeping and Reporting

The following detailed records must be kept and reported:

- **The actual cost** of the project vs. the estimated or quoted costs and reasons for any discrepancy. This report is issued as soon as all invoices have been received.
- **The response** to the mailing. If possible, a detailed record of responses should be kept for at least 60 days after the first response is received. This is especially important if the catalog is used to test lists or the viability of products or a promotional effort. A report on the response is issued at the conclusion of a specified period. Where comparisons to previous similar efforts are practical and pertinent, they are, of course, included. "Back-end analysis" is a specialty all its own. Get professional help if it is needed.

NOTES ON THE CATALOG CHECKLIST

These notes are a supplement to the material presented in this chapter. They are not a substitute for that material.

1. For scheduling purposes, the most important management decision is the date the catalog must be completed and what "completed" means. If meeting the deadline is impossible under normal time or budgeting constraints, management must decide whether or not to authorize the impossible. (Do *not* present managers with an on-time delivery at a cost that is significantly over budget because you "knew" they wanted it that way. Even if they did, it is *their* decision. Some of my best friends have been fired for not understanding this difference.)
2. If the needed quantity becomes a budget problem, here are a few ways to get more catalogs for the same dollars:
   - Use less expensive paper. Often slightly lighter weight paper will save enough on postage to make up the difference.

CATALOG CHECKLIST

Project title/description _____

_____

_____

Overall Supervision by _____

Budget _____ Start-up Date _____

Date _____

Project # _____

Checklist # _____

Deadline _____

Completion Date _____

MANAGEMENT DECISIONS	ASSIGNED TO	DUE	IN	MUST APPROVE	BY DATE	IN	INFO COPY ONLY	SEE ATTACHED
1. Schedule	_____	__	☐	_____	__	☐	_____	☐
2. Quantity	_____	__	☐	_____	__	☐	_____	☐
3. Budget	_____	__	☐	_____	__	☐	_____	☐
4. Theme	_____	__	☐	_____	__	☐	_____	☐
5. Audience	_____	__	☐	_____	__	☐	_____	☐
6. Report(s)	_____	__	☐	_____	__	☐	_____	☐
7. Project Manager	_____	__	☐	_____	__	☐	_____	☐

CREATIVE DECISIONS	ASSIGNED TO	DUE	IN	MUST APPROVE	BY DATE	IN	INFO COPY ONLY	SEE ATTACHED
8. Design Concept	_____	__	☐	_____	__	☐	_____	☐
9. Layout	_____	__	☐	_____	__	☐	_____	☐
10. Copy	_____	__	☐	_____	__	☐	_____	☐
11. Typesetting	_____	__	☐	_____	__	☐	_____	☐
12. Cover Subjects	_____	__	☐	_____	__	☐	_____	☐
13. Photographer(s)	_____	__	☐	_____	__	☐	_____	☐
14. Artist(s)	_____	__	☐	_____	__	☐	_____	☐
15. Insert(s)	_____	__	☐	_____	__	☐	_____	☐
16. Order Form(s)	_____	__	☐	_____	__	☐	_____	☐
17. Envelope	_____	__	☐	_____	__	☐	_____	☐

MECHANICAL DECISIONS	ASSIGNED TO	DUE	IN	MUST APPROVE	BY DATE	IN	INFO COPY ONLY	SEE ATTACHED
18. Paste-up: Cover(s)	_____	__	☐	_____	__	☐	_____	☐
19. Paste-up: Body	_____	__	☐	_____	__	☐	_____	☐
20. Paste-up: _____	_____	__	☐	_____	__	☐	_____	☐
21. Film: Cover(s)*	_____	__	☐	_____	__	☐	_____	☐
22. Film: Body	_____	__	☐	_____	__	☐	_____	☐
23. Film: _____	_____	__	☐	_____	__	☐	_____	☐
24. Print: Cover(s)*	_____	__	☐	_____	__	☐	_____	☐
25. Print: Body	_____	__	☐	_____	__	☐	_____	☐
26. Print: _____	_____	__	☐	_____	__	☐	_____	☐
27. Bindery	_____	__	☐	_____	__	☐	_____	☐
28. Mailing Service*	_____	__	☐	_____	__	☐	_____	☐
29. Postage Check(s)	_____	__	☐	_____	__	☐	_____	☐
_____	_____	__	☐	_____	__	☐	_____	☐
_____	_____	__	☐	_____	__	☐	_____	☐

* Separate checklists are included in Chapter 10 for film work, printing,
and mailing service.

- Use fewer (or more!) pages, provided that they give you the least expensive printing. Adding just 4 pages to a 32-page catalog adds appreciably more than one-eighth the cost. The same costs may be true when printing "only" 28 pages on presses designed for 32. Discuss with your printer the most economical ways to get the job done. If you are unfamiliar with purchasing print, make sure that you learn the whys involved.
- Give your printer a needed quantity and the budget decided upon. If the printer can't meet it, shop around for another.

3. In estimating budgets, make sure that the suppliers know when the services will be needed. If there are likely increases in union rates, nonunion shops will probably have similar raises. Check with the post office for possible changes in regulations as well as postage. As always, try to keep management's surprises pleasant.

4. Try to keep managers from becoming copywriters. Good luck!

5. "Audience" relates directly to #2, the quantity needed, and #3, the cost of getting catalogs to each recipient. Remind management of this inter-relationship, and, where budgets are limited, get the priorities or some other guidance.

6. Anything needed or wanted beyond the budget, costs, and known results. Discuss the practicality of each request if getting the information is not already built into your system. Much of this kind of data is nice to know, but what will be done with it after it's been gathered?

7. The project manager, if different from the overall supervisor, will be *directly* responsible for the supervision of points 8–28. It is this manager who most often appoints as well as supervises the persons involved.

8–9. Who will do each? In some instances, the layout can be done internally, even if a design is purchased outside.

10. How much does the writer have to know about your product or service to do the job? Write technical copy inside, and then give it to an outside writer for review. In accuracy vs. sell, settle for accuracy every time.

11. Discuss with your typesetter the practicality of your producing the manuscript on disk, but having them prepare finished hard copy or film for reproduction. This is often the best solution when the copy is other than standard English or there are numerous last second changes in numbers, prices, or other data.

12. Who decides?

13–14. Commercial artists and photographers tend to do best at specific kinds of projects. Get samples. Negotiate for prices. Try to give "the kid" a chance.

15. Inserts are a practical way to address specific audiences without adding everything to the main catalog. Use them also for testing, as described on pages 67–69. In using different inserts for different parts of your mailing, discuss controls with your mailing service *before* mailing lists are

ordered or anything is printed. Specific codes may be required on each part.

16. It often pays huge dividends to have more than a single order form in catalogs that have a fairly long life. Test.

17. Few catalogs are mailed in envelopes, unless they are accompanied by a variety of loose materials. Often the latter can be bound in. Check. Save!

18–23. Be sure to build in adequate time for in-house review. Everyone who sees anything will want to suggest changes, so ask for corrections and comments from the fewest number of persons safety allows. Nothing gets reviewers more furious than being asked for comments and then being ignored!

24–26. Use in-house expertise if available; get a designer involved if not. On-press approval tends to be a *very* lengthy job. Allow for that in scheduling and budgeting.

27–28. Two excellent ways to let beginners learn the importance of nitpicking detail. Little is likely to go wrong. But everything must be checked— continually—to keep it that way.

29. The postal service will not accept a mailing without payment in hand. In organizations where payment is sometimes slow, get management to set up a system that won't delay the mail.

5 | Conventions, Trade Shows, Consumer Shows, and Meetings

HOW THEY DIFFER AND WHY IT MATTERS

This chapter is about exhibiting[1] at conventions, trade shows, and meetings. In industry jargon, they're all called "shows," but they do have important distinctions.

Conventions

The main purpose of a **convention** is to advance skills, to increase knowledge, or to promote a cause, and sometimes all three. Heart surgeons and political parties have conventions.

Many conventions include exhibits. Your evaluation of such conventions will depend on the interest shown in the exhibits by those attending the convention.

Trade Shows

The main purpose of a **trade show** is to bring together exhibitors with a preselected audience of customers and prospects. Manufacturers of office equipment and T-shirts, as well as breeders of horses and dogs, have trade shows.

Many trade shows also include convention-type activities, but the primary focus is still on the exhibits.

Consumer Shows
(for the General Public)

Auto shows and the larger home and garden shows are examples of exhibits for the general public. They almost all charge admission, and many of them sell products directly from their booths. While the information in this chapter is applicable to consumer shows, it does not deal with them directly, but concentrates on trade shows, conventions, and meetings.

---

[1] The terms "exhibit" and "display" are used interchangeably by just about everyone concerned with either. The traditional distinction of "display" as a verb and "exhibit" as a noun (e.g., to display at an exhibit) is still found in some dictionaries as the primary definition, but is ignored in current practice. Thus, a leading company in the field is called "General Exhibit and Display."

Meetings

A meeting may be a convention, a show, or neither. Check the description in the meeting prospectus before you attend.

WHY YOU CARE

As a new exhibitor or one unfamiliar with a specific show, you don't care what it's called. You want to know what such shows do and how much importance is placed on the exhibits. (See Figures 5.1 and 5.2.) So check the descriptive literature, and then speak to the sponsoring organization—always remembering that they make money only if you decide to go. You'll want answers to at least two questions:

1. **Exhibits-only time.** What times are set aside exclusively for visiting exhibits? (Be aware that many shows which are successful for exhibitors have no such set-asides. Those attending make time. But it's one factor you'll want to consider.)
2. **Conflicts.** What special events by the sponsoring organization, other exhibitors, or anyone else are scheduled? If they do not know, ask for the

Figure 5.1 A 10-booth island display designed by the author from modular units originally designed and custom-built by General Exhibit and Display of Chicago. Note how the placement of overhead signs dominates the immediate surrounding exhibit space.

Figure 5.2 Detail of the island display (Figure 5.1) shown during show hours. Prospects listen to a four-minute presentation at six different stations, then receive a "Good readers are made, not born" bookmark, pin, or other inexpensive premium that echoes the exhibition theme.

previous year's final schedule. This type of activity tends to follow similar patterns each year. (For instance, if noon to 2:00 P.M. is set aside to visit exhibits, is someone enticing away your prospects with a two-hour buffet, or will they gulp a cup of coffee and rush to the exhibits . . . and how can you know?

IS IT WORTHWHILE ATTENDING?

Few exhibitors attend every convention or trade show in their field. Before exhibiting at a meeting of unknown value, ask the sponsoring organization to send you a copy of the previous year's program and, if separate, the list of that year's exhibitors. Call a few exhibitors with interests similar to yours and ask for their evaluation. Are they going back? If so, is it for business or "political" reasons? You'll know whether the same reasons apply to you.

When you've decided where to exhibit, you can start planning what will happen before and after you get there. One thing is absolutely certain: It won't happen if you don't plan.

INSIGHT 29

The First "Secret" of Successful Exhibits:
"Lack of resources" is an invitation to invent excuses. Forget resources and remember goals. In planning your exhibit, keep your focus on your goals and make the resources fit them.

SUMMARY

- Conventions focus on knowledge; trade shows focus on products and services.
- You care not about what it's called—only about what they do.
- Ask previous exhibitors for their evaluations. They paid the bill.

WHY YOU AND THEY ARE THERE

The planning of your exhibit begins with a search for the answers to two questions:

1. Why are they—my clients and prospects—there?
2. What can I gain from being there with them, and how do I do it?

Table 5.1 summarizes some appropriate answers to these questions.

In all probability, a trade show held in Las Vegas in mid-February will get less exhibit attention than the same show held in Iowa City in August. But less is far different from none. Many of the most successful conventions and trade shows are very deliberately held in seemingly distracting locations. That's how they draw such huge attendance. Taking advantage of that attendance despite the attraction of outside interests requires detailed planning. Especially important is the setting of specific goals that will focus your efforts.

HOW TO FOCUS YOUR EFFORTS
AND THEIR ATTENTION

Success with trade shows and conventions is mostly about focusing attention—yours and that of the people you hope to attract and persuade. To demonstrate the problem, imagine yourself at the annual New York or Chicago Premium and Incentive Show. Of the over 1,000 exhibitors, some 27 specialize in T-shirts and caps, 27 more in watches and clocks, 31 in pens and writing materials, and 19 in some kind of food. In addition, 60 exhibitors have a combination of one or more of those products. If you are a buyer deciding among T-shirts, pens, watches, and edibles as a premium, how

Table 5.1   Why Clients and Exhibitors Attend Conferences

Why Clients and Prospects Attend	How to Turn It to Your Advantage
To meet with friends and colleagues.	Become a friend by being active in the organization sponsoring the meeting. The very fact of your being there makes you a colleague.
To learn.	Make your exhibit a learning opportunity by helping *your* customers look smarter to *their* customers.
To make a careful evaluation of exhibitors' and competitors' products and services.	Your customers aren't the only ones who have competitors. Get out of your booth long enough to see what your competitors are doing. Take photographs of their exhibits and any others that seem especially interesting, to learn what they do right.
To get a tax-deductible vacation.	Don't wine and dine guests without a specific purpose in mind. Their goal may be a fancy, free meal; yours has to be more business centered.

do you decide with whom to spend your time? Conversely, if you are one of those exhibitors, how do you get that buyer to spend time with you when he or she can't possibly evaluate every single exhibit? The answer lies in one word: *focus*.

Focus on Focus

The single most effective way to succeed as an exhibitor is to aim for a particular type of prospect and to provide an instantly recognizable reason for thinking that you can solve the problem that took that prospect to the show. If all you want is to draw a crowd, just give a crisp, cool, delicious apple to anyone who comes to your booth. You'll be inundated with visitors. That may be your goal if you are the leading supplier in your industry and are exhibiting to retain and build on goodwill. But if you are new or one of the lesser players, you don't want *visitors*, you want *prospects*. Make that your focus.

Focus on Prospects

It is, of course, possible that everyone attending a trade show or convention is a prospect for your product or service. Booksellers viewing exhibits from publishers or hardware retailers given their choice of different brands of nails seem likely examples. But no bookseller can stock every title, and few hardware stores have more than a few brands of nails. How you bring attention to *your* titles, *your* nails, *your* brand of ice cream, *your* microwaves, or *your* earthmoving equipment depends—often at first sight—on your prospects' view of you. Focusing that view so they see you as a solver of their problems is the key to your success.

Focus on Your Prospects' Problems—and Solve Them

Think of your prospects as buyers who, in turn, must please a specific kind of customer. This is true whether their "customer" is within their own organization (seeking new furniture for the offices or new locomotives for the trains) or outside (buying a new line of children's shoes or a new kind of lawnmower). Pleasing these ultimate customers should be the focus of everything your prospects do at a show. Your success lies not in appealing to them as a buyer, but in assuring their success as a seller. Convince them that you can make them look good to their ultimate customers, and you'll turn prospects into customers, to your benefit . . . and theirs.

INSIGHT 30

Decide who your real prospects are by focusing on what they want from the show and on whether you can provide it. Then look at your display through their eyes. If it doesn't trumpet you as the best answer to their needs, you're looking at either the wrong prospects or an ineffective display.

SUMMARY

- Discover and fill your prospects' needs. It's the most likely way to fill your own.

THE BILLBOARD APPROACH TO SUCCESS AT EXHIBITING

No one has learned better than the producers of billboards how to focus fleeting attention. Just think of the problems of selling *in print* to drivers whose lives depend on keeping their eyes on the road! Here's how it's done:

1. **Use one simple message only** . . . the simpler the better. If ever there was a time for the KISS principle (Keep it simple, stupid), this is it.
2. **Keep it single.** Let everything reinforce the same message. Products, words, visuals, colors, and design all work together to achieve a single goal.
3. **Keep it short.** The fewer words and images you have, the better off you are. Keep it focused. If you can get along without it, do.

What This Book Can Do to Help

Neither this book nor any other guide can design, stock, or staff your exhibit. But it can give you a method for applying the billboard technique to your display from its original concept to your post-show evaluation and at every step along the way. Here's how.

1. Assume that you will be placed in the middle of five exhibitors showing what appears to be a product or service identical to yours. To make things easier, assume that you all have the same amount of space.

2. Assume that a temporarily blinded prospect goes to each of you and asks that you tell her *just one thing*, on the basis of which she'll decide whether or not to return after her vision clears up later that day. That one thing is your "billboard"—the featured words which are part of your display and which tell your prospects that you know who they are and that you can solve their problems.

3. Now assume that a temporarily deaf prospect goes by each of your displays. He'll also return to one of you when his hearing clears up. He sees your signs, but he also sees your entire exhibit. Do they both convey the same message? Do they reinforce each other? Or do they contradict or ignore each other, as if different persons with different goals had been in charge of preparing your display? You have a one-in-five chance of getting the prospect back if you leave it to luck and if your competitors do the same. Since they're unlikely to do that, however, you'd better not count on it either.

INSIGHT 31

Use the billboard technique. Don't be fuzzy, and hope for the most. Be focused and plan for the best.

SUMMARY

- Think of your display as a billboard with room for a single, simple message.
- Know what you want to say and to whom you want to say it. Then make everything send the same signal: "Your problem solved here!"

When You Are Limited to Saying Just One Thing, Make It a Benefit

The Theme. The key to finding the right theme for your "billboard" is to focus on the audience that your prospects need to please, rather than on the prospects themselves. If your prospects don't know what's in it for them, you'll certainly want to tell them, but only after you've established an even more important point—that a greater chance of their success lies with you than with the exhibitor next door.

Think of your prospects as bees, yourself as a flower, and the entire show as a garden. Bees are attracted to certain flowers not because they are going to gorge themselves, but because they're shopping for the nectar that will satisfy the need of the entire hive. Other creatures are attracted to different plants, but you don't care about them. In fact, you're better off if they ignore you and let you concentrate on attracting and satisfying your target audience.

Since, in reality, you hope to attract prospects rather than bees, your nectar is your products or services, plus words that single you out for attention. To make the entire process work, use those words to turn the focus from features to benefits— from what *you* hope to *sell* to what *they* want to *buy*.

The Words. The key to finding the right words for your "billboard" is to translate features into benefits. If you remember that your prospects' success lies in selling your product or service to someone else, you'll find that those words come much easier.

Again, remember that a **feature** is what you have put into your product or service. It's what you know best, so there's a natural temptation to make it your point of focus. Thus, at a Ready-Wear trade show, "hand stitching of every buttonhole" and "worsted wool" are both features. Good features, too. Just don't leave it at that.

Benefits are what the ultimate buyer gets from what you sell. They are what your prospect tells that buyer to prove that he did a good job.

The best way to develop benefits is the "So what?" test. Just ask "So what?" about every feature. Your answer will be the benefits. You'll be astonished at the range of benefits you discover, so be sure to put them all in writing. You don't want them to get lost. "Tailor-made details at half the tailor-made price" and "New worsted fabric that practically never wears out" are benefits. But wait! Remember the "say one thing only" rule! Well, that may be so, but there's no rule about having more than one benefit. The more the merrier, and you'll certainly have literature and subordinate signs that bring out *all* the benefits—and features, too. It's your basic "billboard" that must give one instantly grasped, impact-filled message. Your task is to find the best pollen that will attract the most bees to your flower. Don't confuse them with 31 flavors. They know what they need.

Here are a few more examples to guide you in translating features into benefits. You might find it helpful to check the current literature on your product or service and see whether it is feature or benefit based. You'll want to make sure it's the latter when you use it at your next show.

Examples
- *You* develop a larger computer screen.
  Your prospects want greater productivity through less eye fatigue.
- *You* offer biodegradable paper.
  Your prospects want packaging materials they can brag about.
- *You* offer frozen gourmet dinners for restaurants.
  Your prospects want four-star meals with a nonstar chef.

INSIGHT 32

Features are what you put in. Benefits are what they get out. Features explain and instruct. Benefits attract and sell. Use benefits.

SUMMARY

- Concentrate on learning the real reasons your prospects are at a show, and focus your presentations on meeting that need. (Yes, we said this before, but it's worth repeating.)
- Think of your exhibit as a billboard. It will focus everything you do.

TARGET YOUR PROSPECTS FOR PERSONAL ATTENTION, BECAUSE THERE'S MORE TO EXHIBITING THAN EXHIBITS

How much personal attention you give to specific customers and prospects will depend on five factors:

1. **Identify your targets.** Know the key customers and prospects who are likely to attend. The easiest way to find out is to ask them in advance.
2. **Make two lists.** List one has the clients and prospects you have targeted for special attention, with the reasons they should give it to you (what you have to offer) and what you hope to get out of it. List two has the persons from your company who will attend the show.
3. **Decide what "special attention" means** for everyone on list one.
4. **Focus.** Assign your staff, if any, to specific individuals on list one, with detailed instructions about focusing and goals. Give everyone, including yourself, *objectives you must document*!
5. **Invite the targeted men and women.** Invite them to your "special attention" events. Do it well in advance of the show, and then confirm their acceptance just before the date. (Don't say, "You can make it, can't you?" Say, "I'm really looking forward to our lunch.")

If You're Few and They're Many

If there are just too many customers and prospects to give all of them personal attention, invite them to a grand breakfast in the centrally located hotel. You'll want a private suite or dining room decorated with your products and literature. But don't give them a hard sell. It's breakfast time, and how would you like a sales talk with your cereal!

Since lunch and dinner invitations abound, your "Breakfast Club" is likely to be more appreciated—and remembered—than something fancier and more expensive later in the day.

INSIGHT 33

You and your staff are *not* there to have breakfast! You are there to meet specifically targeted individuals, introduce them to senior management (if that's other than you), generally make them comfortable, . . . and set up a specific time to "do some business" later.

Breakfast is also a great way to give a second invitation to anyone who can't join you at a different time. ("I'm really sorry you can't make it for dinner, but perhaps you can join us for an informal breakfast at the Savoy Drop-In Suite. Anytime between 7:00 and 9:00 A.M. on Monday and Tuesday. I'll send you a reminder before the show.")

It Doesn't Have to Have Food

The wooing of customers and prospects doesn't *have* to be centered around a meal. Be inventive! Consider a sports event, a play, or a disco. They'll relax with colleagues and entertain each other. When they are back home, drop each one a note telling them how much you enjoyed their company and how *they* helped the group have a good time. That will remind them who was their host, something often forgotten in the rush of parties at many trade shows and conventions. Of course, you used the event to focus on your business goals and obtained specific objectives you can document.

There's Always Lunch or Dinner. When the ultimate in individual attention is called for, that usually means lunch or dinner. Here are some suggestions to make those meals more effective as business events:

- **Make reservations in advance**. Check a standard guide of restaurant listings. Since the more desirable places fill up early, make your reservations two months in advance of the show dates. If you are unfamiliar with the location, ask for an approximate time and distance from your hotel. You'll want to remain fairly close for lunch.
- **Fewer is better**. Have a maximum of six persons per table. Invite fewer people, rather than use larger tables. When there are more than six, comfortable conversation is limited to the persons seated next to you. As host, you lose control of the table as a whole.
- Be **"guest wise."** Generally, a ratio of one host to two guests is preferable to the reverse. There are, of course, exceptions, and your own good sense

will tell you when they apply. In assigning guests to hosts, weigh the difference between flattering your guests with attention and intimidating them by sheer weight of numbers.

It is a fact, overlooked at our peril, that much business is done over lunch and golf. That's not because customers or prospects are being "bought." Rather, other things being equal—as they often are—we'd rather do business with our friends, and few things seem to build business friendships faster than a shared activity or a relaxing meal.

INSIGHT 34

NEVER let staff socialize with each other at an event attended by customers and prospects. It is insulting to your guests to have "the help" find itself more interesting than the men and women they invited!

Focus for Individual Attention

Most of this chapter is concerned with your exhibit and you as an exhibitor. But some of your most valuable exhibiting contacts can be made through individual and small-group "business socializing." Like everything else about exhibiting, this requires careful advance planning. You pick the shows to attend because they bring your key customers and prospects to the same location. It's your chance to meet with them individually or collectively, formally or socially, briefly or extensively, as your schedule and theirs permit. Don't pass up the opportunity to cement a business relationship with some personal attention.

INSIGHT 35

Your best prospects and customers are your competitors' most likely key targets. If you don't go courtin', . . . they will.

SUMMARY

- Plan for personal contacts, and then follow them up to make them happen.
- Hold staff—and yourself—responsible for specific targeted results from social events. *Your guests* go to parties; *you* produce business-based events.

YOUR EXHIBIT SPACE

As an exhibitor, you have quite a variety of options for developing your display, but no matter which one you choose, there are certain rules of thumb about the space, generally referred to as "floor space," your exhibit will actually occupy.

Booth Size

Exhibit space is made up of units called "booths," with one booth the minimum space available. At most shows, booths are 10 feet long by 10 feet deep, but always check for variations. If you're attending more than one show and will provide your own exhibit, plan it around the smallest space and build from there.

Booth Height

Almost all standard booths have a maximum height of eight feet at the back of the booth and then drop rather quickly to a 30-inch table height, to permit visibility along an entire row of exhibits. The object is to keep exhibitors from blocking their views of each other by erecting "fences" between their booths. The height rule is often different for "peninsula" and "island" displays, as explained shortly.

Aisles and Visibility

The aisle between rows of booths is generally 8 to 10 feet wide. This width becomes an important factor in planning signs and determining what your audience can actually take in when they see your booth from the middle of an aisle. Work with your display company or other professionals to determine the best size and colors for the signs and their lettering as well as how high they should be placed. (As a general rule, make the top row of letters no more than 6 feet off the ground . . . but there are lots of exceptions.) If local sources for signs seem inadequate, use one of the national suppliers, such as The Banner Barn, in Ocala, FL, 904/867-7860. Call them for a catalog and knowledgeable guidance.

Exhibit Space Configuration

Exhibit space is available in three configurations (see Figure 5.3):

1. **Back wall.** These in-line configurations are any number of booths lined up next to each other. The booths are usually 10 feet wide by 10 feet deep. Occasionally sizes differ, so be sure to check the show guide. The height of the booth is generally limited to 8 feet at the back and table height or 30 inches at the front.
2. **Peninsula.** Peninsula displays have aisles on three sides. Different rules and restrictions apply if they abut another peninsula, versus if they abut two rows of back wall booths. Check the show rules for what is permitted.

Figure 5.3 Sections of floor plan showing three types of booth configurations.

The management will often create a larger size peninsula space upon request by borrowing from abutting back wall booths.

3. **Island.** An island, as the name implies, is surrounded by aisles on all four sides. Special rules apply to islands, but they tend to be quite liberal, as islands are the most expensive spaces to rent and management wants to encourage their use. Height limitations are often highest for island displays, making them the space of choice for tall products or exhibits. Regardless of the height of the ceiling, there are always strict limitations on space you may use. Check before you plan and before you ship your booths.

Hanging Signs

Many shows permit signs that hang above a display. Exhibitors use them to call attention to themselves from locations where their display can not otherwise be seen. Hanging signs are controlled by show rules and fire regulations, but are very effective additional exposure. (See Figures 5.1 and 5.2.)

SUMMARY

- Check the show rules for any display you plan to use. Do not assume that last year's rules still apply. Try to limit surprises to pleasant ones.

YOUR DISPLAY

As an exhibitor, you have five options for developing your display. Which one you select—and many exhibitors use more than one kind—should depend on your goals, budget, and availability of staff, probably in that order.

Custom-Built Displays

Custom-built displays are generally designed, built, and maintained by companies specializing in that field. They (and their cousins, the rental display companies, shortly described), are almost always the most impressive exhibits at a show. The most successful displays are designed with a specific goal in mind, and that is their strength, as long as the exhibitor's focus remains constant. A new focus may require a new display. Generally, displays wear out physically in about five years, so the likelihood of their outliving their usefulness is slight.

Modular Design. For displays longer than 10 feet (a single booth), consider a modular design that is organized around 10-foot or 20-foot units. This gives you flexibility in case of budgetary contraction or expansion: You can subtract or add units without rebuilding an entire exhibit.

What Display Companies Do

Design. Display companies can design your exhibit or consult with you in its design. They are architects, as well as builders, of exhibits. A display company should always be consulted before any design for an exhibit is approved, because of the company's knowledge of exhibit rules and pitfalls.

Construct. Display companies construct exhibits and, equally important, the customized, padded containers for shipping your display with minimal damage. Anyone who has ever watched a display being delivered to an exhibit site knows that "no damage" is but a dream.

Expedite. A display company will act as your agent in all contact with the exhibit site, *except for ordering the actual floor space.* This space is always paid for in advance and then assigned on a first-paid basis. Payment is the responsibility of the exhibitor. Any question as to the size or height of your display, electrical hookups, furniture or other rentals, shipping, setting up and tearing down (dismantling) the display, and shipping the display to the next show or returning it for storage can be handled by the display company as your single source of supply. You will want to know what the charges for these services are, and you might decide to do some of them yourself. Ask yourself what *you* get paid for (even if it's by yourself), then use *them*.

Supervise. The display company can send an in-house expert to supervise set-up—the on-site assembly of your display. You are charged for the supervisor's time, transportation, and living expenses while there, but the ability to expedite the assembly of the display and make on-the-spot modifications and repairs often actually saves the additional cost. And the peace of mind of knowing that supervision is being done by the original construction company is priceless. This same degree of supervision may not be required for dismantling the display, depending on the complexity of its construction, on whether the same crew did the setting up, and on whether the crew was made aware of any repacking problems.

Provide storage. A major function of display companies is to store displays between shows.

Repair. Display companies refurbish, repair, or modify displays and shipping crates as required.

Rental Displays

Many display companies have displays that can be rented and customized to meet an exhibitor's needs. These displays range from impressive island exhibits to single-booth units. They can be very effective where you wish to make a one-shot impact without taking on the cost of designing, constructing, and storing your own display—especially one with limited use.

Costs Involved in Using a Display

For the purpose of establishing costs, a rental display will go through the same steps to get ready for a show as a custom-built unit. The costs involved in this process may actually be higher than the cost of the floor space the display will occupy. Savings are, of course, possible by using fewer booths. In fact, many displays are unitized—that is, made up of modules that can be assembled into various configurations and sizes, depending on the importance of a show. However, there are always some start-up costs, and the savings may not be proportional to the number of booths used. Your display company can give you accurate estimates to help you decide.

A Dozen Cost Factors

1. **Planning meetings**. Take advantage of your display company's expertise by getting it involved at the earliest stages of planning. While it is possible to produce almost anything by using the JTWGCHD system ("Just think what God could have done if He'd had our money"), a conscientious representative will forewarn you about costs, time requirements, and other constraints.
2. **Final agreement** on the display and on modifications, if any.
3. **Removing the display from storage**, unpacking it from its crate(s) (for their own protection, displays are stored in their padded shipping crates), and inspecting, repairing, and modifying the display. Since display graphics—the art and signs—are seldom used the same way twice, a detailed inspection is not done until all modifications and new graphics are agreed upon.
4. **Assembly for inspection** of the complete display as repaired and modified. This is an optional, fairly expensive step. Usually, only the new graphics and major modifications need client approval.
5. **Repairing** the shipping crate and packing the display.

6. **Contacting the trucking firm** and reserving space for a guaranteed arrival time. Depending on the number of days and routes available, the display will be shipped one of two ways:
   - **Direct van.** This refers not to the size of the truck, but to the method of routing. Direct van shipments remain on the same truck from pickup to delivery, minimizing handling and the resulting damage. This is usually the fastest way to ship and, if required, the easiest to trace. It is more expensive, however, than the next method to be discussed, common carrier.
   - **Common carrier.** The shipment may be transferred to a different truck to combine materials going to a common destination. While this is the less expensive way to ship, it generally results in more handling, with possible costly damage.

7. **Shipping the display and unloading it at the destination.**

8. **Assembling the display.** At most shows, only specified carpenters and electricians, not the exhibitor's own staff, may assemble major displays. This work may be supervised by the exhibitor, a display company representative, or an on-site supervisor. Work rules vary widely in right-to-work states. Check before you do anything yourself!

9. **Making on-the-spot repairs and adjustments.**

10. **Preparing for return shipment.** The bills of lading and labels for shipping the display to its next destination or its return to storage are prepared. This paperwork is usually completed in advance by the display company.

11. **Tearing down the display.** The display is disassembled and repacked into the original crates.

12. **Arranging for return shipment.** The crates are checked against the number in the original shipment and, if there is no discrepancy, are returned to storage. Repairs are not made at this time, but await possible modification with the next use of the display.

Off-the-Shelf Displays

Dozens of companies, including many exhibit builders, have standard off-the-shelf displays that can be personalized at little cost, usually by adding the exhibitor's name and some simple graphics. (See Figure 5.4.) Many of these displays are truly portable in that they disassemble into suitcase-size units which fit into the trunk of most midsize or larger cars . . . but measure the trunk before you buy. You'll find the names of the manufacturers in any major city's Yellow Pages, under "Exhibits and Displays." Ask several to send you their catalogs.

The Pipe and Drape Display

A pipe and drape display consists of a curtained backdrop draped from a pipe and holding a sign with the exhibitor's name, plus a table supplied by the show. There is no fancy backdrop. There is no special lighting and no unique graphics—just the exhibitor and the products or services. Some of today's major exhibitors started just this way.

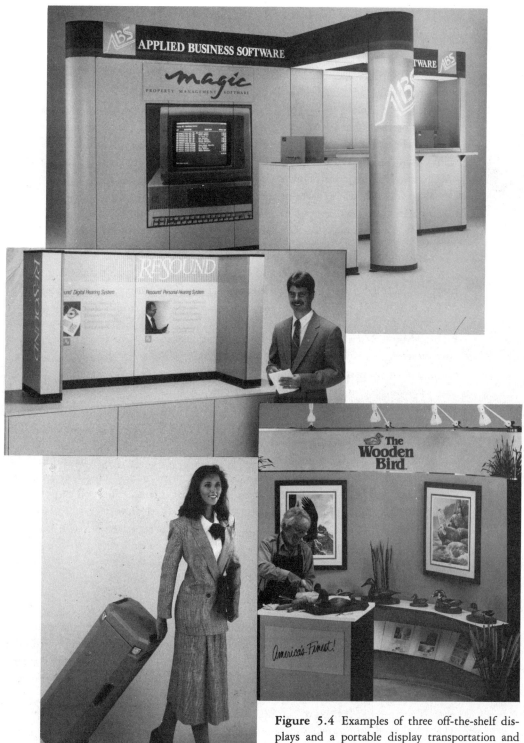

Figure 5.4 Examples of three off-the-shelf displays and a portable display transportation and storage case. (Examples shown are by Skyline Displays Inc. of Burnsville, MN. Many other companies manufacture similar excellent units.)

The One-Show, Leave-Behind Display: An Invitation to Adventure

The leave-behind display is one of my pet projects, which may be why it receives an inordinate amount of space here for something practically no one uses. It is offered for the adventurous who want *more* bang for the display buck!

Many exhibitors have wished for, and some have actually used, leave-behind displays that have much of the appeal of a custom-built unit, yet are so inexpensive that it is cheaper to leave them behind, rather than use them again. Some exhibitors would even pay a premium for the ability to walk away immediately after a show, unconcerned about tearing down, repacking, and shipping the display. That more exhibitors do not use a leave-behind format can be credited to the engineering maxim, "If it 'ain't broke,' don't fix it." But there's nothing in engineering that says you shouldn't even look until it breaks. Maybe you can make it better.

A word of warning: Check with your exhibit headquarters before committing yourself to a leave-behind display. Make a copy of the description of such a display given in this book, and have it approved by them *in writing*. The chances of nonapproval are very slim. But why gamble? Insurance is only a postage stamp away!

Practicalities. With a custom-built or rental unit, much of the cost is made up of fees for storage, shipping, assembly, dismantling, reshipping, repair, and general maintenance. Constructing a leave-behind display that is of low weight and bulk, easy to assemble, and sturdy and attractive is not an impossible assignment for an imaginative designer. Since the display will always be brand new, you eliminate the cost of repair and maintenance. Since it's light and compact, you save a major portion—if not all—of the cost of storage, shipping, and handling. And since it's left behind, you save the total cost of return shipment and subsequent handling. You may, depending on exhibit rules, have to use show personnel for assembling the display, but that would also be true of a custom-built display. You will want to tear down or disassemble your display before you leave, or there's a very good chance that show personnel will repack it and ship it to you at your expense. Just tear it apart, and put a few signs reading "Throw Away! Do Not Ship!" where they can't be missed.

Constructing Your One-Show Display

Triangular Columns. The triangular column, shown in Figure 5.6, is made from a standard sheet of ³/₈-inch-thick, 4 × 8-foot Foamcord.™ This exceptionally strong, yet light, display material is stocked by photostat suppliers. Contact several of them about four weeks in advance of a show. Explain your needs, and then send or Fax a copy of the figure to the likely suppliers. Ask them to quote a price on a job, together with the time they'll need to complete it. Three working days should be adequate. The exact wording on the columns and signs should be provided by you as camera-ready copy—that is, copy of typeset quality that will be photographically enlarged by the supplier you choose. Keep the wording to an absolute minimum. The fewer words, the more likely it is that they will be read and noted.

Figure 5.5 Example of a one-show, leave-behind display. (Original concept and design by Jack Heimerdinger, Plainsfield, IL.)

The one-show, leave-behind display seen in Figure 5.5 cost less than 25 percent of just the shipping charges associated with using the company's custom-built display. The entire leave-behind display was produced on site, where the show took place, eliminating storage and shipping costs. Only two suppliers were needed: one made enlargements of commercial photostats and the other was a "home store" retail outlet. Both were found in the Yellow Pages, as you will in just about any city in which you are likely to exhibit your wares.

To give the columns of the display stability, use the design shown in Figure 5.6. The original board is 8 feet tall, but you need use only 6 feet for the column. That leaves 24 × 48 inches that you can use to make a sign. (See Figure 5.7.)

Your supplier will probably want advance payment, with time to have your check clear their bank. Build that into your schedule. Ask the supplier to arrange for delivery at a specified time to your booth at the show. And get the supplier's emergency telephone number if delivery is on a weekend. It will make you feel better while you wait.

Shelved Cases. Not every exhibitor can make use of the easily assembled bookshelf-type cases pictured between the columns in Figure 5.7, but if you can, they are available at low-cost home furnishings stores for about $100 each. If such a case is desirable, check the Yellow Pages or ask the photostat supply house to recommend a

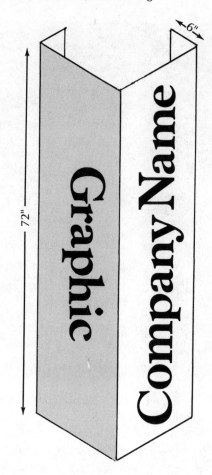

Figure 5.6 Triangular column design.

Figure 5.7 Use a border to "frame" sign copy.

source. When ordering, specify cases with or without doors, and ask how much the cost will be to deliver the units assembled. The supplier can probably also provide inexpensive gooseneck lamps and extension cords for lighting. Use the same delivery instructions as for the columns, but don't worry about emergency numbers. Here, everything is an off-the-shelf retail item.

Tables and Chairs. If tables are needed, rent them from the show, just as you would at any other kind of exhibit. Chairs can also be rented from the show or purchased from the outlet that provides the cases. Purchasing is slightly more expensive, but may have greater eye appeal.

A reminder: Throw it away! Avoid the temptation to save the columns and signs. Unless you can use them again immediately, they will get damaged or frayed or simply be in the way. Throw them out, even though it hurts. The cases, lamps, and—if purchased—chairs are another matter. Before the show is over and you have to rush off, contact a local charity that can use these items and have them picked up. You'll get a tax write-off that will make you proud!

SUMMARY

- Explore all your options, from purchasing custom-built to leave-behind displays, for the shows your attend. There may be a variety of "best" solutions to your display needs.
- Work with an exhibit company if your budget permits. It will let you concentrate on the selling for which your display is just the background.

ORDERING A NEW DISPLAY

The purchase or rental of displays is one of the most exciting projects for any promotion manager. Here, in outline form, is a basic schedule for this project. A special checklist is provided at the end of the chapter.

1. **Getting in-house agreement on the basics of the display.** Get agreement on the following items:
   - Type of display: custom built, rental, tabletop, modular, etc.
   - Number of booths or running feet of display space.
   - Budget. (Get advance cost and time estimates from several possible suppliers, and then add 10%.)
   - Materials and services to be featured.
   - Purpose of the display, beyond showing materials or services. For instance, will there be conference or sales areas or a safe storage section?
   - Visual impact desired, such as high tech or warm and friendly or both.

- Frequency of expected use of all or of portions of the display during a three-year period. Will smaller modular units be used more often than the whole? How many? How often?
- Expected life of the display.
- Approval procedure. Who must be consulted and who will give final budgetary and design approval? When will they be available? Who has approval authority in their absence? (There is little point in waiting till March 9 to approve an exhibit for a show that was over on the eighth.)

2. Putting it in writing. Put the display basics in writing, and get approval of this description from all concerned. If there are disagreements about your description of what was decided on, resolve the difficulties before going any further.

3. Finding an exhibit company. If you have never before worked with an exhibit company or are unfamiliar with those in your area, ask for recommendations from your competitors (this is not a noncompetitive industry), your colleagues, trade associations, or media representatives (they know a surprising amount). Or simply check the Yellow Pages.

Send each candidate a copy of your display basics, and ask for a written response by a specified date. Ask for the following information:

- The candidate's experience with the type of display you have outlined. Have them include pictures you'll return, costs of displays shown, dates of construction, and persons to contact for recommendations.
- Design and construction personnel. Are they employees or outside contractors and designers? The latter is not necessarily negative, but you will want to take it into consideration.
- Where, and by whom, the display will be stored.
- Basic storage charges, with costs for removing the display from storage or returning it after a show.
- Estimated maintenance charges.
- Who the candidate's account executive will be and that person's experience in the exhibit field.

Make absolutely clear that you will not accept a personal presentation in place of the information you have requested, but that you are prepared to answer any further questions the candidate may have.

4. If you have an existing display. For most companies, purchasing a new display is such a large expenditure that multiple bids are mandated, even when they have an excellent relationship with a particular display house. If your company is in such a position, have lunch with your account representative and break the news as gently as possible. No one lives a business life of more threatened security than an account executive, so assure the AE that his or her firm will get "most favored nation" consideration. But ask for exactly the same information you're requesting from everyone else. Few decisions that are at least partly aesthetic can be totally objective, so it is best to begin with a level playing field.

INSIGHT 36

If you are dissatisfied with your current display house or its account executive, try to resolve the problem by going to the senior management of that display house, rather than leaving them out of the picture. Account executives for any kind of supplier sometimes become apologists for their employers, rather than expediters and problem solvers for their clients. That is an excess of loyalty only employers can solve—as they will, but only if you let them know a problem exists. You don't want your account executives fired. You do want them working for you.

---

5. Narrowing the field and final inspections. Narrow the number of candidates to a reasonable number, and then arrange for a personal visit to each. Take along the display construction checklist from this chapter with the candidates' mail or phone responses already filled in. You won't mind their having put their best foot forward, but reality mustn't be too far from what you've already been told.

Satisfy yourself about the ability of the firm you ultimately choose to work together with you. Be prepared to answer some questions about your firm, your credit rating, and your promptness in paying bills. Designing and constructing displays involves such a preponderance of up-front, out-of-pocket costs for the exhibit company, that it customarily gets a one-third down payment before beginning a job, a second third at a specified time during construction, and the final third upon its completion.

Select the finalists—probably three, usually no more than four—and invite them, individually, to visit you for a turnaround inspection in which they will get answers to any questions they may have about you and your project, plus a final project specification form that includes the following:

- General directions, with any modifications from the original version already seen by them.
- The schedule for presentation of their design concept, plus time for at least one revision before a final rendering. Since there is always the possibility of similarities among various aspects of the candidates' designs, put a "hold harmless" clause—their legally binding promise not to sue you or the other display houses as a design thief—in your written agreement with each candidate.
- The date for the presentation of the final rendering and a scale model. The production of a model is customary and, like the customized shipping containers, is included in the overall cost. The model becomes invaluable in visualizing different configurations and the relationships of various elements to each other. Have each presenter specify the following:
  - The date when all copy and graphics to be used in the actual display must be given to the exhibits house.
  - The date when the display will be ready for a first inspection, with adequate time for modifications before shipment.
  - The presentation date for all concerned—the final show and tell.

- The date of shipment of the display to the first show. Certain suppliers may wish to trade a shorter production schedule for more time to prepare a presentation. Don't do this. It's unfair to you, as it forces a faster decision-making process, and it's equally unfair to other candidates who prefer a normal work schedule. Extraordinarily fast production is an invitation to shortcuts and shoddy workmanship. Avoid it wherever possible.

INSIGHT 37

Get at least three bids for creating your display, and pay each company an agreed-upon amount for its presentation. Few of us do our very best work "on speculation."

The three companies chosen for the competition that produced the display shown in Figures 5.1 and 5.2 were authorized to charge up to $5,000 each for their presentation designs. Each was given a maximum budget of $200,000 for a completed 100-foot display. Actual cost estimates from each supplier were not a part of management's decision, since I did not give those to management. To their surprise and delight, the winning display, unanimously agreed upon, proved to be $50,000 less than they had budgeted. (I had told the competitors that within our budget, price would not be a factor.)

SUMMARY

- Put everything in writing.
- Get in-house agreement on basics of the display and the assignment of responsibilities—and don't go further until you do.
- Personally visit likely candidates to inspect all aspects of their operations. Insist on the "show" part of the show and tell.
- Prepare a workable schedule for all concerned, and monitor it continually. When all has finally gone well and your new display is a success, put your thanks to all concerned in writing, too.

NOTES ON THE CONVENTIONS/ TRADE SHOW/MEETINGS CHECKLIST

These notes are a supplement to the material presented in this chapter. They are not a substitute for that material.

1. Why you are at *that* show at *that* time. The answer must determine everything else you do . . . every other point on this checklist. It therefore comes first.

2. The complete-for-everything show budget. If the cost of a new display, whether rented, purchased, or custom built, is included, use the checklist on page 153 for that amount. *Do not let final budget approval delay action on #3 and #4!*

3–4. Unlike real estate, "location, location, location" may not be the most important factor for display booths, but it certainly helps. Find out the why's of space assignments. Just ask! Then be the first to follow the rules and meet the deadlines.

5. This refers to official notification from a show that specific space has been assigned to you. If you plan something unusual in size, shape, traffic flow, or electrical or other service requirements, don't wait for that "official" notification. Make sure to get approval far enough in advance to change if the answer is "no." The show organizers want you to attend and will try to help. Give them the chance!

6. One person at your end deals with one person at the display company's end. Put everything in writing. Get it confirmed. Get the work schedule. Check to make sure that it's being followed.

7. Request reservations *the day they may be ordered*. Find out when is the last moment they may be cancelled. *One* person deals with both of these points.

8. Who is authorized to charge what to your company? What control is there, if any, on those authorized to charge?

9. Display *space* tends to be the least costly of items 9–15. Add more space and place your display within it, perhaps in an island configuration, for extra impact. Even a single extra booth can work for smaller budgets.

10. See the separate checklist for ordering or building a new display. Treat the costs involved as a capital expense, or add them under the total budget in #2. Use #10 for costs associated with maintenance, modification, shipping, setup and dismantling, and reshipping of the display, as well as returning it to storage. For record keeping, separate routine items and one-time costs to make future planning easier.

11. Who goes? Who gets them there? How is it paid for?

12–13. Send, if at all possible, with the display. For both control and huge savings, a single shipment is by far the best thing.

14. Limitations or rules regarding the cost of daily meals. Lodging is handled under #7, but must be recorded here for purposes of budgeting.

15. Estimated or quoted costs for items 16–23. Have a single person *in charge* of hospitality though any number of individuals may have specific responsibilities.

INSIGHT 38

16–23. Have a reason for hospitality. If you can't justify entertaining #16, . . . *stop!* Don't give a party. Go to theirs.

CONVENTION/TRADE SHOW/MEETINGS CHECKLIST

Meeting _____   Date _____
Focus _____   Project # _____
Booths/Space _____   Checklist # _____
Setup _____ Show Dates _____ Teardown _____   Deadline _____
Overall Supervision by _____   Budget _____

EARLIEST DECISIONS	ASSIGNED TO	DUE	IN	MUST APPROVE	BY DATE	IN	INFO COPY ONLY	SEE ATTACHED
1. Exhibit focus			☐			☐		☐
2. Budget approved			☐			☐		☐
3. Booth space/configuration			☐			☐		☐
4. Booth location			☐			☐		☐
5. Space reserved/confirmed			☐			☐		☐
6. Display company notified			☐			☐		☐
7. Hotel reservation requested			☐			☐		☐
8. Direct billing requested			☐			☐		☐
BUDGET DETAIL OK								
9. Booth $			☐			☐		☐
10. Display $			☐			☐		☐
11. Travel $			☐			☐		☐
12. Product $			☐			☐		☐
13. Collateral $			☐			☐		☐
14. Lodging/Food $			☐			☐		☐
15. Hospitality $			☐			☐		☐
PERSONNEL/HOSPITALITY								
16. VIP list			☐			☐		☐
17. VIP responsibilities assigned			☐			☐		☐
18. Hospitality plan OK			☐			☐		☐
19. Hospitality ordered/reserved			☐			☐		☐
20. Hospitality invitations creative			☐			☐		☐
21. Invitation printing			☐			☐		☐
22. Invitation mailing/distribution			☐			☐		☐
23. Hospitality confirmed/cancelled			☐			☐		☐
24. Personnel attending OK'd			☐			☐		☐
25. Personnel notified of plan			☐			☐		☐
and assignments			☐			☐		☐
26. Hotel confirmed/cancelled			☐			☐		☐
EXHIBITING DETAIL								
27. Display design for setup			☐			☐		☐
28. Signs ordered			☐			☐		☐
29. Product ordered			☐			☐		☐
30. Product shipped			☐			☐		☐
31. Collateral ordered			☐			☐		☐
32. Collateral shipped			☐			☐		☐
33. Physical display ordered			☐			☐		☐
34. Physical display shipped			☐			☐		☐
35. Show services & rentals			☐			☐		☐
36. Service & rentals ordered			☐			☐		
37. Set up/Tear down			☐			☐		

© 1993, Fred Hahn

NEW DISPLAY CHECKLIST

Project title/description _____   Date _____
_____   Project # _____
_____   Checklist # _____
Overall Supervision by _____   Deadline _____
Budget _____   Start-up Date _____   Completion Date _____

1. **STYLE:** ☐ Custom Built ☐ Rental ☐ Portable ☐ Pipe & Drape ☐ Throwaway
2. **DATE NEEDED:** _____ 3. **QUANTITY NEEDED:** _____ 4. **BUDGET:** $ _____
5. **SIZE:** _____ Booths/ ____ Running Feet   6. **MODULAR:** ☐ Yes ☐ No
7. **BASIC CONFIGURATION:** ☐ Back Wall ☐ Island ☐ Peninsula
8. **MATERIALS TO BE SHOWN—RUNNING FEET OR DIMENSIONS:** _____
_____
_____
_____

9. **STORAGE SPACE NEEDED:** _____
_____
_____

10. **LITERATURE BINS & OTHER GIVEAWAYS:** _____
_____
_____

11. **EXPECTED FREQUENCY OF USE:**
    (Indicate all or part of display. Be specific.) 1 year _____
    3 years _____
12. **SEATING/HOW MANY & WHERE:** _____
_____

13. **OTHER REQUIREMENTS:** _____
_____

14. **OVERALL "FEEL":** ☐ Contemporary ☐ Traditional ☐ VERY High Tech ☐ User Friendly
    (Check all that apply) ☐ Male ☐ Female ☐ Other

---

15. **APPROVAL PROCESS:DESIGN AND BUDGET**
    First Presentation   _____
    Second Presentation _____

    | | FINAL DESIGN OK _____ Date_____ |
    | Signatures | FINAL BUDGET OK _____ Date_____ |
    | | CONSTRUCTION OK _____ Date_____ |

---

16. Exhibits Co. Candidate _____   Contact _____
    Address _____   Phone _____
17. Years in business _____   18. ☐ Own Designers   19. ☐ Outside Design   20. ☐ Own Construction
21. ☐ Outside Construction   22. ☐ Own Storage   23. ☐ Outside Storage
24. ☐ Photos Received   25. ☐ Cost Information Received   26. ☐ Recommendations Checked
27. Account Executive & Experience_____
28. Other _____
29. Date Visited _____ 30. By: _____ 31. Recommendation (+5/–5) _____

See Attached Concerning Nos. ___ ___ ___ ___ ___ ___ ___ ___ ___ ___ ___ ___ ___

24–25. Are your personnel attending the show determined by hospitality or other needs? Have a reason for everyone's being there—a cash-effective reason!

26. The decision in #24 may be someone else's. The confirmation or cancellation is done by the same person as in #7. Make sure that everything is in writing and everything is confirmed.

27. Exactly how will the display look, and where will the products and collateral materials go? If possible, code every carton or item by number, keyed to a specific location.

28. What do the signs say and where do they go? Ship them with the display.

29–32. Who is responsible? If this person is different from the one responsible for #27, let #27 know if anything is not available. Don't make a half-empty display your convention surprise!

33–36. Generally the responsibility of a single person. When using a display company, let it handle #28, #30, #32 and #34–36. They do it every day, know exactly how, and will save you *lots* of money.

37. Let your display company supervise, if practical. Keep house kibitzers away. Show personnel are expensive and get paid by the hour.

NOTES ON THE NEW DISPLAY CHECKLIST

Unlike the other checklists in this book, this one needs no annotation. The following notes may, however, be helpful:

- Use a separate copy of this checklist for each potential supplier. Fill in #2–14 for each kind of project. Duplicate as needed.

- The type of display (#1) can be determined in advance or by the information provided in #2–14. In either case, be prepared to make some modification from what you want to what is more practical and less costly, even when the display is custom built or left behind and thrown away.

- You'll need #16–31 primarily for custom-built and major rental displays. That's where you require the most detailed knowledge about your supplier. You ask #17 because you do want that company there a year from now, when it's time to use the display again!

- Modify #15 in accordance with the type of display you order. You certainly won't need it for the pipe and drape display, which comes with the show.

6 | Publicity and Public Relations

This chapter aims at helping you generate and disseminate good public relations (PR) for yourself and counteracting any bad PR you may pick up. It does not cover the generation of bad publicity about your opponents—whether they deserve it or not.

INSIGHT 39

Media wastepaper baskets are filled with PR from sources that equate "free" with "too cheap to invest in doing right." Publicity and public relations are *not* "free"! The effort, knowledge, skill, experience, time, and budget needed to prepare effective PR are every bit as great as required for paid advertising. To get such PR, management must understand this and commit the resources that make it possible, because without those resources and that commitment, it won't get it.

Throughout this chapter, certain words and phrases are used repeatedly. Their definitions, as given here, will usually be assumed by your audience. However, it is always safer to confirm such an understanding, rather than take it for granted. Point out that "there are so many ways I've heard (fill in the appropriate term here) used lately, that I'd feel a lot safer if we agreed on a definition in advance." Doing this has saved me endless grief, without forcing anyone to admit to ignorance

PR: Abbreviation for "public relations." "Publicity" is generally understood to be part of the total public relations function.

Medium (plural, media): Any method of communication for getting PR made public. Newspapers, radio talk shows, and word of mouth are all media.

The press: Newspaper and magazine reporters and feature writers; sometimes, depending on the context, the term includes radio and television reporters also.

Electronic media: Radio and television.

Print media: Newspapers, magazines, and newsletters.

Published: Made public by print media.

Broadcast: Made public by electronic media.

Aired: A synonym for "broadcast."

INSIGHT 40

For internal communication, don't fight about what something's called, only about what it is to accomplish and how to get it done. For external communication, you must use generally accepted nomenclature to get across what you wish to communicate.

PUBLICITY AND PUBLIC RELATIONS

How They Differ and Why It Matters

PR professionals can, and do, write and speak endlessly about the differences between publicity and public relations. But for our purposes, an arbitrary distinction is appropriate.

Publicity: Do good and let the world know. A good product, good cause, good film, or good deed all meet this criterion.

Public relations: Limit harm when it strikes and, where possible, neutralize harm or turn it into good.

This chapter has three goals that relate to these definitions:

1. To help you formulate publicity and public relations procedures agreed upon by every level of management.
2. To guide you in doing your own publicity.
3. To urge you to use professional help—from internal or external resources—in major publicity campaigns and in all public relations.

Your Relationship with the Press

The press and electronic news media are in the business of presenting news and otherwise useful information, not of giving favorable free coverage to whoever requests it. The best way to establish an excellent relationship with the print and electronic press is to make yourself a resource for news and to present your stories or story ideas to them in a "news" or "feature" context. How to do this is shown in the pages that follow. Of course, the more news or features you provide to the press, the more valuable you will become, and the more likely it will be that even your lesser stories will get favorable attention. You may even become a source that the press will contact for interesting filler materials when the "hard" news is "light" (sparse).[1] Much more important, you will want the press to know you as a reachable and, especially, *honest* source of fact and opinion about your organization. That's an invaluable reputation to have earned when raw news, without interpretation, can be

---

[1] There are many columnists and feature writers whose coverage is as important as news is to companies and organizations. These writers and electronic commentators live on a constant supply of publicity-type information. It takes a long while to build this type of relationship, but once established, it becomes a very nice bonus for both sides.

harmful to your interests. The opportunity to present your side, in context, when a story *first* appears, is immeasurably more valuable than a dozen after-the-fact correctives (as targets of "dirty politics" have learned to their sorrow).

Be a Pro!

There is absolutely nothing wrong with having your relationship with the media on a personal, first-name basis . . . *provided that it also remains on a professional level*. That media people respect and believe you is much more important than that they like you, although it certainly helps if they do both.

Deciding Who's in Charge

Whether publicity and public relations are assigned to the advertising department or to a separate public relations department depends on both the workload and the experience and PR expertise the departments have. Advertising involves comparatively little direct contact with reporters, on-air personnel, or editorial staffs. As an advertiser, your contact is more likely to be with a sales representative. Your advertising concern is *where* and *when* the advertisement is placed—in which section and on what page of the newspaper or magazine it appears and at what time and in which segment of a series of commercials it runs. You're paying, and your fiddle calls the tune. The ad will appear exactly as agreed on.

Publicity and public relations operate under quite different rules. Unlike paid-for advertising, their goal is favorable coverage by media without payment for space or time. The PR/publicity purpose is threefold. Deciding who will be in charge must be based upon who can accomplish all three purposes:

1. Favorable public notice for what you *do* want publicized.
2. The opportunity to present your point of view on what would otherwise be presented only in a negative fashion. Your hope is to neutralize, in whole or in part, the *approach* to a story, not the story itself.
3. The ability to get instant public notice for certain kinds of news, no matter what the negative consequences to your organization. Tampering with products in a way that may endanger the lives of buyers is a familiar example for which you would want such instant public notice.

SUMMARY

- Your best chance to get published or to get air time is to give the media *news*.
- Your best chance to get trusted is give the media *truth*.
- The best person to handle publicity and PR is the one who can best do both of these, unhindered by persons or departments who do not understand the preceding two points.

THE NEED FOR AGREED-UPON PR PROCEDURES

As the PR person charged with spreading the news, you'll likely get more help than you really want. Everyone wants to spread good news and be the first to pass off blame for the bad. Where news is widely known or suspected, both of these are bound to happen. Even I've been guilty. As a young account executive for an ad agency, I learned from a client's infuriated advertising director that it was not *my* job to reveal our agency's new advertising concept to the company president whom I happened to meet in the hallway, thereby depriving the director of her moment of glory. Fortunately, my apologetic realization that inexperience doesn't excuse stupidity saved us the account.

I never repeated the error, but it's probably impossible to get that kind of self-discipline from nonadministrative employees. They'll spread your news, good and bad, and any attempt to stop them may well be counterproductive. After all, why would you want to hide the story of *their* success and *your* failure? Are you trying to steal all the credit or shift all the blame?

Is It Really a Problem?

The problem with having your news become published through unofficial, word-of-mouth sources is that even when it's reported accurately, you are unlikely to gain the full advantages good news can generate. While bad news can expect ongoing and practically unlimited attention, good news most often gets only a single mention, unless the press is given specific reasons for continuing its coverage. A manufacturing contract presented without an interesting explanation of its civic and human advantages will likely appear on page 37 of the newspaper; a lawsuit will surely be featured on page 1. While you may not be able to change that placement, your PR efforts should get either story to reflect your point of view. The rest of this chapter is a guide both to doing just that yourself and to recognizing whether the PR work done for you by others is likely to get the results you want.

Convincing Management

The first impulse of most people contacted by the media is to feel so important that they tell more than they know. The second impulse is to be so fearful of saying something wrong as to say nothing at all. An agreed-upon, *written guide to media contacts* will guard against both of these extremes.

Since reporters usually try to contact the more senior personnel in an organization, management, too, must agree to follow your procedures in order for them to do their jobs. Here, as in just about every other aspect of organizational life, senior management sets the tone. If the CEO not only signs off on your plan, but actually follows it thereafter, your organization's media problems will be simplified. Since the majority of CEOs reached their position by recognizing the obvious, getting their agreement should present little difficulty. Here's the agreement:

1. **Designate an official spokesperson for PR.** This has the advantage of letting everyone else point to one person as having *all* the facts when, in fact, some of the facts are still in doubt. This becomes especially important when questions contain totally new "information" to which you are asked to react. "(Name) is going to find that out and get back to you immediately" is a perfectly acceptable answer, whether from the president of the United States or the vice president of the local garden society. If your spokesperson is not a well-grounded PR pro, put him or her through a media rehearsal run by professionals and with video playback. Many PR agencies will do this on a fee basis. *Always* do this before known T.V. or other major coverage. Make your blunders during rehearsal, not during interviews or on the air!

2. **Preplan whenever possible.** Good news is seldom a total surprise—although it may sometimes not be equally good for everyone concerned. "How to maximize good news," a few pages on, alerts you to some of the problems, as well as the opportunities, that good news offers. Whether such problems exist or not, discuss your story options at the senior level, and then put the approved approaches *in writing*. Note that what you are putting on paper is *not* "how we can fool our audience into thinking we're better than we are." It *is* "the very real benefits our audience will gain from this event." Plan to make your media guide something you'd feel comfortable about having "leaked" to the press, and structure it accordingly.

3. **When good news does come as a total surprise.** Occasionally, good news does come as a total surprise. A telephone call from a reporter will ask your reaction to something almost too good to be true—as quite often it is. Be honest. Tell the reporter that it's the first you've heard of the event, that you want to double-check to get all the details, and that the reporter will be the very first to get your reaction the moment the news is confirmed. Now check the facts. If the story is true, put your media plan into place exactly as if the story were preplanned, and then contact the reporter who broke it to you. If it is untrue, report that even faster. When it comes to *pleasant* surprises, there is nothing wrong with telling the media that you need some time to check out all the great ramifications. But when it is only a myth, do your best to stop it before it can raise expectations that won't be met.

4. **When bad news strikes.** Where possible, leave the handling of bad news to the professionals. When that proves impossible, do as they would. Whether the event is preplanned, such as a reduction in the work force, or totally unexpected, such as a fire or explosion, the possible legal as well as PR consequences are not for off-the-cuff handling. If management is asked to comment before a PR plan is in place, ask what the media's deadline is and promise to get back to them before then. Whatever that deadline is, keep it! Emphasize that you are trying to get at the facts. Until you do, uninformed comments might mislead the public and unnecessarily jeopardize your organization. Getting the help you need is covered in this chapter.

SUMMARY

- Designate an official PR spokesperson.
- Preplan your media approach whenever your news, good or bad, can be predicted . . . and then follow the plan.
- When good news is a pleasant surprise, admit the fact . . . but check it out before you comment.
- Bad news may have unsuspected negative consequences. Leave the handling of bad news to professionals, unless you really have the experience, qualifications, and authority to respond for your organization.

INSIGHT 41

In announcing what you consider good news, be alert to the possibility that it may be less than welcome to some part of your audience. Your news should be worded with that fact very much in mind!

HOW TO MAXIMIZE GOOD NEWS

1. List every audience to whom news about your company or organization may be of interest. Be sure to include the specialized interest groups you wish to influence or inform.

2. Imagine yourself in the place of each group that, on hearing your news, asks, "What's in it for *me?*" Try to make your news into a benefit specific to that group, especially if the group's first reaction may be more negative than you would wish. The chances are that by practicing this type of empathy, you not only will foresee the negatives, but will be able to translate them into something positive. *Do not, under any circumstances, lie!* In almost every instance, you will be found out, with consequences more dire than those you face for telling an unwelcome truth.

INSIGHT 42

It is extraordinarily difficult for any person or group to think beyond self-interest. Nevertheless, this is the job of the PR person: to get the company or organization to think that way and to tailor the message to the *media's* needs and interests. Management is no better, or worse, about this than employees; the writers of news than its readers. PR has the challenge of understanding and satisfying them all.

3. After deciding how each of your interest groups is likely to react to your news, you can draw some reasonable conclusions to guide further action. Here are some points you'll want to consider:

- **Should there be any official notice at all?** Your news can be announced by a media release, a news conference, or some other official notice. Or it may simply be permitted to happen. Many—probably most—events aren't worth the time and effort needed to make them into a story that's likely to get published. So concentrate on your best bets—the ones that affect the most people or that concern your audience in a very direct way.
- **Who tells your employees?** Decide how, by whom, and to whom to spread the news. Anything that *benefits* employees should be told to them at the earliest possible moment. To avoid distortion, put it in writing. Place it on bulletin boards and mail it to their homes. You want good news shared with the entire family, to help build goodwill toward the employer.

INSIGHT 43

Make the immediate supervisor the first spreader of good news. Resist the temptation so prevalent in politics to have everything good come from the top and everything unpleasant from below. Use the "Army system." The same sergeant who had me dig the latrine also gave me a weekend pass!

- **What to do when it affects the community.** When your news will have a positive impact upon the community (whether it's the neighborhood or the whole state), share that fact *in advance* with the political leadership. Invite the politicos to share in the goodwill the news can generate. If it is important enough, suggest a joint news conference for the announcement. If you're not experienced at gathering the media, they are! Be sure to have a news or media release (see next section) ready for the event. Just as in communicating with your employees, you want to make certain the story reflects your point of view.

  If the political leadership is otherwise occupied, find out whether you can gather the press on your own. Offer a personal interview, but don't be hurt if the press doesn't desire it.

  Just because a very limited news staff can't pay a personal visit does not mean that your story will be ignored. Get it to them in some other way. Mail and messenger are always welcome. Don't, however, FAX without making sure that this method is equally well received. Your attorney and accountant will give you the legal requirements concerning what you *must* tell. Your publicity/PR director will tell you what you *should* tell in addition and how to do it.
- **Investors love good news. Give it to them!** If you are a large enough organization to issue public stock or bonds, you are large enough to use professional help for your communication. Smaller organizations, whether financed by family, financial institutions, or venture capitalists, will want to keep their investors informed, too. As with the giants, the advice, consent, and continuing support of these investors largely depends on what *you* tell

them. But their wrath at being misled is likely to be even more fierce than that of the public investment community. In financial matters, while the truth may not make you free, the untruth may well send you to prison. Unlike our possible amusement at the politicians' "spin control," your investors' insistence upon financial veracity is likely to be unforgiving and with a very long, very accurate memory!

SUMMARY

- Aim your news to influence a specific audience.
- Put yourself in the place of that audience, and consider how your news will be received. If the answer isn't "Great!" why are you sending it?
- Let your employees know when good news happens. The rumors they hear are usually the opposite.
- Let the political leadership share in your goodwill. You need them even more than they need you.
- Keep your investors informed. Be happy when you can share good news with them and prompt to tell them the bad. Reluctance to share any financial data is a dangerous stance!

THE MEDIA RELEASE OR NEWS ADVISORY

A media release is a story that you (a) hope will be newsworthy or otherwise worthy of attention and (b) want to make public. Notice that being newsworthy is the more important criterion. In most instances, print and electronic media get many more stories than they can use. The importance and interest of each story *to the medium's particular audience* will largely decide what gets published or aired. That's why the news must be in the very first paragraph, reinforced and emphasized by a suggested headline.

What Not to Do

Do not begin your release with something like "President Jane Jones of Acme Motors announces. . . . " A great many releases do begin that way because so many companies and organizations think that *that's* the "news" or the most important words. *The media* never begin *any* story that way—unless it's with the words "President Clinton announced. . . . "

INSIGHT 44

News media are swamped with requests for coverage. They don't have the time or personnel to study long press releases to discover whether each one truly contains some news. So put the heart of your news into the first paragraph, preferably into the very first sentence. If you don't catch them there, you're unlikely to keep them looking.

The news advisory or release is the basic tool in your publicity campaign. It's also a tool you should have no difficulty in learning how to use. By way of example, let's create a release about the same senior citizen bicycle invented in the chapter on advertising:

E-Z-Ryder Bike Factory * 123 East Fourth * Wakenaw, KY ①

NEWS RELEASE ②

March 22, 199x ③

To	For additional information, contact ⑤
Charles Smith ④	Jeanette Miranda O'Keefe
Sports Editor	Information Director
Wakenaw Daily Bugle	E-Z Ryder
	789-001-0002

Release date: FOR IMMEDIATE RELEASE ⑥

New bike for seniors hailed by
50-plus test riders ⑦
Warrensville, KY. ⑧ Twenty-nine volunteers, ranging in age from 50 to 81, today test drove the new E-Z Ryder bicycles especially designed for seniors to give them more mobility for both entertainment and basic transportation. While only 5 said that they currently use bicycles regularly, 27 said that they might do so in the future because of the E-Z Ryder's special features. ⑨

"I drove the bike around town for over an hour," reported the most senior of the group, retired Warrensville fireman Chuck Quinzley. ⑩ "I don't know how they made it so easy," he said, "but that's the most biking I've done all at once in the past 10 years."
Ladies version pleases, too ⑪
The 11 women test drivers, who were not asked to volunteer their ages, ⑫ were equally pleased with their bikes. "They must have done something special with the gears to make riding this easy," suggested former science teacher Mrs. Lisa Spengler. ⑬ "I think it made all of us feel a lot younger to be biking around town just like the high schoolers I used to teach."
New patent to Ryder Company ⑭
"Mrs. Spengler is absolutely correct," said Edwyn Ryder, President of E-Z-Ryder, ⑮ when told about her remark. "The gears have just been granted a patent, and we're going to tool up for a major increase in production right here in Warrensville, ⑯ though that won't be ready for about another year. ⑰ Right now, we're going to sponsor some Sensible Junior/ Senior Cycling races in which you have to be over 50 or under 15 to compete. ⑱ Not only are we going to let us seniors ⑲ feel like kids again," concluded Ryder with a laugh, "we're going to beat them at their own game!"

- 30 - ⑳

Photograph herewith. ㉑

Broadcast-quality video available. ㉒
Contact J. O'Keefe for details.

There are 22 points highlighted in this story. Just for fun, take a sheet of paper and jot down what you think is the reason for each point. I'll also give you mine, but just because we don't always agree doesn't mean that you're wrong and I'm right.

More likely, it means that there is more than one good reason for doing something right or for avoiding something wrong.[2]

22 Ways to Get Your Story Printed

1. Make your corporate or association identification clear. Many of us are so used to identifying ourselves with divisions or departments, that we forget the publicity power of our parent organization.

2. "NEWS" is what your recipients want. Promise it with the largest type on the page. Use "Media News Release" when including electronic media.

3. No one wants to publish old news, so make the date of your release absolutely current. If the same release is used for more than a single day, fill in the dates as they are used.

    Use typewriter-style type for the entire release. Make sure that it's a typeface you can match for filling in the date and the recipient's name. If your releases are preprinted before being personalized, rather than auto-typed or computer generated, tell your printers about your personalization plan. They will control the density of the ink to give the appearance of individual typing.

4. There is nothing more direct and personal than an individual's name and title, even when the recipient knows that it's all done by computer. You will, of course, have identified the most likely sources for publication through personal contacts or telephone conversations. If you're not sure whom to address in larger news organizations, ask the editor most likely to be in charge. Not only will you get a name, but you may also interest the editor!

5. Give your recipients a specific person to contact, if possible with a telephone number that cuts through the growing computerized switchboard maze. You're hoping for free in-print and on-air publicity, so don't make contacting you a challenge. Your recipients may not have the time or patience to be so challenged.

6. Your story will usually be held—that is, not published or aired—until the date specified by you. (There are occasional violations of hold dates when the news is "hot" enough.) Most stories are distributed "for immediate release." Others have specific release dates, usually to give weekly or monthly publications the chance to break the news at the same time as the daily media. This is especially important when a key writer won't mention your story once it has appeared elsewhere.

    In some media, specific individuals are so widely read that they won't consider

---

[2] Please send your list to my attention, c/o the publisher, John Wiley & Sons, 605 Third Avenue, New York, NY 10158. We'll credit you (with your permission, of course) for any changes in future editions. A dated postmark on the envelope will control in case of duplicate suggestions.

a story, unless it's given to them before anyone else. When such an "exclusive" is offered, be sure to give it a time limit. Rather than "for immediate release," indicate something like "Exclusive for (name) to (date)." Indicate release after the specified date on all other copies. An exclusive is valuable and should get you a bit more than routine attention in return.

7. Your headline will help determine the kind of attention each medium gives to your story. In this example, we've given the story a human interest rather than a business emphasis. When used, such emphasis should be a well thought-out part of your overall plan. Note that you can supply several stories with different emphases as part of a media kit and then add another story that summarizes all of them. Add a contents page, and not only will the media be grateful, but you're less likely to omit something.

8. This tells where the story takes place, not necessarily where it was written. When a particular local context is important, tell the story from that point of view. A Kansas wheat grower teaching Eastern Europeans how to use an Illinois-built combine typifies both the challenges and opportunities PR faces every day.

9. Note how packed with information this first paragraph is. Make *your* first paragraph tell the story in such a way that if nothing else is published, you will still have made your main point. You'll be happy to find that many releases are printed in their entirety, exactly as they are written, especially by smaller publications with limited editorial and rewriting staffs. But most media will use only a portion of the release. Under the "all the news that fits" rule, stories are written to be cut (shortened) from back to front, so load the beginning. Readers, too, pay more attention to initial paragraphs. Whether they are consciously aware of it or not, they know that scanning just the headlines and first paragraphs will give them the overview that determines whether reading more is worth their time.

Everything after the first paragraph is an expansion on what's just been read. It's our job to make this material so enticing or important that the reader can't resist learning more.

INSIGHT 45

In writing the first paragraph of a news story or feature item, picture an individual whom you most want to inform or influence. Within the format of the media that will get your release, write the initial paragraph so that *that* individual will want to know more. Relate your story or feature to the specific interests, wants, and needs of that special reader, and you will also capture the much broader audience for whom you are looking. You may hope that what you write will be read (or heard or seen) by vast numbers of groups, but groups don't read—individuals do. You'll succeed when you make it worth the while of each separate reader.

10. Take the story from the abstract to the personal as soon as possible. Chuck is someone to whom readers, as well as a radio or television audience, can relate. And note how he gives the product a believable testimonial, a fact that will be reinforced a bit later in the story. Remember that you are writing *news*, not advertising. Keep the plugs for the product soft sell!

11. Your headline and subheads serve two purposes:
- To "highlight" the main points of your story;
- To let the readers spot their own specific interests. No one has time to read everything. Use subheads to make it easy for readers with different interests to find the parts of the story that are important to them.

12. Beware of sexism. Beware doubly of humor. That the female test drivers were not asked to reveal their age may bring a chuckle to some readers, but it would be resented and found not at all funny by many women. It's placed here as a warning of things to avoid, rather than to include. Attempts at humor, unless quoted or put into a totally humorous context, are best left to the professionals.

13. Featuring women and minority groups in a positive manner is permitted and often encouraged. (Be careful, however, not to create resentment by appearing condescending—"Why do you have to point out that *we're* just as good as others?") A photograph usually works well in this regard. Provide a picture that shows the science teacher and gear-guru as African American or Hispanic and you've made your point—without saying a word. Religious affiliations, unless absolutely required by the story, are best left unmentioned.

14. This subhead and the text that follows could easily have been the major focus of the story. They are put here to show how a subhead can signal a change in the direction of the story, even as it downplays the content that follows, by placing it last. It's a handy device for forestalling wild rumors through your own official version.

15. The introduction of the senior corporate officer's testimony signals a change to a more serious emphasis.

16. Note the calming of fears about a possible negative local impact, placed here to minimize the likelihood of such fears. The president *immediately* answers the universal questions, "What's in it—positive or negative—for me?"

17. When promising good things for the future, leave some flexibility as to specific dates. "About another year" is a good deal safer than "One year from today." Notice also that this statement invites an ongoing series of progress reports, with continuing interest and excitement for everyone involved.

18. The story can stop after the previous sentence or continue with a return to the lighter tone with which it began. The media using the story will make that decision.

19. Ryder's identification of himself as a fellow senior—the group to which the major headline is addressed—is an effective way of returning the story to the human interest tone with which it began. It is generally better to maintain one tone throughout a story. However, if, as in this story, you do switch, it is best to return to the tone with which you began, very much as in a symphony or sonata, where the opening and concluding themes most frequently echo each other and a middle section is given more freedom to wander—though not to get lost.

20. The notation "-30-" is a standard way of showing the conclusion of a story and signals that the writer is in the know about even the trivia of his or her craft.

21. When including a photograph with your release, it may be in color or in black and white. The important things are its degree of contrast and its degree of detail. A photograph or other illustration that you hope to have shown in color must, of course, be that way in the original. Standard size for the originals is 8 inches by 10 inches, a format photographic duplication services are set up to handle economically. When ordering duplicates, note that it is customary to give the horizontal size first. Make sure that here, as elsewhere, you and your suppliers are speaking the same language.

About Quantity Photo Reproductions. In a quantity photo service, black-and-white and color copies have different systems of reproduction. Black-and-white photos are made from an $8'' \times 10''$ print, rather than from a negative. If practical, give the service that print instead of your film. It will be cheaper, and copies should be practically indistinguishable from the original. For color reproductions, give the service your negative or transparency along with a print that shows how you wish the photograph to look. If no print exists, tell the reproduction service what the basic colors in the print should be, and then have them make a proof. The cost is nominal and permits you to "color correct" for final duplication. But discuss this with your service if cost is a factor. Almost anything is possible; you must decide whether it's practical.

Quantity photo services are in most major markets. I have used the aptly named Quantity Photo in Chicago for over two decades with superior results.

Type a suggested caption onto a regular sheet of paper, and tape that sheet to the back of the photo. Be sure that both the caption and the illustration can be seen at the same time, as shown in Figure 6.1. For shipping, fold the caption over the photograph.

22. Consider the creation of television-quality film only if T.V. coverage seems assured and worth the considerable investment. You may, of course, gain even more important advantages from your video in financial, zoning, and other face-to-face presentations. A more detailed discussion of electronic media is presented in Chapter 8.

Figure 6.1 Captioning a photo. Tape the caption to the back of your photograph. Make sure the message and picture can both be seen at the same time.

MEDIA KITS

A media kit is a package of materials that both includes and expands upon your news release. It contains photographs, charts, and other pertinent illustrative materials for print media. Less often, it also holds audio and video materials for radio and television. It may contain a variety of background materials about your organization, including human interest stories about the people you want mentioned.

INSIGHT 46

Don't load your media kit just to impress the media with the importance of the sender. More likely, you'll simply try the patience of the recipient. Check for and take out material that duplicates anything else or that is not essentially tied to the story. Your problem, as always, is to get attention and interest, so make the kit complete, but concise. The media will contact you for more background when they do a story that needs it.

HOW TO GAIN LOCAL COVERAGE

For the majority of us, gaining truly national attention, through, for example, an article in *Business Week, The Wall Street Journal,* or *Time*, is unlikely. But don't despair. Send your *major* news releases to them anyway. They may surprise you! More likely coverage, however, lies in your local media—including major cities' neighborhood newspapers—and your regional or national professional and trade publications. They not only want your news; they need it!

In larger communities, such as New York, Chicago, Denver, or Seattle, news of local interest competes for publication with all the news in the world. In smaller communities, including big cities' neighborhoods, you *are* the world. When I was growing up in Chicago, our neighborhood *Hyde Park Herald* told us what was really important—in our schools, our immediate politics, and our business community. I now live in a city of 70,000 bordering directly on Chicago. Here, too, as far as our community's 120-page weekly newspaper is concerned, the world at large hardly exists. Local firms and organizations get the attention that our *Chicago Tribune* neighbor lavishes on Toyota, IBM, and AT&T. Equally important, our local publishers, editors, and reporters live right next door. Since everyone who tells them anything has a "vested" interest in how it will be reported, our "real" news is not only needed, but welcomed.

THREE WAYS TO GET NATIONAL COVERAGE

Essentially, there are three ways you may attain national coverage.

1. Have Fame Thrust Upon You

Practically every day, businesses, corporations, and organizations achieve instant, often unexpected, fame. *People* magazine lauds a product its producer thought would be limited to schools . . . and the phone "rings off the hook." Cold fusion ignites a nationwide debate . . . and a university finds itself in the middle. The nation's favorite van is down-graded by *Consumer Reports* . . . and a manufacturer's nightmare becomes reality.

The examples range from a small start-up business to a Fortune 500 corporation, from an enterprise that is not yet profitable to one that is nonprofit to one that is desperate for profit. But all have one thing in common: the need for expert response. In two of the three examples cited, that expertise was already on staff. In the third, the plug from *People* so totally overwhelmed its recipient's efforts to capitalize on it himself, that he forgot he had expert help on retainer for just such an emergency!

Fame does strike in most unexpected ways. Just don't panic. Do what *you* are good at. Treat a PR emergency—good or bad—exactly as you would a legal or medical crisis. Stay calm. Get help.

2. Find National Media That Want Your News

Trade media are magazines, journals, and newsletters devoted to a specific interest, trade, or profession. They are the most likely national publications to welcome your news, provided that it will appeal to their readers. So many of these publications exist, that even PR professionals need special directories to keep up to date on them. For instance, the Standard Rate and Data Service (SRDS) directory, *Business Publications*, lists 58 magazines and trade papers devoted to metalworking, with cross references to several hundred more in 17 related fields. Other topics in this directory have from 6 listings to 650—and that covers only the English-language periodicals from the U.S. plus selected magazines from Canada.

For PR purposes, the annual *Bacon's Publicity Checker* and *The Editor & Publisher*

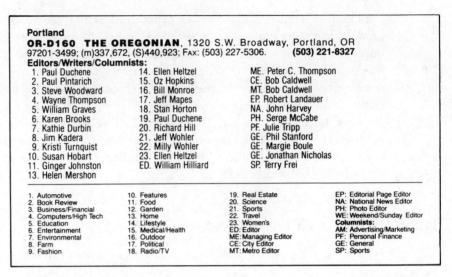

Portland
OR-D160   THE OREGONIAN, 1320 S.W. Broadway, Portland, OR
97201-3499; (m)337,672, (S)440,923; Fax: (503) 227-5306.   **(503) 221-8327**
Editors/Writers/Columnists:

1. Paul Duchene	14. Ellen Heltzel	ME. Peter C. Thompson
2. Paul Pintarich	15. Oz Hopkins	CE. Bob Caldwell
3. Steve Woodward	16. Bill Monroe	MT. Bob Caldwell
4. Wayne Thompson	17. Jeff Mapes	EP. Robert Landauer
5. William Graves	18. Stan Horton	NA. John Harvey
6. Karen Brooks	19. Paul Duchene	PH. Serge McCabe
7. Kathie Durbin	20. Richard Hill	PF. Julie Tripp
8. Jim Kadera	21. Jeff Wohler	GE. Phil Stanford
9. Kristi Turnquist	22. Milly Wohler	GE. Margie Boule
10. Susan Hobart	23. Ellen Heltzel	GE. Jonathan Nicholas
11. Ginger Johnston	ED. William Hilliard	SP. Terry Frei
13. Helen Mershon		

1. Automotive	10. Features	19. Real Estate	EP: Editorial Page Editor
2. Book Review	11. Food	20. Science	NA: National News Editor
3. Business/Financial	12. Garden	21. Sports	PH: Photo Editor
4. Computers/High Tech	13. Home	22. Travel	WE: Weekend/Sunday Editor
5. Education	14. Lifestyle	23. Women's	**Columnists:**
6. Entertainment	15. Medical/Health	ED: Editor	AM: Advertising/Marketing
7. Environmental	16. Outdoor	ME: Managing Editor	PF: Personal Finance
8. Farm	17. Political	CE: City Editor	GE: General
9. Fashion	18. Radio/TV	MT: Metro Editor	SP: Sports

Figure 6.2 Typical *Bacon's Publicity Checker* listing (© 1992 Bacon's Information Inc.). A two-volume set covers U.S. and Canadian newspapers and magazines. A third volume, available individually, covers U.S. radio and T.V. Editorial calendars for major magazines and dailies, updated bi-monthly, are in *Bacon's Media Alerts*. Business and financial editorial contacts for all media, updated midyear, are in *Bacon's Business/Financial Directory*. Print media in Western Europe are covered in the annual *Bacon's International Publicity Checker*. Contact Bacon's Information Inc., 332 South Michigan Avenue, Chicago, IL 60604. (800) 621-0561.

International Yearbook are the most widely used references. Though somewhat overlapping, each has exclusive—and valuable—PR content, and most PR professionals get both. An industry bible, *Editor & Publisher* gives practically encyclopedic newspaper information worldwide, of which PR contacts are only one part. There is also extensive information on newspaper suppliers, news services and syndicates, newspaper organizations, and schools of journalism. *Bacon's Publicity Checker* (Vol. I, *Magazines*, and Vol. II, *Newspapers*) covers U.S. and Canadian print media and includes quarterly updatings designed to be placed directly over out-of-date listings. An example from *Bacon's* is given in Figure 6.2, and one from *Editor & Publisher* is shown in Figure 6.3.

For PR seekers who do not require the quarterly updating provided by *Bacon's*, Morgan-Rand offers biannually updated directories of *TV and Cable, National Radio*, and *Feature News Publicity Outlets*. Contact the company at 2200 Sansom Street, Philadelphia, PA 19103, or call (800)441-3839.

Use Regional and Local References.   In addition to its *Syndicated Columnists Contacts* and *News Bureau Contacts*, BPI Media Services offers handy regional and national guides to the broadcast media. Appropriate listings are taken from their national publications, *Radio, TV, TV News*, and *Cable Contacts*, and combined into regional editions covering all four. These are definitely worth considering for any PR reference library! Contact BPI at PO Box 2015, Lakewood, NJ 08701, or call (800)753-6675.

The Oregonian

(all day-mon to fri; m-sat; S)
Oregonian Publishing Co., 1320 S.W. Broadway, Portland, OR 97201; tel (503) 221-8327; FAX (503) 227-5306. Newhouse Newspapers group.
Circulation: 324,163(d); 317,595(m-sat); 431,989(S); ABC Sept. 30, 1990.
Price: 35¢(d); 35¢(sat); $1.00(S); $159.12/yr (d), $91/yr (S) (mail).
Advertising: Open inch rate $98.97(all day); $98.97(m-sat); $102.72(S). **Representative:** Newhouse Newspapers/Metro Suburbia.
News Services: AP, CDN, LAT-WP, NYT. **Politics:** Independent. **Established:** 1850.
Supplements: Local Northwest, Parade (S).

CORPORATE OFFICERS

President	Fred A Stickel
Vice Pres	Theo Newhouse
Secretary	James Rogers
Treasurer	S I Newhouse, III
Asst Treasurer	D W Palmer
Asst Treasurer	Richard E Diamond

GENERAL MANAGEMENT

Publisher	Fred A Stickel
General Manager	Patrick F Stickel
Business Manager	James Rogers
Controller	D W Palmer
Credit Manager	Betty Kirk
Personnel Manager	Frank Lesage
Director of Community Affairs	Stephanie Oliver
Marketing Service Director	Steve Hubbard
Purchasing Agent	James Brown

ADVERTISING

Director	Brian Bounous
Manager-Retail	Glenn Breniman
Manager-General	John Mannex
Manager-Classified	Tom Jorgensen

CIRCULATION

Director	Patrick L Marlton

NEWS EXECUTIVES

Editor	William Hilliard
Managing Editor	Peter Thompson
Asst Managing Editor	Richard C Johnston
Asst to the Editor	Judson Randall
Asst Managing Editor	R Gregory Nokes
Asst Managing Editor	Sue Hobart
Metro Editor	Bob Caldwell

EDITORS AND MANAGERS

Action Line	Sally Christensen
Amusements	Karen Brooks
Art Dept	Mark Wigginton
Auto	Paul Duchene
Books	Paul Pintarich
Business	Steve Woodward
Cartoonist	Jack Ohman
Editorial Page Editor	Robert Landauer
Editorial Writer	David Reinhard
Editorial Writer	Wayne Thompson
Editorial Writer	Phil Cogswell
Editorial Writer	Jerry Tippens
Editorial Writer	Larry Hilderbrand
Editorial Writer	David Sarasohn
Editorial Writer	Donald J Sterling Jr
Education	Jim Hill
Education	Bill Graves
Fashion	Kristi Turnquist
Lifestyle	Lora Cuykendall
Films-Theater	Ted Mahar
Food	Virginia Johnston
Food	Barbara Durbin
Librarian	Sandra Macomber
Music	David Stabler
News Editor	John Harvey
Northwest Magazine	Ellen Heltzel
Photo Director	Serge McCabe
Political	Jeff Mapes
Radio/TV	Peter Farrell
Real Estate	Steve Woodward
Religion	Sura Rubenstein
Science	Richard Hill
Science/Medicine	Oz Hopkins
Sports	Jeff Wohler
Theater	Robert Hicks
Travel	Milly Wohler
Wire Editor	John Harvey

PRODUCTION

Director	James Rogers
Manager	Ed Hagstrom
Asst Manager	Carol Howard
Plant-Superintendent	Joe Crawford
Systems Manager	Dick Rickman
Communications Manager	Arthur Dummer
Superintendent-Composing	Richard Dorr
Superintendent-Mailroom	James Holman
Asst Superintendent-Mailroom	Ed Spencer
Asst Superintendent-Mailroom	Will Sousley
Superintendent-Plate Making	Dan Tucker
Superintendent-Pressroom	Dennis Russell
Asst Superintendent-Pressroom	Herman Etzel
Ad Services Manager	Larry Wilson
Asst Ad Services Manager	Carl Owens
Asst Ad Services Manager	John Bailey

Market information: Zoned editions; Split run; Total market coverage; SAU.
Mechanical available: Offset; black and 3 ROP colors; inserts accepted — preprinted, free-standing.
Mechanical specifications: Type page 13" x 21½"; E - 6 cols, 2^1/16", ⅛" between; A - 6 cols, 2^1/16", ⅛" between; C - 10 cols, 1¼", ^{1}/14" between.
Commodity consumption (estimated): Newsprint 84,000 short tons; widths 55-54", 40½", 27"; black ink 1,692,600 pounds; color ink 261,800 pounds; single plates used 422,000.
Equipment: EDITORIAL: All-electronic cps —4-CCSI/CPU, DEC/11/70; 213-CCSI Edit/112 BS VDTs. CLASSIFIED: All-electronic cps —4-CCSI/CPU, 3-PDP/1170, 1-PDP/11/84; 100-CCSI/CT97s VDTs. DISPLAY: All electronic cps — CX. 12-CX/Sun Breezer VDTs. PRODUCTION: typesetters —3-Lasercomp Express, 2-Lasercomp MK2i; plate exposers — 2-WL/Lith-Exposer, 2-N/FT40UPNS; plate processors —2-WL/38-D; digital cameras/scanners — 2-ECR; cameras — 2-C/Marathon, 1-C/Spartan III; automatic film processors — 1-P/26RA, 1-P/26ML, 1-C/Powermatic R650, 1-Pak shrink lenses — 1-CK Optical/SQU-7, 1-CK Optical/Variable; digital scanners/separators — CD/646.

Figure 6.3 Typical listing from *The Editor & Publisher International Yearbook* (© 1991 Editor & Publisher International Yearbook). About 20 percent of this listing, giving technical details on printing presses and other mechanical details, is not shown here. Contents cover U.S. and Canadian newspapers in detail, plus basic information about newspapers worldwide. Contact Editor & Publisher International Yearbook, 11 West 19th Street, New York, NY 10011. (212) 675-4380.

As of March, 1993, *local* references seem plentiful. Ask any local media representative whether one exists for your community.

Check 'em All. . . . Only the largest of PR departments is likely to need all of the resources just mentioned. Their publishers offer excellent descriptive literature. Ask for it if you are unfamiliar with a guide. Be sure to request an *actual-size* sample page, too. This will make it much easier to compare styles for their ease and thoroughness of reference.

Local News Welcomed. With endless pages to fill, trade publication editors welcome your local news and features related to their special interest. To the specialist, "local" may have broader implications than even we, the senders of the news, realize—and which of us doesn't enjoy being in the know about *everything* in our field. After all, that's what makes us experts!

For stories that are more than routine, call the editor of the most important publication in your field (probably the one most widely read in your own organization), and offer an exclusive. Of course, you'll put a deadline on their acceptance, one that will permit you a wider distribution if the publication says no to your offer. And do thank the editor for considering the offer. You want his or her goodwill for your nonexclusive releases, too.

INSIGHT 47

Publicists at companies and organizations should do telephone follow-ups with trade media. Get to *know* them. With this group, calling is more important than writing.

---

3. Use National Release Services

The trade term for a national release service is "mat release service," although "mats" stopped being used to duplicate printed materials about 1970, when they were replaced by photographic-quality originals, or "slicks." Ask your newspaper representative to tell you about mats. It's a fascinating story.

What National Release Services Do. Several services provide the nation's media with a constant stream of stories, articles, features, and cartoons of such broad interest that they can appear almost anywhere, yet be of local interest. Depending on the season, these items may include stories on gardening or snow blowers, June wedding dresses or Thanksgiving turkey stuffing, or child safety seats in automobiles or new gears for seniors' bikes. The subject list is endless.

Unlike news services that employ reporters and charge media for the use of their stories and features, release services get their materials from public relations offices and get paid to distribute them for free use by the media. But don't be alarmed. The media hasn't sold out. Everyone involved knows the sources and the rules. Release services accept only materials that have wide appeal. Otherwise their primary audience, the editors looking for interesting "fillers," will stop considering what they submit. Release service customers, the companies paying to have their stories distributed, will remain customers only if the materials they distribute actually appear in print. What you, as a customer, are paying for is a combination of professional preparation, specified distribution, and a reasonably friendly reception in editorial offices. You eliminate the expense of an up-to-date mailing list and the duplication and distribution of your individual stories or features.

Who Uses Release Service Materials. Some release service materials find their way into electronic media and newspapers of major cities, especially in specific interest sections, such as gardening, homemaking, automotive, and cooking. The most widespread use of these materials, however, is in smaller communities. There they are appreciated not only for their content, but because they can be used exactly as received, without new typesetting or editing—a not inconsiderable benefit in a budget-conscious office.

How to Learn Where Your Story Appears. Clipping services are in the business of reading practically every newspaper and magazine and, for specified fees, "clipping out" items that mention a specific subject. When you receive from them the stories you've ordered clipped (some 10 days to 3 weeks after they're first published), each has attached the name of the publication in which the story appeared, its circulation, and when the story ran. For organizations that wish to document the local, regional, or national success of their PR efforts, these services, listed under "Clipping Bureaus" in major-city Yellow Pages, are about the only way of keeping track of those efforts. Analogous services also exist for radio and T.V.

INSIGHT 48

Remember why you want national media PR:
1. To serve a specific purpose beneficial to your firm or association;
2. To have *national* material to duplicate and distribute to the audience you hope to influence;
3. To let the market for your product or service know it is there or is coming.

GETTING MORE PR FROM YOUR PUBLICITY

- Any mention about you in a national publication—even a trade journal— will get reported in your local press . . . provided that you make it known to them. Do it!
- Employees love to read about themselves and their successes. Post such stories prominently on special "Good News Bulletin Boards" . . . then invite everyone to post their personal good news there also—weddings, births, graduations, anniversaries, divorces, or whatever. Let them decide!
- Mail copies of your national coverage to persons important to you or your organization. Be sure to include local political leaders, the financial community, and your employee and union newsletter.

INSIGHT 49

Few publicity stories have truly national appeal. Don't sink your time and dollars into expectations that just won't be realized. Feeding an ego as big as the world is an appetite few of us can—or should—afford.

SUMMARY

- Local media want and need your news, especially when you give it a local angle. Your audience is always interested first in themselves and secondly in everything that affects them.
- Think of your trade media as another local market, with the "locality" being its specialized interest. Then write accordingly.
- For national coverage, use the rifle rather than the shotgun approach. Get to know specific media contacts, and then translate your news into a story or feature that meets *their* needs and preferences. Trust hard work and creativity rather than luck.

WHEN NOT TO DO IT YOURSELF

We began this chapter by defining the task of public relations as being "to limit harm and, where possible, to neutralize harm or turn it into good." That "harm" is the way we are viewed by a specific part of the public and the actions they might take because of that perception. Thus, PR has two tasks. One is to forewarn its own company or organization against, and possibly prevent, harmful PR consequences that can be foreseen. The second and more frequently called upon task is to neutralize the public's perception of something—foreseeable or not—after it has occurred. Notice that the focus is on "something," rather than "us." An aircraft failure caused by a usually harmless lightning bolt may cause the same wreck as poor engine maintenance, but the public's perception of mechanics, the flight crew, and the airline affected will be markedly different in the two cases. And if you think this is too radical an example to apply to *you*, consider the fact that it is the expected PR emergency for a specific industry. For an airline, public relations surely should not be handled by amateurs—just as the PR critical to *you* demands equally expert attention. So when you are in need of PR:

- **Consider the stakes**. Are you trying to climb from a 60-percent to a 65-percent market share or halt a precipitous decline?
- **Consider the personalities**. Is the CEO more likely to accept PR guidance from an "objective" outside pro than from inside staff . . . especially when the results are painful as well as necessary?
- **Consider the location**. Will you be an outsider who raises suspicions, whereas local expertise would gain a friendly welcome?
- **Consider your own abilities**. Balance what you can do, and do well, against what *only you* can do, and direct yourself accordingly.

But let's not be "firemen," waiting to be summoned to PR disasters. Public relations and publicity can and should be used to create goodwill—among employees, customers, clients, and the community as a whole. This may mean sponsoring or helping to publicize a golf tournament, a health fair, a scout outing, a contest for kids, etc. It may also involve, depending on policy, making public your charitable contributions or involvement by management in public service. You probably do much more good than anyone suspects . . . so let the world know!

YES, YOU CAN DO YOUR OWN PR . . . SOMETIMES

Doing your own publicity can be both rewarding and a great deal of fun, and nothing I have said here should keep you from it.[3] There are, however, times when your expertise should concentrate on finding PR professionals who can handle a project better than you can and then making sure that that's what they do.

The biggest mistake made by firms when hiring outside PR professionals is not to tell them the *whole* story. Usually, professionals are called in to help overcome a bad image, a falling market share, or unfavorable publicity. Many firms think that they won't get a good job out of the pros if they really tell them *all* the "bad news." So they send them into battle unaware. Of course, they do learn, the hard way—from the media! They wind up looking foolish, and their employers look worse. Think of the pro as your good-guy hired gun. Don't arm him or her with blanks!

INSIGHT 50

When assigning any task, search for someone who's better at it than you. And don't worry about being shown up: Organizations are desperate for managers who recognize talent and tend to reward that more liberally than just doing a good job yourself. Managers get promoted. Good workers get more work.

NOTES ON THE PUBLICITY/PUBLIC RELATIONS CHECKLIST

These notes are a supplement to the material presented in this chapter. They are not a substitute for that material.

1. The audience(s) you want to reach and which—if any—to address specifically, rather than as part of the whole. Differentiate between the same message keyed to different interests and different messages.
2. Both what the message is to say and what it is to accomplish. Set realistic PR goals, not those for advertising.
3. Link the project(s) to #1 and #2. Define the media for each audience in relation to the "cash value" of achieving each goal. Not only dollars, but staff and staff time are limited, too.
4. Almost anything can be done—given that nothing else is needed. If due dates demand an absolute concentration of effort on one particular project, make sure that management knows that no other project can receive attention.

---

[3] For a much more detailed treatment of do-it-yourself PR, get *The Publicity Kit* by Jeanette Smith (Wiley, 1992).

PUBLICITY/PUBLIC RELATIONS CHECKLIST

Project title/description _____ Date _____

_____ Project # _____

_____ Checklist # _____

Overall Supervision by _____ Deadline _____

Budget _____ Start-up Date _____ Completion Date _____

Project Focus (Mark A–Z in order of importance): ☐ Managers ☐ Other Employees ☐ Immediate Community
☐ Broader Community ☐ Stockholders ☐ Other Financial ☐ Suppliers ☐ Customers ☐ Clients
☐ General Press ☐ Trade Press ☐ Financial Press ☐ _____ ☐ _____ ☐ _____

MANAGEMENT DECISIONS	ASSIGNED TO	DUE	IN	MUST APPROVE	BY DATE	IN	INFO COPY ONLY	SEE ATTACHED
1. Audience(s)			☐			☐		☐
2. Focus			☐			☐		☐
3. Project(s)			☐			☐		☐
4. Time Line			☐			☐		☐
5. Cost–Quotes/Actual			☐			☐		☐
6. Project Supervision			☐			☐		☐
PRODUCTION								
7. Components			☐			☐		☐
8. Copy			☐			☐		☐
9. Layout			☐			☐		☐
10. Type			☐			☐		☐
11. Duplication			☐			☐		☐
12. Camera-Ready Art			☐			☐		☐
13. Printing			☐			☐		☐
14. AV Practice			☐			☐		☐
15. Audio Creative			☐			☐		☐
16. Video Creative			☐			☐		☐
17. AV Duplication			☐			☐		☐
DISTRIBUTION								
18. Phone Contacts Assigned			☐			☐		☐
19. Phone Contacts Made			☐			☐		☐
20. Media Kit Packaging			☐			☐		☐
21. Lists Ordered (mail/phone)			☐			☐		☐
22. Shipping Assigned			☐			☐		☐
23. Postage OK			☐			☐		☐
24. Personal Contacts Assigned			☐			☐		☐
25. Personal Contacts Made			☐			☐		☐
26. Mailing Lists Checked			☐			☐		☐
27. Phone Lists Checked			☐			☐		☐
28. Legal Clearance			☐			☐		☐
REPORTS								
29. Quotes/Estimates			☐			☐		☐
30. Actual Costs			☐			☐		☐
31. Checking Bureau Assigned			☐			☐		☐
32. Results Received/Distributed			☐			☐		☐

5. A centralized budgeting control, especially for multimedia projects such as items 12 through 18. Not how individual budgets are set, but how expenditures are tracked and monitored. Don't do these projects without such a system!

6. Note here if this is different from the overall supervision and how both work in developing items 1–5.

7. Spell out each project's components. Not, for instance, just "Media Kit," but every detail. This includes the type of outer envelope along with its size and message; the color of the pocket folder and the number of pockets it has; any special design or standard format; and what each pocket contains and in what order. Mention also any additional enclosures—both new and existing—and the order in which they appear. Specify *everything*.

8. Writing for PR is a specialized skill. Frequently, it can be found or developed in-house. Since its message is most often aimed at print and electronic media, experience even on high school or college newspapers, or radio, or T.V., is invaluable.

9. When PR requires layout or type, treat them with the importance given to everything else that represents your organization. If it's not worth doing right . . . why do it at all?

10. Most PR projects can be produced by desktop publishing.

11. This is for the simpler quick-print projects and office duplication. For more ambitious outside printing, use #12 and #13.

12–13. When PR requires the creation and production of major new printed pieces, use the separate checklists included for such projects. Their use is determined not by the quantity printed, but by the complexity of the work.

14–17. Practice for likely contacts with electronic media with a *realistic simulation*, especially if you are new to radio and T.V. broadcasting. Unless you're a pro, do not do this cold! (For creating and producing your own taped materials, use the information and checklist from Chapter 9. Don't even think of doing it yourself without reading that chapter first.)

18–19. Most PR telemarketing involves in-house invitations and follow-up on news material. Only when the list or effort seem overwhelming, use the information or checklist in Chapter 8. That's why they're there.

20–27. These are a project reminder more than a personnel assignment in most instances. Save personal contact (#25) for something really worthwhile and for media who ignore everything else. If you're a beginner, ask colleagues who in the media that is. It's never a secret.

28. Consider every claim and promise a legal commitment. If in doubt—and even when not—get legal clearance.

29–30. Official report on estimates and decision on approvals. Due dates for this are established as part of #4.

31–32. Consult with several checking bureaus regarding what it is possible to learn about results. They're most often the only way to check on PR *distribution*. Gauging PR *effectiveness* is beyond the scope of this book.

7 | Presentations

While selling as such is not the subject of this book, I do want to share some tricks of the trade that I have used in "selling" myself to management as their employee, their consultant, and their agency. There was nothing tricky, secret, or underhanded about this. The techniques are taught in presentation classes and many in-house seminars. Those of you who have not had the opportunity to participate in either should find this chapter of exceptional value.

INSIGHT 51

Practice your presentation! Put it on audio—even video if lots of movement is required. You won't look or sound nearly as bad as you feared. Listen and correct any problems that you detect. Do this as often as is required. Don't try to remember your dialog word for word; you're not in a play. Instead, get the concepts and flow of the presentation. I *always* listen to my tape one final time, just before the presentation. I've given hundreds. It works!

START WITH AN AGENDA

Start your presentation with a timed agenda that everyone can see. Leave it unobtrusively in view throughout your presentation, or distribute it before you begin. Almost every presentation has a time limit. The agenda permits the control you must have to cover all three parts every presentation should have:

1. **Review the Problem.** Be very specific about this. While the problem has received *your* total attention, some of your audience may be hearing about it for the first time. Even those who assigned it to you have been occupied with other matters and can use the reminder. You may also find—and this *has* happened to me—that the problem has changed, but they forgot to tell you. ("We didn't tell you that our cross-country bike was changed to a senior citizen model?") To avoid this, request a preview of any group presentation with a key insider. You'll learn what is "obviously" wrong in time to make necessary changes. Of course, you may choose not to make them, but at least you'll be forewarned on *what* you have to sell.

2. Present the Proposed Solution. But don't just jump into your show and tell. First tell the members of your audience *why* you are presenting your solution to *them*. Tell them the decisions you will ask *them* to make based on the presentation. Are you going to ask for approval of copy and layout? Of media or direct response plans? Of tentative or final budgets? Of time lines? Of all of these? Some of them? Just one? Something else?

Remind everyone of what has already been approved, by whom it was approved, and what they will be asked to decide today. Do *not* make the last of these a surprise at the very end of your meeting, or you may find that they've concentrated on something quite different. ("You mean we're supposed to OK the layout? I thought all we were here for was to OK the budget. You'd better leave those sketches, and we'll get back to you next week.")

3. Ask for Approval! Ask for *formal* approval of the decisions that have been made—generally those previewed in Point 2. In any presentation, the presenter is a salesperson. Failing to ask for approval, for "the order," is the most common error made in selling. Don't *you* suggest that you'll come back for a decision next week. Ask for that *positive* decision *now*. Say "As you can see, the layout does exactly what you asked us to prepare, so if we can get your approval on that today, we can have the copy and definitive budget at our next meeting in two weeks," *not* "You'll probably want to think about this and discuss it amongst yourselves." Let *them* make that suggestion!

INSIGHT 52

Many managers are more comfortable making financial decisions than esthetic judgments. So give them some alternatives on the budget. In promotional matters, present options only when they are requested. Then explain which one you expect to work best. Tell why; managers appreciate that kind of help. Try to base your explanation on fact— your experience *is* a fact!—and they will almost always decide your way.

LOCATION AND VISUAL AIDS

Where to make a presentation and what visual aids to use are important considerations. The following techniques work equally well for the advertising director "selling" management and the sales representative selling the ultimate customer. The emphasis here is on advertising and promotion, but can easily be adapted to any sales presentation for a product or service. The mechanical and technical considerations especially are exactly the same.

Location

1. **Whose turf?** Where you give your presentation determines much more than the obvious mechanical choices between, for instance, a slide projector and a flip chart. It can also determine the comfort level of your audience, especially when that audience numbers fewer than the presenters. The very reason we would like to invite our audience onto *our* turf—the fact that we feel more comfortable there, rather than in alien "executive country"—should warn us against doing so. Perhaps the executive feels just as uncomfortable surrounded by us strange creative types. What back on the executive's own turf would become a careful consideration of copy and art might well turn into an abrupt "I don't like this. Do it over." Outnumbered and outspecialized, the best defense is offense. Why invite that!

INSIGHT 53

Make your presentation where your audience—and not you—feels the most comfortable. When your audience does want it on your turf, suggest a preview by a key person first. You may still get the same "No," but at least you'll learn why.

---

2. **What space?** If at all possible, inspect the physical location where your presentation will be held. For an audience of one, or a small group meeting in someone's office, a prior inspection may be impossible. But you can still ask how the audience would like your materials presented. For larger audiences, you need either *exact* specifications or, preferably, a personal visit to check on the following:
   - **Comfort.** Decide what your audience will be doing, if anything, other than just listening and watching. Is there some practical way to get the audience involved, and what will you need to do it: Tables? School-type chairs? Writing materials? Samples? How you handle this without stealing your own thunder is covered shortly.
   - **Lighting and visual aids.** How much control will you have over outside and inside lighting? Where are the electrical outlets and what is their capacity? (Beware of extension cords that are an invitation to tripping/falling/breaking/suing.) What projection equipment is available? What is its condition? Should you take your own? And what about a spare bulb in either case! Where will the presenter stand, sit, and move, and is that practical? Are the site and equipment available for rehearsal? It's an absolute necessity if a new presenter is involved. You can't remember *everything*. Use our checklist or make your own!

3. **Which audience?** Suppose you have a 20-person conference room, an audience of 5, and a flip chart that can only be seen close up. Their favorite chairs are scattered throughout the room, and they're not about to move out of them. Now suppose you

have a meeting room set up for 100, but only 10 of your invited audience show up. Both of these situations are, unfortunately, all too common. Fortunately, you can be prepared—with slides and a projector for the first audience and a more personal flip chart for the second.

INSIGHT 54

Before any presentation, consider the worst case scenario, as well as some that are only bad. Be prepared to turn them into best. When it comes to *your* abilities, make all your surprises pleasant ones!

---

4. How about sound? Now that your audience can see you, can they hear you too? Consider and check the following:

- What are the amplification requirements for the presenter and the audience? Play a tape of the presenter's voice, and then wander around the room, listening for spots where it can't be heard. Will you amplify the sound there or block off that spot?
- If sound is a problem, appoint someone to monitor it during the presentation and play conductor for the presenter. Who? How?
- Check on outside sounds, including house music, paging calls, and telephones. Can they be turned off during your presentation? Be sure *you* know how, if you may do it.
- In locations with several halls, can your neighbors blast you out? Play the same tape next door and be forewarned.

Visual Aids

In making a presentation, you have a choice of one or more of at least eight different visual aids. Their advantages and disadvantages should be part of every presenter's personal hands-on experience.

1. **Desktop material.**
   - *Advantages.* Of notebook size and often in notebook or small flip-chart format, desktop material offers the most personal of standardized presentations. Catalogs, flyers, and fact sheets also fit into this format—as will anything that can be examined by prospects and buyers from the comfort of their own desk.
   - *Comments.* Desktop material may be difficult for several people to see at the same time, so have additional copies available if the prospect wants to share the presentation. Better yet, have a somewhat larger version of the same presentation with you for just that situation. You retain more control and gain extra points for foresight.

2. **Actual samples or models**.
   - *Advantages*. Nothing sells like a hands-on demonstration. It's how we are convinced to buy anything from cutlery to cars to computers. If it's practical to show and try—they'll buy. Do it!
   - *Comments*. If samples or models are taken to the prospect's turf, Murphy's law will surely take hold. Whatever can go wrong will. So don't go armed with explanations and excuses; go with the ability to fix the problem before the prospect finds fault with you or your product.

3. **Larger flip charts**.
   - *Advantages*. Flip charts serve as a prompt or script, since what they say *must be* read exactly as it is written. You can point to a chart or illustration and talk about what it means, but if textual matter is to be read by the audience, *read it aloud*. Do not expect the audience to read a written message while you are expanding upon it with a spoken message. The reason we can read subtitles in a foreign-language film is because we *don't* understand the somewhat different vocalization. There, the sound is merely background; it conveys emotion, not comprehension.

INSIGHT 55

In any presentation where words are seen and heard at the same time, make both sets of words exactly the same. Showing one message while speaking another is a sure way of losing both.

   - *Comments*. Almost all flip charts have too much material—too many words in a typeface that is too small—to be read or understood. Keep it big and simple. In wide rooms, you cannot get enough distance from your audience to let *everyone* see your presentation. Get there early, try various locations, and then make sure that the key people sit where you are visible.

4. **Individual pages**.
   - *Advantages*. Unlike a bound flip chart, individual pages can be easily added or removed, arranged into any sequence, and left in view to build an increasingly dramatic visual presentation. They can be moved and shown to the entire audience, no matter how it is seated. Placed on a lightweight board, they can be circulated for closer viewing and tactile reinforcement.
   - *Comments*. Pages left in view must have a place to stand, hang, lie, or otherwise be visible.[1] Be sure that your location makes this possible—that

---

[1] Stikky-Wax "Sure Clips,®" available at stationery stores, hold papers on practically any surface without harm to the surface or what is held. Instantly affixed and removed, they are an excellent solution to many presentation problems.

you're not at a podium surrounded by empty space, standing illustrations on a stage only the first row can see. Plan ahead to avoid having to improvise.

5. **Chalkboard and other on-the-spot creations.**
   - *Advantages*. These are excellent when a presentation can be built on audience participation that is limited to *brief* statements. Responses to the presenter's question, "What are your most important considerations in awarding this contract?" are usually predictable. But elicited, noted, and considered on the spot, they have a personal relevance that many types of visual aid lack.
   - *Comments*. Using a chalkboard requires an ability to "tease out" participation without creating ill will. This is probably not a good method in multilevel corporate presentations, where participants may be bashful about appearing too smart . . . and fearful of seeming too dumb. Use it with care!

6. **Slides.**
   - *Advantages*. Slides make a brilliantly lit statement or illustration that forces focused attention. They are one of the least expensive of all presentation devices, are easily portable, and are practical for almost any size audience. Slides are easily keyed to a prerecorded vocal accompaniment, too.
   - *Comments*. Slides are most effective in a dark or dimly lit room, which is not always available. Also, with computer-generated full-color slides, there is a tendency to confuse audiences through an overuse of colors, words, and typefaces. Slides *that are to be read* are best shown with a frame drawn around them or as reverse type (white or yellow surrounded by black or a very dark background). Keep individual slides to 12 words or less. Read them to the audience *exactly as they are shown*. Change text slides at least every 10 seconds. Illustrations and charts can remain in view as long as they are being discussed.

7. **Overhead transparencies.**
   - *Advantages*. Overheads are similar in effect to slides, but have definite advantages in specific applications:
     - Overheads can be shown in fully lit rooms.
     - The image can be written on or otherwise modified as it is being projected.
     - Blank overhead originals can be used for on-the-spot creations.
     - For one-time or limited use, overheads can be produced instantly on standard office copy machines, including full-color copiers. Copies for repeated use are best when done by photostat or photographic duplicating services.
   - *Comments*. Overheads are an excellent projection device for those who prefer not to work in the dark. They make multimedia presentations practical without turning the lights on and off repeatedly. For assured excellence in projection, use your own machine or double-check a rental model. Have a *correct* spare bulb on hand, and make sure that you know how to change it.

Single-color overheads made on office copiers cost less than slides; full-color copies may cost more. True full-color projection may require originals produced on photographic film. With outside production of overheads, get a sample made from *your* original, not theirs!

8. Video.
   - *Advantages*. Videos are surely the best way to demonstrate action and motion, present individuals who couldn't make it to the presentation, preview new T.V. commercials, and generally demonstrate that you're at home with current technology for today's audience.
   - *Comments*. Videos are by far the most expensive method of presentation. Chapter 8 discusses videos in more detail.

9. Talking heads.
   - *Advantages*. Besides using the preceding visual aids, there is the plain old-fashioned method of "talking heads"—just you, speaking to an audience of one or hundreds. You have no props, no visual aids, no distractions, and no other helps, except your words and your ability to convey them. As in the most elaborate of multimedia presentations, the three "tells" are your best approach:
     - Tell them what you're going to tell them.
     - Tell them.
     - Tell them what you've told them. (And tell them why. Surely your job is to sell something—even if it's only yourself!)
   - *Comments*. In purely verbal presentations, limit the things you're "going to tell them" to no more than three. That's about the most things audiences can keep in mind as you proceed.

NOTES ON THE PRESENTATION CHECKLIST

These notes are a supplement to the material presented in this chapter. They are not a substitute for that material.

> This checklist has been prepared for a presentation organized by you. If you are an invited presenter rather than the host, learn who your audience will be, what they expect you to present, and where the presentation will take place. Also check #6 and #7, then go to #15-on.

1. If the supervisor will not be at the presentation itself, delegate on-the-spot supervision to one other person only. Don't wait until you get there. Do this in advance and let *everybody* know.
2. Which is decided first, who is invited or the number the location can accommodate? Decide before the selection of guests begins.

PRESENTATION CHECKLIST

Project title/description _____   Date _____
_____   Project # _____
_____   Checklist # _____
Overall Supervision by _____   Deadline _____
Budget _____   Start-up Date _____   Presentation Date _____

PROJECT SUPERVISION	ASSIGNED TO	DUE	IN	MUST APPROVE	BY DATE	IN	INFO COPY ONLY	SEE ATTACHED
1. Project Supervisor	_____	___	☐	_____	___	☐	_____	☐
AUDIENCE								
2. Selection	_____	___	☐	_____	___	☐	_____	☐
3. Invitations	_____	___	☐	_____	___	☐	_____	☐
4. Telephone Contacts	_____	___	☐	_____	___	☐	_____	☐
5. Badges	_____	___	☐	_____	___	☐	_____	☐
6. Handouts	_____	___	☐	_____	___	☐	_____	☐
7. Premiums	_____	___	☐	_____	___	☐	_____	☐
LOCATION								
8. Find Location	_____	___	☐	_____	___	☐	_____	☐
9. Price Approval	_____	___	☐	_____	___	☐	_____	☐
10. Inspect/Approve	_____	___	☐	_____	___	☐	_____	☐
11. Confirm	_____	___	☐	_____	___	☐	_____	☐
12. Decoration/Materials	_____	___	☐	_____	___	☐	_____	☐
13. Food/Drink	_____	___	☐	_____	___	☐	_____	☐
PRESENTATION								
14. Presenter(s)	_____	___	☐	_____	___	☐	_____	☐
15. Transporation	_____	___	☐	_____	___	☐	_____	☐
16. Lodging	_____	___	☐	_____	___	☐	_____	☐
17. Script/Script OK	_____	___	☐	_____	___	☐	_____	☐
18. Create Visuals	_____	___	☐	_____	___	☐	_____	☐
19. Produce Visuals	_____	___	☐	_____	___	☐	_____	☐
20. Create/Produce Audio	_____	___	☐	_____	___	☐	_____	☐
21. Projectors (specify)	_____	___	☐	_____	___	☐	_____	☐
22. Audience Materials	_____	___	☐	_____	___	☐	_____	☐
FOLLOW-UP								
23. Who/What	_____	___	☐	_____	___	☐	_____	☐
_____	_____	___	☐	_____	___	☐	_____	☐
_____	_____	___	☐	_____	___	☐	_____	☐
_____	_____	___	☐	_____	___	☐	_____	☐
_____	_____	___	☐	_____	___	☐	_____	☐

3. For repeated presentations, prepare a standard invitation.[2] But remember, "standard" is *not* a synonym for "plain": Old Faithful showers us with standard wonders several times a day.

4. Telephone contacts make responses to written invitations jump in number. Don't rely on either one alone. Synergy works!

5. Have name badges. Make sure that the presenters use them, too. It's the best way to get everyone on a first-name basis. Of course, make sure that that's what they want, too!

6. Upon the audience's arrival, give out handouts, or place them on chairs or tables before the presentation begins. If nothing more, give the audience the timed agenda, translated into a benefit-loaded schedule.

7. Give out as premiums a tote bag in which to carry everything home . . . writing materials to use at the presentation and later . . . something special to key into the event—all with your name and logo. That way, they'll still be reminded of you even when they're at home.

8. This item works in conjunction with #2. Is there knowledgeable local staff to find and inspect a particular location? Hotel and motel floor plans are generally available. Use them.

9. Price is often negotiable, especially in facilities that include other services, such as food and drink. Ask also for special signs, a reserved parking area, special service, etc. Make a list!

10. For major presentations, have the project supervisor visit the site, even when it's the only location available. The best of floor plans may not forewarn you of *avoidable* hazards to your presentation!

11. Get specific, written agreement on dates required to confirm, change, and cancel your presentation. Phoning is fine, but make sure to get written or FAXed confirmation that your order was received.

12. Get advance approval for anything you'll attach to walls, ceilings, windows, or floors. Often, the house rules (such as requiring the use of specific fasteners) make sense . . . and are easy to follow, too!

13. Do *not* provide alcohol at events from which people will have to drive away. Get legal advice even for a wine tasting!

14. Use the best presenters to give the presentation, the most knowledgeable to answer questions. If one person must do both tasks, the project supervisor will decide who it is to be.

15–16. Take care of travel and lodging arrangements from where your presenters are, to where they'll stay, to where they're going. Even if no one stays overnight, they'll need a place to freshen up before and after the presentation. Make that part of your negotiations in #9.

17. Personalize your talk where possible. Review it with someone who'll know whether you've got it right, especially the pronunciation of names. For

---

[2] Include a homemade map that is *not* totally dependent on reading city street signs. Give *exact* mileage and local landmarks, and mention the nearest gas station. Do not leave guests, as I once was, lost in a wintry Wisconsin storm, with every sign hidden under an inch of ice.

anything other than the routine, rehearse on location, even if you have to get there while others are just waking up.

18–20. Will you create new visuals? New copies of existing materials? Special sound effects or music synchronized to sound tracks? Make a list. Find out how long each takes (and costs?) before it is approved.

21. Use your own equipment. Have a spare—and a *long* extension cord.

22. For materials distributed during or after the presentation, in addition to #6 and #7. Who decides what materials to use? How do the materials get there? What happens to materials that are not used?

23. They came. They saw. They listened. They left. Who is in charge of follow-up? To do what? To report to whom? If the answer is "No one," why were you there?

8 | Telemarketing

Telemarketing is the planned use of telecommunications equipment with a set purpose or goal. What it is *not* is simply picking up the phone—whether to answer or call out—with no set directions as to what is to follow. Like audiovisual communication (see Chapter 9), telemarketing is expensive and easily done wrong, with its success depending as much on management commitment as on in-house or outside expertise. Much of telemarketing, such as giving information and taking telephone orders, can be done in-house. More specialized aspects are usually better done by professional telemarketing service bureaus. What is required for successful use of either option is what this chapter is all about.

SCOPE OF TELEMARKETING

Telemarketing was the fastest growing legitimate economic activity of the 1980s and shows every sign of continuing its growth into the nineties and beyond. Just how its dollar totals should be counted is one of the more pleasant industry debates. (For example, do you include the phone call that ordered the Boeing 747, as well as the one that ordered the 79¢ ball-point pen that signed the confirmation?) Whatever the totals, there's general agreement that telemarketing had a sevenfold increase in revenues in the eighties—from about $70 billion to $500 billion, with growth continuing into the nineties at an explosive rate.

TECHNICAL AND PRACTICAL FACTORS

Under the broad categories of "inbound" and "outbound" telemarketing, there are at least a dozen kinds of activities. Before exploring them in detail, let us consider the technical and practical factors that apply to them. These *must* be agreed upon before any telemarketing project is begun. Often, they also control the decision to work in-house or go to an outside service bureau.

- **Time-line.** When will the project begin? How long will it continue? How many calls will you get or make? How much time is allowed per call? Beware of confusing quantity with success! Would you really rather get 10 calls per hour at $15 in sales each as opposed to 6 calls averaging $45?
- **Personnel.** How will telemarketers *and clerical staff* be acquired, trained, and supervised? How many workers will you need for peak hours? For

regular and slow periods? How much will you pay? To whom? On what basis?

- **Location.** Is the location safe before and after standard office hours? Telemarketing is often a 24-hour service. Is there public transportation nearby? Parking? A place to purchase food? Where will telemarketers work, rest, eat, have their coffee breaks, and use toilets?
- **Mechanical.** What equipment must be acquired, installed, and maintained? For how long? At what cost? By whom? If its use is short term, can it be leased? If not, can it be resold? For how much?
- **In-house vs. outside.** For in-house telemarketing, how do you know the answers to all the preceding questions? For outside service bureaus, get written quotations from at least three suppliers. You're looking for the best supplier, not necessarily the cheapest.
- **Management commitment.** Success in telemarketing does not just happen. It demands, from management, a commitment to a plan that permits the costs of learning. It works best—and often works only—when it is integrated into the marketing plan from the very beginning. It is seldom successful as desperate first aid when everything else has failed.

WHAT TELEMARKETERS DO

As defined in the introduction to this book, marketing is concerned with *what* is sold, *where* and *how* it is sold (by mail, phone, radio or T.V.; in retail stores; through personal calls; etc.), *how* it is priced, and *how* it is promoted. Telemarketing can have a minor or major role in every one of these concerns. Determining your own use of telemarketing is best begun by seeing what outside service bureaus have to offer. Examining them not only opens the mind to new and exciting views of research, sales, and promotion, but also is a very practical overview of what is required to do telemarketing in-house.

Total Service Agencies

"Total" telemarketing service agencies, unlike most telemarketing service bureaus, work as all-around "marketers," rather than specialists. They work on *everything*, from analyzing a client's initial concepts for a product or service through managing the ultimate sales campaign. In this regard, they do exactly what is done by standard manufacturers or service organizations themselves. What they add, however, is their marriage of "tele" and "marketing" to produce a hoped-for synergetic whole. Essentially, they are *multidisciplinary promotion services* that combine product and price testing with electronic, direct mail, telephone, and print selling, plus order fulfillment, and collecting. They bring together a half-dozen disciplines that are more often found in-house or at separate outside organizations. Since the vast majority of clients are unwilling to give anyone that much control over their business lives, most telemarketers provide equally expert, if more limited, services.

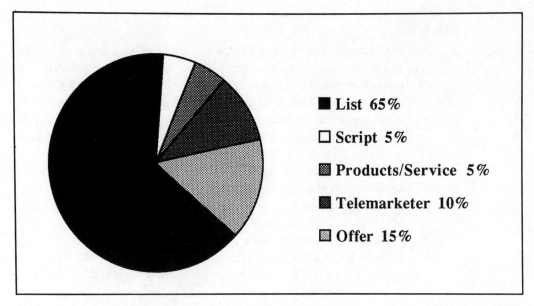

Figure 8.1 Components of a telemarketing program. (Chart courtesy of Hugh Gollogly, Jr.)

Standard Telemarketing Service Bureaus

Standard telemarketers are "standard" only in that they have a variety of different specialties. Their competitors are each other, not the total service agencies, which do something quite different. The services standard telemarketers provide (see Figure 8.1) can usually be bought individually, as well as in combinations or as "packages." They include the following:

• **Consultation at the marketing plan stage.** What is feasible by telemarketing? What are some alternatives? How long it will take to plan, test, and do, and what will it cost? These are best discussed before a marketing plan is even begun, not after it is set. Many telemarketers will meet for this discussion without charge. Some will have a fee if they do not get the project. Ask!

• **Consulting on what the project is to produce.** Shall the telemarketers do nothing but take the order? Deliver a message? Answer a question? What else, if anything, is practical and affordable? What can you get from the person on the line, once they are there?

• **Scripting, testing, and training.** Writing for telemarketing is an art in itself. But successful scripting is more than that. It's testing to see whether the script works, modifying where necessary, and then training a staff to be suitable for a particular project. In telemarketing, the importance of *how* something is said, as well as *what* is said, is a fact of life. It's also a continuously changing fact that only monitoring and testing will keep current.

- **Serendipitous supervision.** Some telemarketing operators are better than others. Sometimes it's innate talent. Often it's subtle improvements in the script that the individual operator is not even aware that he or she is making. But *supervisors have to know* that something good has happened, test it with others, and if it works for them, too, give credit to its originator. That is the kind of supervision you search for in building your in-house abilities, as well as evaluating outside services.

- **Continuing evaluation and reports.** Every telemarketing project will become more and more proficient as its operators become more comfortable and efficient with their assignments. Evaluations and reports, however, begin with the first call. On an agreed-upon, often daily, basis, they should tell the following:

  - Number of operators involved, and for how long
  - Number of calls made or received
  - Average time per call per operator
  - Results
  - Operators' comments, both impressions and "hard" facts
  - Service bureau or departmental evaluation and recommendations.

How Telemarketers Charge

Telemarketing, in-house or from a service bureau, has three sets of costs. For outside organizations, these usually require partial payment in advance, to help cover up-front expenses. Since telemarketing programs can be—and often are—cancelled before even the first call is made, specified cancellation fees are included in most agreements. The three costs are for the following services:

1. **Planning and consultation.** Know exactly what you wish to discuss, have a written agenda, and make sure that every point is covered. Once a service bureau has been selected, it charges for planning and consultation meetings. If there's a per-person rate for visiting you, ask the charge for visiting the service bureau instead. Even if that won't be practical for you, it will make them aware of *your* budget concerns.

2. **Writing, testing, and training.** Preparing scripts, testing, revising, and retesting them, and training operators all precede the first call. Just as with preparation of copy and layout for an ad, 90 percent of the planning and creative thinking will have been done and will be charged for, even if the actual program is cancelled.

3. **Calling, refining, reporting, evaluating, and recommending.** Most telemarketers charge for their inbound and outbound calling by the hour. The success or completion rate, especially on outbound service, practically demands honor-system billing, with frequent, detailed supporting documentation. If your initial evaluation of a telemarketing service makes you uncomfortable about this, consider other

telemarketers until you find the right match. Evaluating, refining, reporting, and giving recommendations on the ongoing projects are usually, but not always, included in the hourly rate. Make sure.

TYPES OF TELEMARKETING

There are several types of telemarketing with which you're most likely to be involved. All can, of course, be given to outside service bureaus. I have emphasized the opportunities and problems each brings the do-it-yourselfer.

Inbound Telemarketing

In inbound telemarketing, the inquiries and orders received by phone or FAX are increasingly important to direct response selling. Where speed in fulfilling orders is vital to business success, the toll-free telephone—and, increasingly, the toll-free FAX—has practically replaced ordering by mail.

Simple Product Ordering. Taking orders by phone has always been the most widely used of all telemarketing activities. Simple product ordering, whether from a catalog with thousands of items or in response to a television commercial offering a product that is "not available in retail stores!" *can* be handled in-house. Whether they *should* be depends largely on traffic flow. While you might be able to handle gigantic bursts of telephone activity economically for two weeks every two months, how would you staff for such a contingency? Outside help is unlikely to wait the other month and a half without seeking more dependable employment. Here are some approaches that work:

• **Stagger your promotions,** where practical. For instance, mail, advertise, or broadcast your products to one quarter of your audience two weeks apart. You'll need only a fraction of the staff to handle the responses, and you'll be able to give them all full-time work and decrease turnover, with its recruiting and training costs.

• **Promote the products more often** to the same audience. Even the most successful of promotions leaves the vast majority unsold on *that* item at *that* time. If you can't find new products or services, use what worked before. Run exactly the same promotion twice and even three times. But, of course, test first!

• **Use an outside service bureau.** These organizations *are* staffed to handle sudden bursts of activity with trained telemarketers who'll learn and remember your ordering system the next time it comes on line.

A catalog or other promotion may bring orders for years. Many service bureaus can continue to handle these orders as well as in-house personnel could, throughout that time. Through a system known as automatic phone distribution, callers are given to specific telemarketers who know a particular product line and have become even better at selling it as time goes by.

Relationship Selling. This is not the illegal "bait and switch," but legitimate and often appreciated "cross-selling" and even "up-selling." Relationship selling works best when the selections are comparatively limited (say, an 80-item catalog rather than an 800-item one) and the conversation is presumed to be with an expert in the field. Thus, a skilled telemarketer might suggest the scarf or glove shown on page 12 to go with the jacket ordered from page 17 . . . brushes or cleaning fluid to go with a specific paint . . . or an additional fall flowering plant when one is ordered for spring.

Supervise relationship selling as if your life depended on it. If potential customers are turned off by it, your business life may cease as well.

Free Information. In offering telephone information about a product or service, a number of factors have to be evaluated on an ongoing basis:

- **How the call will be charged.** Options include a local, regional, or national toll-free service, to accept collect calls, or to have the caller pay.[1]
- **Who will get the initial call** and to whom it will be transferred if the first telemarketer can't answer the question.
- **When phone help will be available,** especially to do-it-yourselfers and for products likely to be used evenings or weekends.
- **Limits on types of telephone information** regarding how to *use* a product, rather than the physical product or service itself. This involves both the time you need to spend and possible legal ramifications (for example, telling a caller how to use battery jump cables to start a car). Check your insurance for appropriate coverage.

Charges for Information and Other On-Line Services. Fees for giving immediate telemarketed *services*—though not for information on products—are becoming common. The development of 900-number systems has made it possible to charge practically any amount—from pennies to dollars—to the telephone from which a call originates. Thus, a technical service bureau can charge just enough to keep nuisance calls within manageable limits, a legal or accounting service can cover the cost of an initial telephone consultation, and a children's storyteller (or adult sexual fantasizer) can charge whatever the traffic will bear.

---

[1] When both paid and toll-free calls are available, practically no one chooses to pay, even for local calls, as I discovered when I used a wrong number in a client's promotion. The number had been taken from a previous brochure. To our surprise, the client wasn't nearly as shocked as I was. He had not had a paid call since toll-free service began, he told me. Hence, toll-free numbers were the only numbers his staff checked before printing. (I did not tell him that, once alerted, I corrected a second wrong number on another brochure. At my suggestion, the client now uses *only* toll-free numbers in his promotional materials. At least *they* are checked.)

The fact that telemarketing knows how to do all this does not, of course, mean that all of it *should* be done. The resulting conflicts between protectors of the First Amendment and laissez faire capitalists on the one hand and protectors of children's welfare and morality on the other seems certain to grow more heated. Whatever the outcome—and it will vary among communities—*all* of telemarketing, no matter how innocent, will be affected. Consider the long-term consequences before joining either side. Your power to turn off *their* messages may well be their right to turn off *yours*!

Outbound Telemarketing

Outbound telemarketing can be simply making your calls in a routine or mechanical fashion. For this, live operators and computer-generated dialing can deliver the same *message*. But very few of the simpler automated dialers have any built-in "judgment." Many of them are operated from a one-person office or a home. The costs are comparatively modest and allow the system's owner to be away, handling leads or projects the calls have brought. But this type of automated dialing has led to annoyances and even dangers; for instance, the tying up of lines by calling every number in a hospital, police, or industrial network. Such automatic dialers have now been outlawed in many communities and some states. More sophisticated—and expensive—systems call specific numbers only and are an important part of true telemarketing.

True telemarketing is much more than mechanical or routine calling. It includes ongoing data-based analysis on which actions are based. The true telemarketer knows what is being said on both ends of the line—not only what message is sent, but how it is received and responded to. Together with the possibility of ongoing changes and improvements in communication, this knowledge is key to much of telemarketing's success. It also can—and indeed, at times, must—signal failure. When telemarketing will not work—at least, not on a cost-effective basis—the telemarketer must recognize this and be willing to stop the operation. Telemarketing must be used as a self-monitoring tool!

Outbound Sales Calls. Placed as "cold calls," without preparing the prospect, outbound sales calls are the most difficult of all telemarketing efforts. Cold calling requires knowledgeable guidance and continuous positive reinforcement. When these three factors are kept in mind, it will succeed in many instances. However, don't expect results without professional help.

Requests for Donations. Even when placed cold, requests for donations for community, religious, fraternal, or educational organizations imply a common interest and usually get a friendly hearing. But take care in using professional service bureaus for such efforts. Their fees often absorb the lion's share of what's raised. A volunteer effort may not produce nearly the gross as a service bureau would, but it will probably increase the net amount vastly. Get a pro to help with the message; let dedicated amateurs make the calls.

INSIGHT 56

Make fund-raising efforts and other telephone requests for donations a group effort if at all possible. The group will cheer each other up and on during the inevitable dry spells that might cause volunteers at home to give up calling.

Warm-Ups for Mailing. A call to key customers or prospects (or both) lets them know that a very special mailing is coming. It's a proven way of increasing attention to what will be received, but consider these questions before you begin:

- If asked about it on the phone, what can you tell the listener about the content of the mailing? If the answer is "Nothing," why not?
- What if the person called wants a faxed copy of the offer . . . right now?
- What happens after they do get the special mailing? Will they be called again? If the mailing isn't worth a second call, what made it worth the first?

Do *not* use warm-up calls unless the offer is truly special. It's a very expensive way to have your audience disregard your subsequent mailings.

Qualifying Leads. Culling valuable prospects from an undifferentiated group is one of the most valuable services telemarketing can supply. But success in qualifying individuals depends both on what is asked and how it is scripted. It very much demands a skilled hand in both areas with freedom to modify the message and its delivery if the initial response is unsatisfactory. That is, after all, one of the major advantages of telemarketing: the ability to switch approaches midstream. It is imperative to have agreement on the desired results, but also to be flexible on how they are to be achieved. To that end, begin by defining:

- What *exactly* it will take to qualify a lead.
- What *exactly* follows when someone does—or doesn't—qualify.
- How you will handle overwhelming success—or failure.

Qualifying the qualifications. Allow for all possible responses, especially if you are new to telemarketing. Your actual follow-up will show very quickly whether your identification of those who qualified is valid. But don't leave it at that. Give a random selection of nonqualifiers the same positive selling effort. Experienced telemarketers will insist on this as a check on their *real* success. Take nothing for granted. Learn at least *what* works, even if you can't tell *why*. Build a file that can be used as a data base. A decade from now you want 10 years' experience, not 1 year's 10 times!

Pretesting Mail. Telemarketing is *not* direct mail. What works *and is affordable* in the one may not work in the other. But the advantages of using telemarketing to *pretest* direct mail offers is proving its worth to many direct marketers.

- Testing by mail gives only yes and no answers. But telemarketing can tell you *why*—both *why* they are *not* ordering and *why* they *are*. The latter especially may not be at all what you expect. It can turn a merely good mail response into a bonanza.

- Testing by mail can take months, from concepts and copy to production, printing, and mailing and then waiting for and analyzing the response. Skillful telemarketers can get their results in weeks!

INSIGHT 57

Consider testing by telemarketing as giving you an expanded instant focus group. It won't work for color or taste, but for many options, it gives a hundredfold increase in participants for about the same cost.

- Skillful telemarketers can change their trial script right in the middle of a message. Properly trained and supervised, they can refine or reposition the offer . . . instantly. Immediate feedback and response can help discover the best target markets, the most likely lists to reach it, and the most persuasive offer to convince it—almost while you wait!

Postsale Follow-Up. I was not surprised when my doctor phoned to make certain that a new medicine he had prescribed for me had no unwanted side effects. I *was* surprised when the salesman from whom I had bought a washing machine, as well as the dealer to whom I had taken my car for a tune-up, both called to make certain that I had been *completely* satisfied.[2] All of these are examples of postsale telemarketing, one of the easiest[3] and simplest ways to create goodwill and encourage repeat business. Practically everyone is surprised and delighted by such a call. Word-of-mouth advertising—we all like to brag about our importance as customers—is often an additional benefit.

Surveys and Other Research. Why people are willing to speak so freely and frankly on the telephone with absolute strangers has always perplexed me. But they are! Practically any statistically valued information can be gotten this way. Household names like Gallup and Roper, as well as hundreds of other research organizations, provide the expertise needed for complicated research that requires sophisticated analysis. Many *business* surveys, however, can be do-it-yourself projects. Decide what you need to learn, decide who can give you the answer, get a statistically valid list of names, and call. Here are a few things to help bring do-it-yourself success:

---

[2] The mechanic to whom I had gone previously sent a computer generated follow-up. Unfortunately, it was so poorly printed, that it was practically impossible to read and hardly spoke well for his attention to detail. (See page 101 for more about messages—subliminal, liminal, and accidental.)

[3] A message from the nurse to the effect that "Dr. Doctor asked me to call . . . " does just as well. The *mechanic* didn't call; his supervisor did—in person.

- **Have a written script** of the entire conversation, not just the questions. After about the 10th call you'll forget your own name!
- **Tell them immediately the reason for your call** and about how long it will take. (For example, "Good morning. I'm Charlene McCarthy from the Scofield corporation, and I'd appreciate just three minutes of your time to ask about your likely need of toothpaste in the next six months."
- **When calling competitors** who are unlikely to share information, give the project to some graduate students, who can honestly say, "I'm a graduate student at ZLU, and I'm doing a survey of . . . "
- **Establish an in-house research arm** with an identity, address, and telephone that is different from yours. The more important the statistical validity of the responses, the more you will need experience or help in telemarketing, setting up surveys, and analyzing data. For just a general "feel of the situation," do it yourself!

FINDING THE HELP YOU NEED FOR IN-HOUSE OPERATIONS

Setting up in-house, whether business to business, business to consumer, or consumer to business, *must* begin with a telemarketer experienced in *successful start-up operations of that kind*. Just knowing how to run a program is not enough; starting up is the key! This telemarketer is not necessarily the person who can or will run the ongoing operation, so consider a consultant. Here's how to find one:

- **Check with local direct marketing associations.** If you are unfamiliar with where they are, the Direct Marketing Association, Inc., will tell you. Write Direct Marketing Association, Inc., Dept DM Clubs, *Associations Networks*, 11 West 42nd St., New York, NY 10036-8096. Or call (212)768-7277. If you write, enclose a self-addressed, stamped envelope. Then join your local club. It'll help you even if you're not a member, but the continuing contacts alone are worth the price of admission!

- **Check with local or regional telemarketing service bureaus.** Some may recommend themselves. All will know appropriate consultants. None will want to see you—and telemarketing—fail!

INSIGHT 58

Consider starting up with a service bureau, even if you plan to go in-house. It will give you instant professional telemarketing, plus invaluable research on your work flow and staff needs, while your own facilities and personnel are put into place.

• **Check with telemarketing users, including your competitors.** Every start-up operation needed help. Telemarketing is so new, that they may well remember where they got their initial help or know of other sources you can use.

• **Check professional magazines.** Three industrial publications include annual directories of telemarketing products and services: *Telemarketing*® magazine [(203)852-6800], *TeleProfessional*™ magazine [(319)235-4473], and *Inbound/Outbound* [(212)691-8215]. As a comparative novice, subscribe to all three. The resulting flood of mail and (we hope) calls, will keep you alert to everything new in the field.

• **Find a mentor.** Search for someone whom you can call for advice when disaster strikes—or who can warn you before it happens. Practically everyone loves to find a new audience to hear about *their* pitfalls and how *they* solved them. Your business, direct marketing, and advertising associations are ideal sources. Join. Participate. Learn.

Finding the Right Service Bureau

The process of finding a service bureau is the same as that just discussed for finding a consultant. The problem isn't in the finding; it's deciding on what you need to find. Begin, as always, with a list. Figure 8.2 is an example.

A million names outbound is wholly different from inbound responses to a million catalogs. The first may be completed in 30 days, and you risk comparatively little in working with start-up telemarketers who'll go all out to prove their worth. The second may bring inquiries and orders for 30 months. For inbound service, longevity is all important. Your 800 number, once published, takes on a life of its own. Consider also what happens when the initial rush of calls tapers off. Can and will the service bureau handle a few calls as well as many? How? For how long? At what cost?

Few, if any, telemarketers can do everything. Define what you need, and then hunt for it with a rifle, rather than a shotgun.

Testing Telemarketers

Elsewhere in this book—for convention displays, catalogs, and major direct mail projects—I suggested a contest among possible suppliers, *with everyone paid for their work*. Telemarketing also seems to lend itself to direct head-to-head testing, but first, consider the following:

• What is the size of the universe you will test, and what percentage of it gives an adequate response? Telemarketers consider 100 to 300 hours of outbound calling a reasonable test. If six of those called can be *contacted* per hour, that's 600 to 1,800 completed calls on which to base your decision. Should you want to match the 5,000 to 10,000 used in direct mail, your hours also will jump into the thousands. (That's 5,000 to 10,000 for *each* competing service!) If there is going to be a major difference

ABOUT US:

☐ What the telemarketer must know or learn : _____

_____

☐ Outbound need : _____

☐ Size/source of lists : _____

☐ Inbound need : _____

☐ Source of calls : _____

ABOUT THE TELEMARKETER:

BUREAU_____Date_____

Account executive _____

☐ Experience with similar lists _____

_____

☐ Service bureau age: _____ Years of continuous telemarketing

☐ Service bureau specialization

_____ % business to business

_____ % business to consumer

_____ % consumer to business

_____ % other : _____

☐ Maximum number of operators available for project _____

☐ _____ years pertinent experience of account executive

☐ $_____ guarantee to service bureau

☐ $_____ hourly rate

References:_____

☐ _____

COMMENTS_____

_____

By_____ Date_____

Figure 8.2 Sample service bureau evaluation checklist.

in the rate of contact or number of positive responses, it will show up in the smaller quantities. They'll also let you "roll out" (i.e., put into use) your entire list much earlier.

• One of the key things in evaluating a test is the type of analysis provided. Is it both quantitative and qualitative? Are the service bureaus making any recommendations as to the market? The product or service? The offer? Or are they simply calling? You really shouldn't do any testing unless you want to learn as well as sell. Telemarketing has the ability to gather vastly more information, and do it more quickly and cheaply, than testing by mail. Determine what you hope to learn. Make a list. Give it to each of the service bureaus being tested. Let *them* decide what's practical. After all, it is a test.

• Where significant differences in success appear, use the winner. More likely, the competitors will be evenly matched. In my experience, even that result has made a decision quite easy. Working with any outside service means forming a partnership toward a common goal. When all other factors seem equal, select the partner who you are convinced has the most to contribute and is willing to give that as part of your relationship.

NOTES ON THE TELEMARKETING CHECKLIST

These notes are a supplement to the material presented in this chapter. They are not a substitute for that material.

1. Suggest a brief professional updating on what the state of the art makes possible. Don't let management limit its options by not having asked that question first.
2. Set specific, though generous, budgets, especially for getting started. Definitely get outside guidance if you are new to this medium.
3. Set time lines for management as well as staff: When testing must be done, reported, and evaluated. When after-the-test decisions must be made, with agreement as to what that involves and on the budget to make it possible.
4. Not necessarily an either-or decision. Often, both are required, at least for getting started.
5. Consider separate managers if *major* in-house staff and a service bureau are both required. Telemarketing—even its supervision—is a totally time-intensive job!
6. Why the inbound services are established and what they are to achieve. Spell out the details against which evaluations can be matched.
7–9. Who pays for each call; also, why and how they are paid for. If different types of calls (routine orders, requests for technical data, simpler how-to questions) require different personnel, will they be available when callers

TELEMARKETING CHECKLIST

Project title/description _____ Date _____

_____ Project # _____

_____ Checklist # _____

Overall Supervision by _____ Deadline _____

Budget _____ Start-up Date _____ Completion Date _____

MANAGEMENT DECISIONS	ASSIGNED TO	DUE	IN	MUST APPROVE	BY DATE	IN	INFO COPY ONLY	SEE ATTACHED
1. Purpose	_____	___	☐	_____	___	☐	_____	☐
2. Budget	_____	___	☐	_____	___	☐	_____	☐
3. Time Line	_____	___	☐	_____	___	☐	_____	☐
4. In-House/Outside	_____	___	☐	_____	___	☐	_____	☐
5. Project Manager(s)	_____	___	☐	_____	___	☐	_____	☐
INBOUND								
6. Types & Purposes	_____	___	☐	_____	___	☐	_____	☐
7. 800 number(s)	_____	___	☐	_____	___	☐	_____	☐
8. 900 number(s)	_____	___	☐	_____	___	☐	_____	☐
9. Regular	_____	___	☐	_____	___	☐	_____	☐
OUTBOUND								
10. Types & Services	_____	___	☐	_____	___	☐	_____	☐
11. Phone Lists	_____	___	☐	_____	___	☐	_____	☐
IN-HOUSE								
12. Location(s)	_____	___	☐	_____	___	☐	_____	☐
13. Personnel	_____	___	☐	_____	___	☐	_____	☐
14. Equipment	_____	___	☐	_____	___	☐	_____	☐
15. Training	_____	___	☐	_____	___	☐	_____	☐
16. Budget	_____	___	☐	_____	___	☐	_____	☐
SERVICE BUREAU								
17. Selection	_____	___	☐	_____	___	☐	_____	☐
18. Script Approval	_____	___	☐	_____	___	☐	_____	☐
19. Schedule	_____	___	☐	_____	___	☐	_____	☐
20. Reporting System	_____	___	☐	_____	___	☐	_____	☐
21. Billing System	_____	___	☐	_____	___	☐	_____	☐
22. Cancellation Option	_____	___	☐	_____	___	☐	_____	☐
23. Budget	_____	___	☐	_____	___	☐	_____	☐
INBOUND/OUTBOUND								
24. Data-based Records	_____	___	☐	_____	___	☐	_____	☐
25. Evaluation(s)	_____	___	☐	_____	___	☐	_____	☐
26. Reports	_____	___	☐	_____	___	☐	_____	☐

© 1993, Fred Hahn

are likely to phone? Who monitors what actually happens? Who's authorized to make it all work?

10–11. What outbound telemarketing is to accomplish and the data available to help make it happen. Do *not* count on getting usable telemarketing data from *any* computer—especially your own—without first seeing it happen. Don't settle for assurances or promises. Demand a demonstration.

12. Consult your telephone company telemarketing expert—there is one!—before setting up in house. Telemarketing experts may even have solutions to which you have not yet discovered the problems.

13. Don't start up without a *telemarketing start-up specialist* who's been through it all before . . . several times. This is critical to everything you'll do, from finding people to write the scripts and answer the phones to figuring out who works where with whom on what. Think of them as test pilots . . . there to get you safely launched.

14–15. Match equipment and training to what you need now. Allow for future expansion in long-range planning, but concentrate on making the present successful first if you want that future to arrive.

16. Do as was suggested for direct mail. Separate budgeting for start-up, testing, and ongoing telemarketing. Start-up is probably a capital cost. Testing is advertising. Ongoing telemarketing is sales. Money for start-up and testing is spent no matter what else you do. Don't let it distort posttesting success . . . or failure. Analyze, too, the effect on budgets of changing from in-house to an outside service bureau or vice versa. Keeping within budget is seldom the only reason for such a decision, but it is certainly a major one.

17. Personal rapport is vital in your working relationship with the account executive, especially during start-up. Let management set parameters for the decision on which bureau to choose. Let the actual choice be made by the project manager.

18. Read scripts for what they say, not the details of how they say it. Don't try to do the telemarketer's job. It's why you went to an outside service.

19. Allow for the learning what works best that can be achieved only on the phone. Discuss needs and scheduling with the service bureau before promising results to management.

20. The frequency and detail of reports, evaluations, and recommendations from the bureau. Who must see everything? Summaries? Only decisions?

21. How the service bureau bills. What work—if any—they do before payment is made. What adjustments—if any—must take place in your system, as well as theirs.

22. Get unmistakable written agreement. ("Unmistakable" means that both parties understand the same thing the same way.) Establish routine checkpoints for continuation of the service. Set an automatic halt for review if specified goals are not met. Include an option for instant cancellation, with a basis for calculating costs incurred.

23. Most service bureau charges are known. They are easily estimated for purposes of budgeting.

24. Build customers as well as sales. Meet with data-processing personnel to learn whether and how a data base is being built. Take the same precautions as in #10 and #11. Check!

25. Much telemarketing is a team effort. It's telemarketing *plus* mailing . . . *plus* space and electronic advertising . . . *plus* selling in person . . . *plus* more and different prospect/suspect/customer contacts. Differentiate here and elsewhere between "prospects" on whom you spend more effort and dollars and "suspects" who are not worthy of that much attention. Relate all this to evaluation, where appropriate.

26. Note especially what has been learned that may apply to future efforts. Check later whether the learning is actually passed on . . . and applied.

9 | Audio and Audiovisual Communication

FINDING AN AUDIOVISUAL "PARTNER"

If, like most of us, you're a novice at purchasing audio and video services, you'll need someone at the creative and production end who will become your "partner"— someone whom you can trust to give you your money's worth, especially when you have no way of knowing what that is. Selecting such a person has to be based on finding an organization that can demonstrate a consistent level of results over an extended period of time within an established price range. Shopping by cost is easy: You can always find someone who will do it for less. But not knowing whether you can *use* what you'll be buying is where disaster awaits. An advance deposit with progressive payments is standard practice. You seldom can allow time to do a project over. You have little recourse if you do not like what you get.

The Longevity Factor

Don't hesitate to work with a start-up company that can demonstrate its ability at a lower than expected cost, *if what they produce won't be changed in the future*. Many new audiovisual suppliers have undercharged themselves out of business before they learned the true cost of what they were doing! For long-term projects, work with suppliers who've shown their ability to survive a few years.

The Basic Skills

Your audio or audiovisual projects require four distinct skills:

1. **Preproduction.** The script with sound (such as a slamming door) indicated and a cartoon-style storyboard visual concept.
2. **Production.** Recording or videotaping the project—on location, in the studio, or both.
3. **Postproduction.** In-studio editing.
4. **Duplication.** As required.

Each of these skills can be, and often is, provided by different organizations, especially when overall supervision of the project lies with an advertising agency experienced in audiovisual production as well as creativity. I myself took a different route, both as an employee and as the owner of an agency. I looked for, and found, audiovisual companies that could provide three of the creative functions, from scripting through editing. Duplication, like printing, is quite a different specialty, best given to experts in the field.

Finding Suppliers

In larger markets, if no other guidance seems available, begin with the business Yellow Pages under "Recording Services" or "Video Production Services." In smaller communities, you're unlikely to find the same level of experience or sophisticated equipment, but you will be able to find *someone* who can help. Begin by deciding how "big city" you really have to be. Your commercials will actually be seen on television. Instructional and informational "infomercials" are shown on monitors using the same screen. Your audience, without consciously realizing it, expects the technical quality they get from that screen every day, in regular programs, other commercials and feature films. The ability to approach that quality within your budgetary and creative restrictions is what your initial search is all about.

A Wealth of Suppliers

Audio and video production facilities are practically everywhere. Community colleges, some high schools, many hospitals, local radio, T.V., and cable companies, and, of course, local audio and video production companies all offer their services. And look for special promotions in which radio or T.V. stations—including some in the largest markets—offer to create and produce your commercial without additional charge, provided that you purchase a specified amount of broadcast time. You may even get to use their work on another station! In all probability, though, their end product, while competent, will be very packaged—one of a limited number of set solutions to any promotion problem. If what you want is some variation of "Good morning! We're so and so. Here's our address. Come in or give us a call," this may well be all you need. Much local automotive, home builder, and retail on-air promotion is done exactly that way.

The use of on-air personalities in audiovisual projects requires quite different considerations. Broadcasting—especially local television—demands mechanical skills. Its expertise lies in sending a signal to listeners, subscribers, and viewers. With the exception of some news and sports, few television broadcasts originate locally. Local staff have neither the need nor the talent for much creativity. Radio's call-in and disk jockey personalities do tend to be excellent sales "voices," especially on their own programs. Elsewhere, however, use local talent with caution.

Selecting by Budget

For longer "infomercials," that is, informational programs or commercials that delve deeper into your product or service, you must use people who are, first and foremost, creative. You need a true recording or video production company. As a novice purchasing audio or video services, begin with the Yellow Pages of a major market. Call several suppliers with the largest ads, several more with medium-size ads, and several with simple listings. Ask all of them which of the writing, shooting, and editing services they offer. When they tell you "all three," ask for their typical budget. You do *not*, as yet, know enough to work with someone who answers "Anything you wish to spend." You do want to see samples from several suppliers who work within defined ranges, to learn what specific budgets can buy. The $5,000, $15,000 and $75,000 end products should be obviously—perhaps even dramatically—different. Which one you need may be a pleasant surprise. (A little more than the $5,000 one? A lot less than the $15,000 one? Find the suppliers of the $10,000 products, and check them the same way.) If your budget is in the $50,000-plus range, don't go to the $15,000 supplier because they offer a seeming bargain. You won't be satisfied, no matter what the results. Don't look for "just transportation" when you really want a competition sports car, and don't expect to get the latter for the price of the former, no matter what you're told. Search for two things: the best creative ability to understand audiovisual problems and the technical know-how to produce the solutions *within your budget*!

SUMMARY

- Much audiovisual production works on the honor system. Find suppliers who will act as "partners," guarding your interests as well as their own.
- If you are unfamiliar with costs, preview work by suppliers in various price ranges. Establish your budget *after* you see what different dollars can buy.

THE CLIENT AND AUDIOVISUAL CREATIVITY

Begin with introspection: Let the producer or production company know how clients see themselves. Are the clients so serious about what they do, that the least touch of whimsy is out of character? Do they feel branded as stodgy and want a lighter image? Generally, senior managers don't review anything until it's completed. The last thing your audiovisual supplier wants to hear *from them* is "but that's not *us*." There has to be a knowledgeable person from the client's side directly involved in *ongoing* creativity, not to tell the producer how to run the train, but to help redirect it when it's on an obviously wrong track.

What Audiovisual Creativity Is All About

In low- to medium-priced audiovisual organizations, the writer, director, and producer often are one and the same. But whether there is one, two, or a team, audiovisual creativity is the ability to use *media* to tell a story. It begins with the ability to create a script—to write the words that are spoken while sound effects, music, and visual images are received by the audience. It demands from the producer and director technical expertise in acting, filming, and editing. It requires visualizing what the entire project will achieve as individual segments are produced and then making it happen.

For on-location shooting, the writer and producer visit the site to learn whether filming there is practical, both for reasons of safety and to remain within the budget. Once reassured, they put their imagination to work. Immediately, they start seeing shots, hearing words, and visualizing action. Suggested scripts from the agency or the client are actually helpful at this stage. Far from hindering the writers, they tell them what the client wants and how they see themselves in relationship to that project. It focuses creativity within specified limitations, rather than letting it expend time, energy, and costs on efforts that are sure to be rejected.

INSIGHT 59

Give your audiovisual producers suggestions, directions, and even scripts as a base on which to build. If *their* creative ability can't improve on *your* efforts, ask yourself whether you're really that good, whether you need a different supplier, or whether someone else should decide between you.[1]

Openness to Criticism

No audiovisual professional expects a first script to be accepted without change or comment. It's for discussion. Both client and scriptwriter are like chefs given the same ingredients. One may not recognize the full possibilities, while the other may take them a bit too far. The key is to be open to each other's tastes. Argue, and even fight about the scripts, but just don't forget the audience for whom you are "cooking."

Amateur vs. Professional Talent

How and where your audio or video product will be used may well determine whether amateur talents are an option. Not only do amateurs tend to get frustrated quickly, but contractual obligations for professional talent may be a factor. Your producer, charged with finding the talent, will be aware of these factors. When the option to use amateurs does exist, you can screen them from among actors, musicians, singers, and dancers in colleges, local drama and music groups, and fraternal organizations. Often, it's not a question of talent as much as it is of a client's wishes and priorities.[2] Keep in mind that what does make the professional different is the ability to follow directions: To a professional, doing or saying the same thing 10 or 20 times or more isn't deadly boring; it's part of the job. The result doesn't deteriorate with repetition; it gets better.

---

[1] In having third parties check a script, don't let them know who wrote it. I have my own advertising copy checked, and I always let the editor think it was written by someone else. It's the only way to get honest, fearless criticism.

[2] Try not to impose talented relatives on your producer. One of my more costly commercials needed a quartet I did not budget for to outsing a client's daughter attempting to turn a simple radio spot into grand opera.

INSIGHT 60

Amateurs require inspiration. Professionals do it with a headache.

SUMMARY

- Differentiate between producing your idea and being open to alternatives. Be honest with yourself, and let the producer know *before* they begin.
- Be candid about how you see yourself. Be open to achieving your aims in unexpected ways.
- When either professional or amateur talent is an option, let the producer decide. "Talented" relatives tend to cost most of all.

ON-LOCATION SHOOTING

A sound stage set and modern video techniques can put you on top of Mt. Everest or leave you battling a shark 3,000 feet under water without abandoning the comfort of the studio. But if you are to show your earth-boring machine inside a coal mine, or the vast inventory of a department store or supermarket, video equipment must go where they are—and probably inconvenience a great many people to get the job done.

Management Commitment

Production within a studio is comparatively easy. However, for on-location shooting, management must be absolutely committed to the project. Video makes natural interiors turn blue. Thus, true colors require an immense amount of lighting, specially placed for shooting. Distracting extras, whether people or things, must be removed from the picture. Work, traffic, and possibly sound must be stopped or redirected. Electrical cables must be permitted in strange places, and imperfect strangers must be allowed to give orders *to everyone*, whether they're in the video or not . . . and get their releases if they are.

INSIGHT 61

Consider asking for a written release at the time of employment granting permission to picture that person in promotional materials. Many organizations do this. However, check with your attorney first.

Without on-the-scene cooperation, on-location shooting can become literally impossible. So be committed, and make that commitment known!

Endless Shooting

On-location shooting for the average piece, no matter what its length, will be from one to three days. Generally, there's a minimum crew of three: the producer/director, the camera operator, and an expert all-around assistant.[3] Their task is not only to shoot the project, but to *overshoot* everything—the clock on the wall, the view from the window, the notices on the bulletin board, the receptionist's smile, the loading clerk's wave, the office, the hallway, the factory sweeper, and the jeweler's polishing—whether it seems to have a connection with the final piece or not. Though seemingly random, this shooting is far from haphazard. It provides a wealth of raw, "cutaway" footage to be found and inserted wherever there is a need for a smooth transition between scenes. (Lack of such footage becomes obvious only when transition shots are missing or the same ones are endlessly repeated.) For the postproduction editor, there is never too much variety in *good* raw footage.

THE ART AND CRAFT
OF AUDIOVISUAL EDITING

It is in postproduction editing that your project is actually created. The process involves a series of steps, some mechanical, some judgmental, and some both.

Time Code

Most often, video editing begins with the placing of a small time-code "window" onto each frame. The window shows the hour, minute, second, and frame for that video and looks like this: 03:16:32:05 . Video is edited to 1/30 of a second. That is, there will be 30 frames *for each second*. But first comes the decision to edit for picture or sound. If the visual is the important thing, make the sound match it. If, on the other hand, you begin with a script that must be followed, tune the video to the sound track. Either is equally possible, provided that the postproduction editors know what is needed.

Sound Editing

The sound of your project—especially the spoken words—demands the same attention and skill as the picture. Decisions must be made on using the sound from the location or from studio recording. Everyone speaking on camera will require a teleprompter, a device that lets them *read* a script on camera, just as T.V. news broadcasters do. Teleprompters and tiny lapel microphones that assure good sound take a bit of practice, but have made in-house stars out of many an unlikely candidate.

---

[3] If cost is no object, or the project demands it, a crew can expand to include makeup artists, hairstylists, carpenters, and electricians—indeed, almost any specialist you can name. The reason movies often list a hundred or more credits is that every single person named was *needed* to do *that* film. What "that" means for your project will determine *your* crew and *your* cost.

Sound editing involves first finding the best available sound from on-location shooting and then knowing *and using* sound-quality techniques to improve, or "sweeten," what your location gave you. Incidental, ambient sounds, such as a door closing or footsteps approaching, almost always require "sweetening." Fortunately, they're also the easiest sounds to fix. Voices have fewer options, unless in-studio "lip sync" recording was planned and allowed for. Music if any, can wait for the final combination of words and pictures.

Visual Editing

As in sound editing, in visual editing all the steps are determined by the producer. Generally, it is the producer/director who views raw footage and determines which sections fit the script best, how to handle transitions, and when to add special effects or enhancements. The client can, and often does, work along with the producer/ director, but must recognize that the job is immensely time consuming. It begins with viewing *all* the raw footage to eliminate technically unusable shots or those for which superior versions exist. Suppose you start with 10 hours of film. This first assessment, with stops and starts to make notes, review some sections, take personal and meal breaks (although I have never worked with a/v editors who actually stopped for lunch, rather than eating a sandwich while working), will take at least two days. Now, having eliminated what is obviously unusable, the really creative editing begins. Everything that remains is viewed twice—or three or four times. In audiovisual editing, as in much advertising and promotion, "Everything takes longer than it takes!" But it does get done.

Final Editing

Final editing almost demands the presence of both the producer and the client. Audiotapes for radio commercials or information and training are easily edited and changed by simple cut-and-splice techniques. Video is different, however: Once the sound and picture are brought together in final form, any change, no matter how seemingly trivial, may require starting from scratch. Audiovisual editing is not done on actual film; rather, it is done with electronic impulses, from which a final film is created. To make changes, sound and pictures must once again be synchronized from a dozen different sources. You must make synchronization decisions during editing, not afterwards, or else not only will everything take longer than it takes, but it will surely also cost more than it costs.

INSIGHT 62

About animation: Disney-type animation costs about $2,000 per *second* for the animation alone. That's $7,200,000 for a one-hour feature film, a comfortably low cost by film standards. For a 30-second commercial, it's $60,000, and perhaps twice that by the time the project is done. Don't try and do it for less. If budget is the problem, stick with quality and do something else.

SUMMARY

- On-location shooting is invariably disruptive. Management must make its commitment known and enforced *before* the crew appears on the scene.
- Editing is often more costly than shooting. Keep it in control by being there when it happens, not correcting it after it's done!

THE ART AND CRAFT OF DUPLICATION

The majority of audiovisual production companies do not have facilities or equipment for duplicating large quantities. Where only a few copies are needed—perhaps a dozen or fewer—these companies can undoubtedly do the work. Many producers will provide such duplication as a low-cost service. Others have much higher pricing—from 2 to 10 times more, in my experience—than regular duplication companies. So check all of the following costs before you decide:

- **Setting up**. Preparing tapes and equipment before duplication can begin.
- **Duplication**. Make certain that your duplication company knows how the finished product will be used and can provide that service. Anyone can duplicate for a VCR. For anything else, from installing antipiracy protection to knowing T.V. requirements abroad, find and use specialists.
- **Labeling**. Preparing camera-ready type and art, if any, plus duplicating labels both for the cassette itself and for individual audio- or videocassette containers.
- **Containers**. Boxes for audiocassettes. Use softer "albums" or more sturdy "library cases" for videocassettes.
- **Handling**. Putting everything together as a finished package.
- **Shipping**. Be sure to specify how the complete packages are to be shipped. Many duplication companies routinely ship air express, unless instructed *in writing* to use a less expensive method.
- **Scheduling**. Your responsibilities, as well as theirs, should be specified in writing. And what happens if either one of you is late?

Finding the Duplication Service You Need

Audio and video duplication services are either small- or mass-quantity suppliers. Unlike printers, a middle size hardly exists. Since they may seem much alike to the uninitiated buyer, here are some guidelines:

1. Have your audio or video producer recommend a duplicating service (perhaps itself). Get a quote on the project *based on your producer's specifications* before production begins. If quantities and dollars are low, you can probably stop right there. For large quantities or large dollars, get additional quotations.

2. When evaluating new audio or video duplication companies, have them produce a sample copy from *your* original if time permits. Let them know that you will

compare it with one or two other suppliers and that you will use it as you would a printing proof to check the complete run.

3. In my experience, audiocassette services are fairly comparable to one another for *voice* duplication. If music is a critical part of the sound, however, get help in the evaluation. But keep a perspective on what it is that you are producing and the extraordinary cost of perfection when a good product will do!

4. In my experience, videocassette duplication services repay the evaluation effort. An obvious "winner" has always been easy to determine. When cost has been a factor, less expensive labels and containers have produced major savings. Consider purchasing them yourself only if your suppliers' sources fail to give them an obvious price advantage. (They're not purchasing just for you; they should get larger quantity discounts.)

5. For mass duplication—from thousands to millions of copies—go to a major national company. Before 1990, videocassettes had to be duplicated in real time; that is, a two-hour tape took two hours to copy. Larger producers had to have thousands of duplication machines to handle this. After 1990, high-speed duplication of videocassettes (as had been the case for audio) was finally perfected, with quality every bit as good as the previous real-time system. If quantities warrant, ask your producer to recommend such sources, or check Allied Film and Video at (312) 348-0373. This firm has offices and facilities from Florida to California.

SUMMARY

- For small quantities, the cost of a new setup may be more than the cost of duplication. Check with your production service before you go elsewhere. Get *total* costs from both—for the finished package, not just the tape.
- To evaluate audio or audiovisual duplicating ability, comparison shop by having *your current project* copied. It's worth the extra cost and will give you a proof against which to check the production run.
- Mass duplication needs a mass producer. Check several, not just the one closest to home.

NOTES ON THE AUDIO/ AUDIOVISUAL CHECKLIST

These notes are a supplement to the material presented in this chapter. They are not a substitute for that material.

1. The purpose of the project from management's point of view—especially *what* it is to achieve. *How* that is to be accomplished is best left by management to the pros.

AUDIO/AUDIOVISUAL CHECKLIST

Project title/description _____   **Date** _____

_____   **Project #** _____

_____   **Checklist #** _____

Overall Supervision by _____   **Deadline** _____

Budget _____   **Start-up Date** _____   **Completion Date** _____

MANAGEMENT DECISIONS	ASSIGNED TO	DUE	IN	MUST APPROVE	BY DATE	IN	INFO COPY ONLY	SEE ATTACHED
1. Purpose	_____	___	☐	_____	___	☐	_____	☐
2. Client Self-Image	_____	___	☐	_____	___	☐	_____	☐
3. Budget	_____	___	☐	_____	___	☐	_____	☐
4. Project Supervision	_____	___	☐	_____	___	☐	_____	☐

CREATIVE

	ASSIGNED TO	DUE	IN	MUST APPROVE	BY DATE	IN	INFO COPY ONLY	SEE ATTACHED
5. Focus	_____	___	☐	_____	___	☐	_____	☐
6. Audience(s)	_____	___	☐	_____	___	☐	_____	☐
7. Desired Response(s)	_____	___	☐	_____	___	☐	_____	☐
8. Supplier Selection	_____	___	☐	_____	___	☐	_____	☐
9. Client Script Ideas	_____	___	☐	_____	___	☐	_____	☐
10. Client Contact/Supervision	_____	___	☐	_____	___	☐	_____	☐
11. Script/Storyboard Approval	_____	___	☐	_____	___	☐	_____	☐
12. Suggested Length	_____	___	☐	_____	___	☐	_____	☐
13. Creative/Production Time Line	_____	___	☐	_____	___	☐	_____	☐

PRODUCTION

	ASSIGNED TO	DUE	IN	MUST APPROVE	BY DATE	IN	INFO COPY ONLY	SEE ATTACHED
14. On-Site Contact	_____	___	☐	_____	___	☐	_____	☐
15. Production Supervision	_____	___	☐	_____	___	☐	_____	☐
16. Editing Supervision	_____	___	☐	_____	___	☐	_____	☐
17. Actual Length	_____	___	☐	_____	___	☐	_____	☐

DUPLICATION

	ASSIGNED TO	DUE	IN	MUST APPROVE	BY DATE	IN	INFO COPY ONLY	SEE ATTACHED
18. Supplier Selection	_____	___	☐	_____	___	☐	_____	☐
19. Supplier Contact	_____	___	☐	_____	___	☐	_____	☐
20. Label Copy with ID	_____	___	☐	_____	___	☐	_____	☐
21. Label Design	_____	___	☐	_____	___	☐	_____	☐
22. Distribution	_____	___	☐	_____	___	☐	_____	☐
23. Duplication Time Line	_____	___	☐	_____	___	☐	_____	☐
24. Report(s)	_____	___	☐	_____	___	☐	_____	☐
_____	_____	___	☐	_____	___	☐	_____	☐

2. Be open about the self-image you wish to project. If there are different suggestions within management, rank them. More than one may fit in.

3. Be certain that management knows what its proposed budget can actually buy. If the budget is too limited for the quality desired, rethink your audiovisual needs.

4. The project supervisor is charged with managing #5 on. Where supervision is delegated, the project supervisor makes the assignments.

5–7. The how of #1, addressed to a specified audience to achieve a specific response. Put #5 through #7 into writing before evaluating suppliers. If you are unsure about focus—soft sell or hard sell, for instance—leave it until after #8. Just be sure which options do exist for you. Not everything will work.

8. It's not a question of which suppliers are best at what they do, it's who's best at what *you* need done. Evaluate your potential supplier from that perspective! (Our son's rock group was best for his friends. It was a disaster as a dance band for us parents.)

9. Nothing presents the client's self-image more clearly than his or her ideas for scripts. The more detailed, the better they are. Urge management to participate, perhaps in a brainstorming session. Most of us know we're not scriptwriters. Keep it informal.

10. The client's one contact person—and keep it at one only!—with whom outside services may deal. Audiovisual production is just too difficult, time consuming, and costly to fix to permit uncoordinated instruction.

11. Who *must* be involved? Who *may* be involved? Surely, not everyone who *wants* to be involved!

12. This is primarily an "infomercial" decision that's often determined by the needs of the sales department. For on-air commercials, determine all the likely uses (say, 60-, 30-, or 15-second spots) before writing begins. It's much easier, and much less costly, to plan now, rather than as an afterthought during editing.

13. This time is determined by the client's needs, the supplier selected, and the variety of the end product. (A 30-second commercial made from a 30-minute infomercial may take as much time as the infomercial.) Order duplicates to be made by #18 *now*, based on the #13 schedule, and notify everyone if there are delays. Everything in AV generally takes longer than you expect.

14. Designate who is authorized to act for the client during on-site shooting, especially at the client's site. Also, appoint a backup. Audiovisual producers get paid by the day . . . whether we make it possible for them to work or not.

15. Designate a project supervisor for management who makes on-the-spot filming and taping decisions. Others may have to be consulted, but the management's project supervisor *decides*.

16. After filming and taping, editing achieves the final project. A number of product specialists may be present, but, again, only the management's project supervisor speaks for the client.

17. For "infomercials," the actual length is determined during editing. Do not let this vary by more than 10 percent from the projected length in #12 without approval. Sales personnel, for instance, may not be able to use something twice as long, no matter how good it is. Even public service announcements often must fit set time slots. Don't just do. Check!

18. Hold final approval of the production and duplication suppliers until you know that they are mechanically compatible with each other. Have them speak to one another. Make them explain what they decide.

19. This standard purchasing procedure is best left to the purchasing department. Of course, the management project supervisor retains approval on all aspects of quality.

20–21. Duplication services are generally the best source for labels and labeling. If special designs are wanted, let your duplicating service know. But find out the effect on production time. Consider routine, but quick, labeling for immediate needs, with customized labels thereafter.

22. When the duplication supplier also ships the goods, find out the supplier's routine way to distribute them. Many send everything by air express, unless ordered to do otherwise in writing.

23. Don't spare the details for larger projects or multiple shipments. Something will be forgotten if it isn't specified here.

24. Note especially what has been learned that can be applied to future efforts. Put it in writing so that others may learn, too.

10 | Moving a Project from Camera-Ready Art Through Film, Printing, and Distribution

FILM SEPARATION AND PROOFING

Almost all modern printing begins by photographing the camera-ready art; that is, the material that is to be printed. That photographic image is then transferred onto a printing plate from which the actual printing is done. If colors are to be used in printing, there are two options:

1. Select from or have the printer create a special color. Thousands of such colors exist.
2. Print by one of several color systems in which all printed colors are a combination of just four inks. "Process printing," which uses the four "process" colors, is the best known such system.

It is the job of the filmmaker (known as a "color separator") to create the films from which the printing plates are made. What follows tells how this is done.

From Paste-up to Film

To reproduce something in color—say, a color photograph as part of a printed piece—the filmmaker begins by separating the original image into its four process colors. The use of special cameras and filters for this purpose is almost obsolete. Computerized high-tech laser scanners[1] now scan the color image, first interpreting the colors into process inks, then printing dots onto film electronically by means of a "laser gun."

INSIGHT 63

Discuss the capabilities and limitations of a separation scanner with your film supplier *before art or photography is assigned*. It's a lot easier and cheaper than attempting to fix the product after it is delivered.

Creating the Original. In preparing film for one or more colors, each color must end up on a single piece of film, which is then used to make the printing plate. But that film can seldom be made from just one camera shot or laser scan. Each of the preliminary shots must be stripped into position and contacted onto the final film. It

---

[1] Color images to be scanned are fastened to a rotating circular "drum." If your art makes this impossible, discuss options with your color separator as early as possible.

is not at all unusual to have a dozen or more preparatory contactings to create the film that will actually be used in printing!

Stripping. In stripping, the filmmaker takes two or more pieces of film and tapes them together. We can think of this as "film paste-up." Stripping can also be used to move elements closer together or place them further apart once they have already been transferred to film.

Contacting. Contacting involves two different processes: creating an original film or copying that film at some later time.

INSIGHT 64

For clarity and legibility, *always* mark your paste-up "SHOOT ALL TYPE AS LINE." Without this instruction, type may be screened routinely, giving it the appearance of a series of fuzzy dots rather than continuous lines. Your color separation filmmaker knows this, but is not permitted to avoid it without your instructions!

Contacting for new generations. The final film used for the printing plate is known as the first-generation film. If contacted (copied), the result is second generation. Second-generation film is used when the first generation may not be cut for repositioning or is not available, but a copy is. This frequently happens when the original film is part of another project and must be maintained in its current form. However, a copy can usually be made through the contacting process. If that copy must be transferred once again by contacting, the film becomes third generation. Ask which generation a particular film is, because each contact will lose some of the fidelity of the original. Think of it as a copy of a copy of a copy, etc.: The more generations, the further removed is the film from the original source. However, the more careful and talented the film house, the less is the loss overall. Expect a loss of 2 to 4 percent per film generation. That's hardly noticeable until the third or fourth generation, but it's definitely a factor thereafter.

Film Ownership. Specify on your purchase order *your* ownership of the film upon payment. This does not require you to take physical possession of the film unless you want to do so. It does, however, give you complete freedom to use and move your film as you wish.

Proofing the Film Before Printing

Once the film is ready for printing, it is used to make one or more prints for a final check. The sample that is checked is called a *proof*. For catalogs and other material that will be folded, the filmmaker provides at least two kinds of proofs for the same project:

Color Proof. When two or more colors are to be printed, a color proof shows how the printed piece will look and how it compares with any original art or photographs. This comparison should be made under industry-specified controlled lighting of 5,000K, which sounds unnaturally bright, but is actually the intensity of typical workplace lighting. The purpose of the controlled lighting is to give specified, uniform conditions for comparisons, rather than the random light sources that are available wherever you happen to be. Your filmmaker will have such a light source.

For multicolor projects, it is quite common to begin with a *random proof*. This shows, to size, the illustrations and photographs only, before they are placed into position. These are viewed and corrected for color density and detail. Any substitution or other change at this point is less costly than after everything is in place. After corrections are made, a second random proof is done only if the changes are major. More often, the second proof shows everything in position, that is, as it will appear in print. This proof is checked again, both for the specified corrections and for any other changes and corrections that may still be needed. Most often, none of the latter are needed, and this is the proof that goes to the printer.

INSIGHT 65

Accidents can happen any time anyone works with film. Don't just check for your corrections—check *everything*. But don't change anything unless *absolutely* necessary. The process is costly and requires equally careful checking every time.

The proof is accepted, dated, initialed, and marked "OK for printing" or "OK as corrected." (*Note the difference!*) It becomes the guide against which the project is checked while it is actually being printed. In reviewing proofs, be mindful that "what you see is what you get." Do not give your approval until you are satisfied with what you see!

Of course you will let your print production and art departments take the lead in proof checking and approvals. If such departments are not available, use your design source. It is *their* area of *expertise*. It is *your* area of *responsibility*.

Single-Color Proofs and Folding Dummies. Where only one color will be used in printing, the color chosen and the sophistication of design will determine how closely the proofing must match the printed piece. An exact proofing match of a specific color (or something as close as the filmmaker can provide) is more costly than a routine monotone, but like multicolor proofing, it is the only way to *know* what you will see when you print.

The folding proof is produced in one color on paper that is thin enough to fold easily. The proof is folded or formed into the exact shape and format of the final printed product. It is this folded proof that lets you see how facing pages actually look when all the elements are present and that lets you check whether all those elements are the way they were specified.

We check the following elements on folding proofs:

- Are all pages present and in consecutive order?
- Do elements that run across the center of facing pages (across the gutter) line up?
- Does the index or table of contents reflect where the elements are? If not, which one is wrong?
- Do all the elements work together? Do the materials fit into envelopes? Are items that bind together the proper size and shape? Etc.
- Are comparable elements positioned properly? Are all page numbers (called "folios") in the same spot? Is the use of page or section headings consistent? If not, was this deliberate? Do all cross-references check out? Do the captions match the pictures? Are both in the right place?
- Is all mailing information present and accurate? Is all ordering information present and accurate? Telephone numbers? Addresses? Legal and self-protection requirements (e.g., "Printed in USA," "Prices subject to change," etc.)?

This is your final chance to see the job as a whole before printing. Take the opportunity to *check everything*.

A Continuous Process

The preparation of film for use in advertising or printing and the printing itself are so interrelated that we shall treat them as continuous, with the film checklist and the notes that follow a part of the basic information. That is, in other chapters, checklist notes are supplemental; here they are a significant part of the text.

The proof delivered by the color-separator film house and accepted by the printer carries an implied guarantee that the film will produce what the proof shows. Many printers inspect all film and proofs carefully before agreeing to accept the film. Once accepted by printers, any problem in producing what the proof shows is to be solved by them and the supplier of the film, not by the client. Be mindful, however, that the printer is matching a proof, not original art! The time to settle questions concerning the artwork is when it is first seen by whoever makes the film. If the filmmaker does not forewarn you about how art will actually reproduce and suggest ways of doing it better, he or she may be the wrong person for the job. Note that certain colors or inks probably cannot be matched in standard process printing. They simply will not reproduce as seen. So warn your colleagues. And for the sake of your printer's sanity and yours, do not try to "fix" it on press!

NOTES ON THE FILM PREPARATION CHECKLIST

Unlike notes on most other checklists, these notes are not *a supplement to the material presented in the chapter. Rather, they are an integral part of the chapter.*

1. **Project manager**. The direct technical supervisor. If the client has no one

FILM PREPARATION CHECKLIST

Project title/description _____   Date _____
_____   Project # _____
_____   Checklist # _____
Overall Supervision by _____   Deadline _____
Budget _____ Start-up Date _____   Completion Date _____

	ASSIGNED TO	DUE	IN	MUST APPROVE	BY DATE	IN	INFO COPY ONLY	SEE ATTACHED
1. Project Manager	___	_	☐	___	_	☐	___	☐
2. Start-up	___	_	☐	___	_	☐	___	☐
3. Completion	___	_	☐	___	_	☐	___	☐
4. Tentative Schedule	___	_	☐	___	_	☐	___	☐
5. Supplier Selection	___	_	☐	___	_	☐	___	☐
6. Final Schedule	___	_	☐	___	_	☐	___	☐
7. Film/Printer Contact	___	_	☐	___	_	☐	___	☐
8. Prefilm Art Check	___	_	☐	___	_	☐	___	☐
9. Prefilm Paste-up Check	___	_	☐	___	_	☐	___	☐
10. Random Proofs	___	_	☐	___	_	☐	___	☐
11. Final Proofs	___	_	☐	___	_	☐	___	☐
12. Dylux Sample	___	_	☐	___	_	☐	___	☐
13. Delivery	___	_	☐	___	_	☐	___	☐

in this capacity on staff, use the person or studio that prepared the camera-ready art.

2. **Start-up.** The date the color separator can begin processing materials. (Note that if illustrations or photographs have been delivered without specifying their final sizes, the color separator cannot begin working on them.)

3. **Completion.** The date the client is responsible for approving the final proofing. Be sure to allow for at least two proofings on *everything*.

4. **Tentative schedule.** The schedule prepared before the film house is selected. This is generally done at the very beginning of the project, during its planning stages. For anything complicated or more than a few pages, have a color separator give a ballpark *time* estimate to help your planning. The separator probably can't estimate costs without more facts.

5. **Supplier selection.** If you are new to the field or to the geographic location, here are workable suggestions for selecting a film supplier.
   - Find out whom your company or organization has used in the past. Don't change without a reason.
   - Call several printers in the area and ask for their recommendations.
   - Ask the nearest local direct marketing association. To find it, call the Direct Marketing Association in New York at (212) 768-7277. Ask for the "DM Clubs and Association Network."
   - Ask the promotional director of some local businesses.
   - Check the Yellow Pages under "Color Separators."

   For simple one- or two-color projects, almost anyone recommended should do. So shop for price and schedule. For full-color or complicated projects, call first to learn the kind of work the various suppliers do. (Think twice before having a podiatrist do brain surgery or a brain surgeon look at your feet.) Get references. Check! Get samples. Give your final candidates written specifications, including deadlines.

6. **Final schedule.** Prepare a schedule that you, your color separator, and your printer can meet to get the project done on time. If all else fails, negotiate.

7. **Film/printer contact.** Film must be prepared to match the printer's need. Choose your printer as early as you do the film house, and have both agree on how the film is to be delivered (for instance, as 4-, 8-, or 12-page units). But first, ask other printers how their film is normally supplied, and ask color separators how their film is normally prepared. In case of conflict, get the cost of fixing the difference before film work is assigned. Your higher priced supplier may turn out to be a pleasant surprise.

8. **Prefilm art check.** The color separator should check the drawings, paintings, and other original art so as to foresee problems in duplication and to discuss their solutions. (It is sometimes better to begin with a color photograph, rather than with the original.) Also, the color separator should select the most reproducible photograph or transparencies when

several are available. Often, the choice is between contrast and detail. In printing, the printed photographs and drawings are called halftones because they are made up of dots of various sizes lined up in rows, with from 65 to 300 dots per inch. The fewer the dots, referred to as line, screen, halftone, or any combination of the three ("65-line screen," "120-line halftone" etc.), the less detail can be shown. But specific lighting and camera settings also control results. Without instructions, color separators tend to work for a middle ground. For advertising and promotional purposes, I almost always prefer high contrast. When numerous illustrations will be used, have the separator shoot and proof samples in a range of modes before you make a decision on which to use.

For rapidly disappearing letterpress printing and for rougher stock newspapers, 65- to 85-line halftones are standard. In general commercial offset work, 120 to 150 dots are typically used. Two hundred- to 300-line reproduction is used only in the highest quality printing, almost always to show detailed illustrations to exceptional advantage. For any advertisement or for your own commercial work, check on the maximum number of lines *the printer can use*. Each printing press works best at a specific line value. Know what that is, and make certain that no finer screening is ordered from the filmmaker. Fewer lines may give you less of an impact, but it is never a *printing* problem. On the other hand, over 10 percent more than the maximum number of lines for a particular press tends to produce random ink blots that reduce rather than enhance detail.

9. **Prefilm paste-up check**. Except on the simplest of projects, do not just ship a paste-up to the film house. Rather, take your paste-up artist or art director with you to meet with the color separator and go over *each* instruction. Ask the filmmaker to point out potential difficulties in making the film *or in printing*, as well as costs not covered by the estimated total. (Marking type for more than two colors is a typical problem—not for the filmmaker, but for the printer. Often a two-color substitute can be found after the difficulty is noted.)

10. **Random proofs**. When transparencies are the art against which proofs are compared, they are generally placed on a "light box," which illuminates them as if they were projected onto a screen. *No printed proof can possibly match the intensity of the colors this produces!* Visualize the originals that the transparencies show, and make *that* the basis for judging.

INSIGHT 66

Color separators expect to do two random proofings for advertising agencies, but only one for most other clients, and quote accordingly. Specify your likely needs when you describe the project, and have those needs reflected in writing in the quotations.

11. **Final proofs**. Final proofs show the project as it is to be printed. The corrected illustrations are in position, and everything should match what was asked for on the paste-up checked in #9. Make sure to:
    - Compare the corrected illustrations against the previous version, using the uniform lighting source.
    - Check the proof against every instruction given on the paste-up. Literally check them off to make certain that none are missed.
    - Make a final inspection of every color, to be certain that no obvious errors were made. (For instance, green will turn into blue if yellow has been erroneously located on the film.) If the color of the products is important, have someone who knows about colors check with you. We often see what we expect to see—especially the 10th time we look at it!

    Four-Color Proofing. Four types of proofs are possible for most four-color projects. If you are unfamiliar with any of them, ask to see a sample of a project done in all four ways, with the cost difference for each. The four types of proofs are:
    - **Match print**. This most closely matches what will be printed. It is not as popular as it should be, probably because many clients prefer the flashier Cromalin.™ Match print is the most costly of the four proofing techniques.
    - **Cromalin**. This is the most popular full-color proofing process. It produces a very high-gloss surface that can be somewhat deceptive in its feel as a printed piece.
    - **Color key**. This technique results in layers of film, one showing each printing color, positioned on top of each other to reflect what happens in the actual printing process. The colors are slightly muted through effects of the film itself. This was the original color proofing process and is the least expensive of the color systems available.
    - **Reading or Dylux™ proof**. In this technique, proofs are used to make the samples described in #12, for a final check of all copy, and for the positioning of all illustrations. Depending on the colors used, this proof can be made from just one or two of the four colors used in printing.

    Two-Color Projects. In many two-color projects, single-color reading proofs are adequate. Where only the color of the type is affected—for instance, red headlines or blue handwriting—color is often indicated as a grey, less dense image that is still easy to read.

    Illustrations. Where illustrations are to be shown as "duotones," that is, in two colors, one of which most often is black, at least a color key should be used for proofing. The two ways of achieving the final color have quite different effects:
    - **Fake duotone**. The illustration is printed in the darker of the two

colors and then covered with a light layer, or screen, of the second color. This is the easier way to print and is less expensive for film.

- **True duotone**. A halftone image is made on film for both colors and is then printed with all the care used in full-color projects. True duotones require specialized knowledge and skills by the film house. The technique does not simply use the same film for each color. To give instructions to the film house and to help check results, you need an art director who is familiar with the process.

12. **Dylux sample**. This is the *only* preview of how the final project will look in its actual size and with all pages or elements in proper order. All other proofs are presented with wide margins for notations and can be very deceptive. (Dylux is a trade name, and your printer may use a different process. Check for nomenclature.)

    Everyone with whom I have worked has had a near heart attack when I have dared to fold or cut a Cromalin to see what a page actually looked like, although it was never what they thought they had seen in the untrimmed version. (Cut very carefully with a sharp razor, and you can tape it back together almost like new. Remember, I gave you absolution: "Hey! It's not a sacred relic! It's just a proof!")

13. **Delivery**. You are responsible for providing the address of the destination. Let the color separator be responsible for shipment or delivery to media and printers. The last thing you want to hear is "It was perfectly fine when you picked it up." So don't!

ON WORKING WITH YOUR PRINTER

My first full-time job, at age 16, was as a printer's helper at a company that prepared the newspaper advertisements used in Chicago by Montgomery Ward. The preparation of the ads and the printing itself were essentially unchanged from the way Johann Gutenberg had set type and printed his Bible five hundred years before. Individual letters, cast in lead, were selected from a large wooden tray that held the alphabet in specific compartments whose locations we had to learn, much as we learn touch-typing today. Once composed, or set, type was locked into a frame with metal wedges. Ink was applied, paper placed on the inked type, and a roller moved over the paper, pressing it just hard enough to produce printing. This method, called *letterpress*, had grown in sophistication, speed, and applications for five centuries and is still the way printing is done in much of the world today.

Other Methods of Printing

In the United States, two newer methods, *offset* and *rotogravure*, now do almost all commercial printing work. Both have two major advantages over letterpress:

1. An easily handled printing plate replaces the heavy and bulky metal type. Thus, storage for reprinting that once took a warehouse can now fit into a closet!

2. Illustrations are produced photographically rather than through the metal etching process required by letterpress. For fairly simple projects, this makes possible practically instant transformation from paste-up to printed piece.

Even newer methods of printing are now in research, development, or use. Computerized systems that can personalize direct mail will undoubtedly do the same for advertisements printed in magazines and home-delivered newspapers. The same teenager who helped set metal type ten years later ran an office-sized offset press as part of his first job in advertising. Nothing about printing has surprised me since.

NOTES ON THE PRINTING/BINDERY CHECKLIST

Unlike notes on most other checklists, these notes are not *a supplement to the material presented in the chapter. Rather, they are an integral part of the chapter.*

1. **Printing budget.** The portion of quoted or estimated costs allocated to printing, even if printing and binding are given to a single supplier. You will want this figure for future comparison shopping. Be mindful of probable savings in getting a printing-binding "package" price.
2. **Start-up date.** When the project will actually go to press. Dates materials must be received by the printer are covered in #7.
3. **Completion date.** When the *printing* portion of the project is to be done. Any bindery work that is to follow is checked off in #12 on.
4. **Project manager.** When in-house technical expertise is available, use it, always asking to be a spectator *permitted to learn*. When printing decisions are thrust upon you before you feel quite ready for them, ask the printer to be your guide. Never involve yourself in how-to questions, however. Remember the client's magic words: "I know what we have to achieve. I couldn't begin to tell you how to get there."
5. **Tentative schedule.** This schedule is generally prepared at the beginning of the project, before suppliers are chosen, and helps guide in their selection. Some flexibility must be built in, depending on the complexity of the project.
6. **Supplier selection.** Follow the same procedure as that suggested for selecting a film supplier on page 221 and then add the following considerations:
    *   **Sheet or web printing.** Sheet-fed printing uses precut individual sheets. Web printing uses paper taken from huge rolls. Web printing almost always prints on both sides of the paper at the same time, with folding continued as part of the same printing process. Commercially, web printing is used for larger quantities—generally, no less than 25,000 for printing one or two colors and 50,000 for full color.
        Sheet-fed printing has many advantages of its own. It tends to

PRINTING/BINDERY CHECKLIST

Project title/description _____   Date _____
_____   Project # _____
_____   Checklist # _____
Overall Supervision by _____   Deadline _____
Budget _____   Start-up Date _____   Completion Date _____

PRINTING	ASSIGNED TO	DUE	IN	MUST APPROVE	BY DATE	IN	INFO COPY ONLY	SEE ATTACHED
1. Printing Budget	_____	_	☐	_____	_	☐	_____	☐
2. Start-up Date	_____	_	☐	_____	_	☐	_____	☐
3. Completion Date	_____	_	☐	_____	_	☐	_____	☐
4. Project Manager	_____	_	☐	_____	_	☐	_____	☐
5. Tentative Schedule	_____	_	☐	_____	_	☐	_____	☐
6. Supplier Selection	_____	_	☐	_____	_	☐	_____	☐
7. Final Schedule	_____	_	☐	_____	_	☐	_____	☐
8. Paper	_____	_	☐	_____	_	☐	_____	☐
9. Inks/Colors	_____	_	☐	_____	_	☐	_____	☐
10. Varnish	_____	_	☐	_____	_	☐	_____	☐
11. Shipping	_____	_	☐	_____	_	☐	_____	☐
BINDING								
12. Bindery Budget	_____	_	☐	_____	_	☐	_____	☐
13. Bindery Start-up	_____	_	☐	_____	_	☐	_____	☐
14. Completion Date	_____	_	☐	_____	_	☐	_____	☐
15. Project Manager	_____	_	☐	_____	_	☐	_____	☐
16. Schedule	_____	_	☐	_____	_	☐	_____	☐
17. Folding	_____	_	☐	_____	_	☐	_____	☐
18. Binding	_____	_	☐	_____	_	☐	_____	☐
19. Shipping Dates & Methods (skids, cartons, etc.)	_____	_	☐	_____	_	☐	_____	☐
20. Postage	_____	_	☐	_____	_	☐	_____	☐
21. Reports	_____	_	☐	_____	_	☐	_____	☐

© 1993, Fred Hahn

be much more flexible in quantity, number of pages to be printed, size of the pages or printed sheet, stock to be used, and number of suppliers than does web printing. The "quick print" shops found almost everywhere are sheet-fed printers, as are commercial printers in smaller communities.

- **Check for the right printer for each job.** No one printer can do everything! Visit the plants you asked for quotations. If you are unfamiliar with anything you see, ask. If the plant is not spotless, leave.

7. **Final schedule.** Prepare a schedule that you and your color separator, printer, bindery, and distribution supplier can achieve to get the project done on time. If all else fails, negotiate. Remember to differentiate between how and when!

8. **Paper.** Selecting paper, or "stock," is one of the most critical aspects of any printing project. There are literally thousands of different stocks, many available in a variety of thicknesses or "weights." The lower the weight, in units of pounds, the thinner the stock. Thus, paper used in most office copy machines is 50-pound offset, or 50# stock, which means that 1,000 25" × 38" sheets weigh exactly 50 pounds. To keep life from being too simple, different kinds of stock use different weight criteria, but each is consistent within itself and shows thinner to thicker (light to heavy weights) as smaller to larger numbers.

INSIGHT 67

Before making a final decision on paper, get stock samples and dummies—that is, actual-size samples—from the paper merchant or printer. Have *them* label each paper type and weight. Include that sample stock when you order. Let your order read: "80# cover and 70# body *as per samples herewith*" if you don't want 70# cover and 80# body and want no excuses for getting them confused.

Buying Paper Yourself. Paper and other stocks can be purchased through the printer or, for large jobs, directly by the client from wholesalers or paper mills. If you are inexperienced in purchasing paper or judging among suppliers, get expert help. Merchants are listed in major cities' Yellow Pages. Information is available from your advertising or direct marketing organization or trade publications in the graphic arts.

Here is a short checklist for purchasing paper:

Paper Supplied by Printer

☐ Availability
☐ Cost
☐ Alternative comparable stocks, including their availability and cost

Paper Supplied by Client

☐ Minimum order required
☐ Cost of specified paper and comparable stock
☐ Delivery schedule and guarantees
☐ Storage and handling
☐ Responsibility for quality
☐ Insurance
☐ Alternatives if delivery or quality fails

Many organizations and companies purchase their own paper. Others take advantage of their printers' house stocks, purchased in huge quantities at equally huge discounts. But when only one stock will do, allow enough time for its acquisition. Paper can seldom be manufactured overnight, no matter who orders it. If it's not on hand, it must wait until the manufacturer's production schedule says it's ready to be purchased.

There are many types of paper, including the following:

- **Cover stocks.** These are heavier papers used for catalog covers and similar projects.
- **Offset or matte papers.** These have a duller finish, though not necessarily less white, than that of the glossy alternatives. Most books and newspapers are printed on offset stock.
- **Enamel papers.** These are glossy papers used in many magazines and promotional mailings and on book jackets and other retail packaging. Printed on enamel, color illustrations achieve more sparkle, and even black-and-white illustrations seem to have more life. Enamel papers range from having a lesser gloss, used where materials have to be read as well as seen, to having practically mirrorlike finishes, called "chrome coats," where attention-getting ability is the major criterion.
- **Textured stock.** Few things are as underused as textured papers to give an immediate impression of elegance and good taste. Their very touch conveys prestige. Perhaps a fear that textures will cause difficulties in reproduction is why they are not more used. However, this fear is most often groundless, whether reproducing type or illustrations. Ask to see printed samples, and then be pleasantly surprised at how little more it costs for this added impact.
- **Colored stock.** The more popular offset stocks tend to be available in dozens of colors, at a somewhat higher cost than white. Most enamel stock, unless specially prepared by the paper mills, is white only.

Advantages and disadvantages of color. The major advantage of colored over white stock lies in its being different—in its standing out from the majority of paper people look at. The disadvantage lies in the way printing on color mutes type and illustrations, especially photographs. (Since many art directors are interested in how something looks, rather than how easily it can be read, be especially mindful of this problem.)

Fortunately, there is a solution that produces both unmuted illustrations and color stock: printing the color and leaving the areas to be illustrated white. To do this, you need merely instruct the filmmaker to use a "screened," light tone of one or more inks that are already part of the job. The process is quite simple and adds little to the overall cost of printing. For example, you can mark the paste-up, "Screen entire background 10% blue, but drop (remove) color behind all illustrations." This not only gives your illustrations their maximum visibility, but also frames them in color for even more impact.

9. **Inks/Colors.** One of my favorite memories is of Don Eldredge, then a Rand McNally vice president, screaming at an art director who had just shown him a proposed layout, "This is the last time I'm going to tell you. There is no such color combination as black and blue!" Eldredge knew exactly what colors he wanted, why he wanted them, and what their effect was likely to be in the marketplace. So should you! Before agreeing to radically different colors, ask to see a few samples using those inks on your kind of paper. Quite often, even the person making the suggestion is surprised.

10. **Varnish.**[1] Varnish on paper has the same results as its use on wood: protection, durability, and special visual effects.

   • **Protection.** Touching unvarnished printing, especially on enamelled, glossy stock, tends to leave fingerprints on the paper. The darker the ink, the more obvious the fingerprints will be. Catalog covers are the most common example. Adding an inexpensive, easily applied coating of varnish totally eliminates this problem. Many four-color (full-color) printing presses have a fifth-color unit that can be used for this purpose. More often, varnish is applied on a single-color press, after the ink has dried. Both methods are effective. Using the latter, however, permits an actual fifth color in the printing. Few of us are able to resist that temptation.

   • **Durability.** Fingerprints are far from being the only danger to unvarnished printing. Scuff marks, caused by pieces rubbing against each other during shipping, can make anything appear used or damaged, much as if you were asked to accept a new car with a blotched paint surface. I have seen thousands of presentation folders thrown out because their buyers had not known about press varnish. You do. Use it!

   • **Special effects.** Varnish can be glossy or dull. No explanation will be as effective as seeing the difference, so ask your printer for samples. Either will give protection. More important is the use of "spot varnish," which adds a striking gloss to a portion of the page, usually its illustrations. In trade terms, "spot" can be any size and any

---

[1] Much more expensive plastic coatings are possible, but almost always unnecessary. I never used them on any printed piece.

quantity, as long as it does not cover the whole page. Here, too, seeing is much better than describing, so ask several printers for examples and costs. Comparatively few of them have a wide range of samples.

11. **Shipping.** Many printers have their own bindery departments. Those with major mail order clients may also have an in-house lettershop. This can eliminate the time and cost of one or two shipping and handling moves: from the printer to the bindery and from the bindery to a mailing service. In getting quotations, factor in all these variables. I have always been willing to pay slightly more to keep everything under one roof—with one supplier held responsible.

12. **Bindery budget.** The bindery portion of the estimated or quoted costs, even if printing and binding are given to a single supplier. You will want this figure for future comparison shopping. Be mindful of possible savings through a printing and binding "package" price.

13. **Bindery start-up.** Start-up does not necessarily or often occur the moment printing is done. Be there, or ask to see the first completed pieces. Show them to the lettershop as a final safety check.

14. **Completion date.** Specify what "completion" means: the day a job is finished at the bindery or the day it is received at the next destination, usually the letter shop mailing service. Go for the latter.

15. **Project manager.** Costly outside creative direction should not be needed here. Do-it-yourself management again comes into its own.

16. **Schedule.** Whether work is done by the printer or contracted with a separate bindery, get a schedule that shows the following:
    * The time and cost (if any) for shipment from the printer to the bindery.
    * The time and cost of specialized outside services, such as die-cutting or embossing, before bindery work can begin. Have the print shop run those portions first. They can be finished outside while the rest of the printing is being completed.
    * The time and cost of all standard bindery work.
    * The time and cost (if any) from the bindery to the lettershop and all other destinations.

17. **Folding.**[2] Before ordering folds on pieces that are to be mailed, especially if they will be placed in an envelope, show them to the bindery and to the lettershop. Almost any fold is possible; some, however, may be very expensive because they cannot be made by a single run through the folding machines at the bindery. Your lettershop will tell you if a folded piece can be handled by their automated equipment. Some folds can't! Don't lock in your paper-folding ingenuity without assurance from both the bindery and the lettershop.

18. **Binding.** For multipage promotional pieces, such as catalogs and brochures, there are three binding or fastening options:[3]

---

[2] A variety of folds available through most printers and lettershops is shown on page 37.
[3] A variety of binding options is shown on page 120.

- **Press glue**. Pages are glued together at the spine as they are folded. When printers have this equipment, and unfortunately few do, it is an excellent—and inexpensive—way of binding 24 or fewer pages.
- **Saddle stitch**. Pages are folded and stapled together with a metal fastener through the spine. For thicker saddle-stitched projects, allowance must be made in filmwork and printing to have uniform-sized pages. To get an immediate view of the problem, fold several dozen same-sized pieces of paper in half, and then look at the front. The "v" formed by the folding becomes more exaggerated with each sheet you add.
- **Perfect binding**. This is the system used on most paperbound books. Where thickness permits (different binderies have their own minimums), perfect binding is the method of choice for appearance and ease of printing. Where it is used, it produces a flat spine that should be imprinted as if it were a book. Many perfectly bound catalogs are filed vertically, on bookshelves, rather than in filing cabinets.

19. **Shipping dates and methods**. Discuss with your lettershop, warehouse, and other bulk destinations how they want their shipments sent to them—in cartons, on skids, etc.—and how each unit is to be marked. Get their instructions in writing. Discuss this with the bindery before you approve. If the bindery suggests a better way, let the bindery people discuss it with the people at the destination. As always, don't pretend to an expertise you do not have. But learn and get it!

20. **Postage**. How much postage and other shipping costs must be paid in advance? Where? When? How is the proof of mailing or shipping documented and recorded?

21. **Reports**. In a brief form, reports are for management. A more detailed version is for do-it-yourselfers. Give yourself time to review such reports at a later date. All too often, they are done, filed, and forgotten. Remember a critical difference between a professional and an amateur: Where a professional has, say, 10-years' experience, an amateur has 1 year's experience 10 times.

ON WORKING WITH YOUR LETTERSHOP

Lettershops began as mail-handling services that could print your letter and reply card or order form, address the letter on the bulky mechanical systems then in use, insert the pieces into envelopes, often by hand, seal the envelopes, and deliver them to the post office. Many lettershops maintained and housed their clients' mailing lists, because their sheer bulk and weight, and the cacophony involved in creating or correcting individual metal addressing plates, made them unwelcome elsewhere. Today's lettershop is still your partner in getting your mailings stuffed, addressed, and delivered. But what a difference the computer age has brought to you and to them! The lettershop distribution checklist that follows will help you both in evaluating potential suppliers and in scheduling their responsibilities—and yours—once they are selected.

Three-Column Format

The lettershop/distribution checklist is not complete in itself, except for the simplest of mailings. Its purpose is to guide you through at least one preliminary and final planning meeting with your lettershop. Additional checklists and schedules will be needed for creative design, printing, acquisition of mailing lists, and your in-house handling of responses and their evaluation. Make liberal use of the third column, "SEE ATTACHED." Where possible, use the other checklists in this book. Where none exists, use them as models and make your own.

Evaluating the Lettershop

Whether it calls itself a lettershop, mailing service, or something else, the important thing is not only what a service promises to do, but whether or not it actually does it. For your evaluation, visit prospective suppliers while they are working. Note especially the degree of supervision they operate with, the relationship of supervisors to line workers, and the esprit de corps in the shops. Lettershop work demands unflagging attention to detail by *everyone* involved. Look for that first. Where it exists, the rest is likely to follow.

NOTES ON THE LETTERSHOP/DISTRIBUTION CHECKLIST

Unlike notes on most other checklists, these notes are not a supplement to the material presented in the chapter. Rather, they are an integral part of the chapter.

1. **Discussion of project specifications.** Your lettershop can be an unexcelled source of *free consultation* on the mechanical aspects of direct mail. Involve it in your preliminary planning. If you are not a direct mail pro, tell the lettershop people! Ask for guidance in mechanical and postal specifications that will help your more detailed planning as you proceed. For lowest mail-handling costs and postage, envelopes must be of a certain size, with flaps in a certain position, larger materials must be folded in certain ways, and addressing labels can not be affixed to specific areas of the envelope. Your lettershop can be invaluable in helping you plan. Even if you are a pro, the one way to keep up in this volatile industry is to ask.
2. **Dummy copy for estimate/quotation.** Show your dummies—samples of the exact size and stock you plan to use—to the lettershop. Discuss with them possible cost-saving changes and get estimates or quotations. Estimates are just that—an *approximation* of what the project will cost. *Quotations* demand *exact specification* of every item on this checklist.
3. **Date mailing is to get to recipients.** The date mail *must* be received by the recipients controls all your decisions. Tie-ins with scheduled events or traditional promotion times are obvious examples. Fourth of July sales are announced in June. Seed catalogs arrive in January. Every business product has its own season, and some bloom all year long. Do not, without

LETTERSHOP/DISTRIBUTION CHECKLIST

Project title/description _____   Date _____
_____   Project # _____
_____   Checklist # _____
Overall Supervision by _____   Deadline_____
Budget _____   Start-up Date _____   Completion Date _____

SUBJECT	PLANNING	FINAL	SEE ATTACHED
1. Discussion of project specifications	_____	_____	_____
2. Dummy copy for estimate/quotation	_____	_____	_____
3. Date mailing is to get to recipients	_____	_____	_____
4. Scheduling	_____	_____	_____
5. Quantity to be mailed	_____	_____	_____
6. Source and type of lists	_____	_____	_____
7. Merge/purge and other list control	_____	_____	_____
8. Type(s) of addressing	_____	_____	_____
9. Personalization–wanted/required	_____	_____	_____
10. Class of mail (first/second/third/fourth)	_____	_____	_____
11. Date(s) printed materials must be at lettershop and how delivered (skids/cartons/etc.)	_____	_____	_____
12. Printing and bindery work to be provided by lettershop	_____	_____	_____
13. Date mailing list(s) required by lettershop	_____	_____	_____
14. Outgoing mail permit(s)	_____	_____	_____
15. Incoming mail permit(s)	_____	_____	_____
16. Postage amount(s)	_____	_____	_____
17. Date(s) postage is required	_____	_____	_____
18. Lettershop charge(s)	_____	_____	_____
_____ _____	_____	_____	_____

ELEMENTS OF MAILING	QUANTITY	SUPPLIER	ID#
Self-Mailer			
Outgoing Envelope			
Reply Envelope			
Reply Card/Order Form			
Letter			
Flyer/Brochure			

careful testing, mail anything out of season. The reason everyone in your industry mails at the same time is . . . because that's when everyone decides what to buy.

4. **Scheduling.** Based on your "must be received" dates, work through this checklist with the lettershop. Most suppliers will have standard cost, expedited, and EMERGENCY schedules and rates. Note that your lettershop has no control over your outside suppliers. Item #11 especially will demand its own schedule. Try for the lettershop's standard time line. Not only does it have the lowest costs, but if anything does arrive late, it has built-in time for expedited or emergency action. If you begin on the fastest track and something goes wrong, how can anyone make up the time?

5. **Quantity to be mailed.** The total quantity of your mailing is not the only question to be decided here. Will you test? If so, what quantities and what potential rollout? Different equipment and planning may be needed for different-sized lists. Can your lettershop do both economically? If not, should you try to find a different shop that can or use two suppliers? If two shops are used, who will supervise the second—your primary lettershop or you? There are lots of questions. *Now*, in the planning stage, is the time to get answers.

6. **Source and type of lists.** If anything more than simple affixing of labels is required, discuss with your lettershop what it can do, how much it costs, how long it takes, and how the list must be supplied to make it all possible. Before agreeing, contact your sources of lists to see whether they can meet those needs and at what cost. Do not pretend to expertise you do not have. Let lettershops speak with sources of lists and translate for you.

7. **Merge/purge and other List control.** The operations here are computer generated. They cannot be provided economically—if at all—from printed lists already on labels. Before any of these operations are specified, give your lettershop a contact at the location of each list source and let the lettershop determine what is *possible*. You must decide what is *practical*.

   • **Merge/purge.** A way of eliminating duplicate addressing when using more than one list. Merge/purge is a computerized system that can save you money and mountains of printed material. But it does have a price. Check on its possible savings vs. mailing to duplicate names. Check it in an area that would get a lot of mail and see how much you would save. You do not actually have to mail anything! Just run the test lists through the merge/purge system, and compare before and after totals.

   • **Merge only.** It is often less costly to create a single large list, (without purging duplicate names), than it is to handle several lists individually. Although this list will include all the duplicate names, it may qualify more of your list for postal presort discounts. Merge only definitely is less expensive *as a system* than merge/purge.

   • **Test selected items.** The *nth* name, zip code, or other selection from larger lists may be less costly when done by a lettershop rather than the list source. Let both quote, but get *all* costs involved.

- **Coding of source list.** If the lists are delivered uncoded, it still may be possible to code them. Check.
- **Presort and zip code qualifications.** Sorting from alphabetical order into zip code, combining for individual mail carrier delivery, and refining into zip code plus four extra digits may all generate substantial savings. Not every mailing needs this much sophistication, but find out what your lettershop can do, the costs, and savings in postage.

8. **Types of addressing.** You can address on labels, simulate typewriter or handwriting, and address onto envelopes, reply forms, or letters that show through windows. There are lots of options, different requirements, and costs. Know *why* as well as *how* if you decide to test.

9. **Personalization.** Practically everyone loves to see their name in print, no matter how obviously it is mass produced. New computer technology is making personalization increasingly more versatile and less costly. Learn what your lettershop can do and what they will need—and charge—to do it. Test.

10. **Class of mail.** Check with your post office, as well as your lettershop, on the requirements and costs for different classes of mail. Then find out whether your list sources can supply what's needed. You may need postal permits, or you may be able to use the lettershop's. Most *business* mailings will produce essentially the same results no matter how they are mailed, but don't take it for granted. For *your* mailing, . . . test. Believe the numbers.

11–13. **Deliveries to the lettershop.** Determine the specific dates by which outside materials must be received by the lettershop to maintain the dates and costs that were quoted. On-time delivery is *your* responsibility for printing, bindery work, and mailing lists. Many lettershops can provide printing or binding in addition to mailing services. Consider outside shipping and handling in your costs. Find out the lettershop's capabilities, especially in regard to personalizing materials you might not otherwise give that special touch.

14–15. **Mail permits.** New mail permits may be required, depending on where and how you mail your material. Check with both the post office and the lettershop at the beginning of your planning, and then incorporate the permit numbers into your printing. Certain preprinted permits may simulate an *undated* first class meter. Let your lettershop be your guide.

16. **Postage amounts.** Make out your check to the postmaster rather than to your lettershop. It must be deposited in its entirety at the post office. A refund of any overpayment requires a written request, while underpayment *by any amount* may cause refusal of the entire mailing. If you mail regularly from the same post office, establish a bulk rate account there, and always deposit a bit more than you think you'll need. For a one-time

mailing only, ask your lettershop how best to handle the postage. Deposit postage at the post office before it receives the mailing. If a check accompanies the mailing and there is any question raised about it, the mailing may be refused.

17. **Dates postage is required.** Deposit checks at the post office several days in advance of the mailing, to give them time to clear. (A cash payment may require references!)

18. **Lettershop charges.** *Any* change between what your lettershop saw for estimating and what it actually receives may change costs. Get samples to the lettershop so it can confirm or requote prices in advance of the actual mailing.

INSIGHT 68

Code *every piece of every mailing*, whether that piece changes within the mailing or not. Place the code where it can be seen (on the outside, not the inside of the brochure). It's the best—and often the only—way of getting the right pieces into the right envelope addressed with the right list. Code reply cards and order forms *on the ordering side*. For test mailings, copy each reply (that's why you put it on the ordering side) before it goes to the order fulfillment department. Use those copies to check any computer analysis reports. This time, don't believe the numbers. Check!

11 | Finding the Right Advertising Agency[1] and Other Promotional Resources

The selection of an advertising agency is based on one of four circumstances:

1. You have never had an agency and are convinced that you need one now.
2. Your previous agency has resigned.
3. Your previous agency has been or will be fired.
4. You wish to evaluate your current agency against other resources.

The process suggested in this chapter works equally well for an external or in-house advertising agency, an advertising department, or any other advertising or promotional resource.

THE JOB DESCRIPTION

No matter what the urgency of your need, precede the search with a job description as carefully considered and detailed as one for an executive vice president or other senior officer.

- Put in writing *exactly* what the job involves, including an objective basis for evaluation.
- Specify what you, as a client, will contribute to help make the desired results happen. Your agency, as well as you, needs assurances of resources to get the job done![2]
- Detail the compensation—how much you will pay.

Of course, the job description is just a beginning. You and your more likely candidates must discuss it—often phrase by phrase—until there is agreement not only on what it says, but on what it means. For example, every such description contains the words "assist with marketing." But what is "assist"? What is "marketing"? How does one get compensated for marketing?

---

[1] If all else fails, call 708-866-9009 and ask for Fred!

[2] In my experience, the most frequent reason for the "failure" of an advertising or promotion campaign has been a client's refusal to continue a multistep program when success planned for step six had not yet been reached at step four. Don't plan steps if only the long jump will do!

COMPENSATION

Begin with the budget. Everything that follows will be determined by the dollars available for it. Agencies and other promotional resources—whether they admit it or not—are structured to work within specific budget ranges. Those handling accounts of $50,000 or less probably could not provide the service demanded by clients spending $500,000 or $5 million. A $50,000 account represents one-half of one percent of its billing to a $10-million agency. It means a 10-percent increase to the one billing $500,000. Find the right-size pond in which to swim.

INSIGHT 69

An advertising agency is a business. Unless there are overriding reasons to the contrary, put your account where your financial contribution is meaningful to that business' success. You certainly don't have to be the biggest fish in their pond; just be one that they'll *know* is gone if you're landed by someone else.

MAKE FIGURES MEANINGFUL

Differentiate between your advertising and promotion budget and your agency budget. To the client, $100,000 for direct mail is detail enough. For your candidate agencies, the critical facts would be $80,000 for *client-purchased* film, printing, and postage, with $20,000 for agency copy, art, and supervision. Think of your possible client-agency union as an arranged marriage where compatibility will matter beyond anything else. Of course you want to feel comfortable with your mate from the very beginning, so put that in the job description, too. But always remember that you have a *business* relationship, with mutual profitability as its only likely continuing bond.

WHAT ADVERTISING AGENCIES CAN DO

Advertising agencies excel in the ability to tell a story convincingly in a variety of media, address that story to its most appropriate audience, and get that audience to take some specific action based on what they have seen, or heard, or both. Where the product or service is new, different, or simply superior, the descriptive job is comparatively simple. It's making oneself seen and heard through the competitive clutter that calls on all the agency's creativity. Any of us can tell you that something is bigger, better, faster, cheaper, safer, or healthier. It's getting our audience to pay attention, believe what we say, and do something about it that becomes difficult.

The difficulty is compounded when you and your competitors' products or services are essentially the same. It grows even more so when even the client recognizes that the problem lies in the product or service itself, yet advertising is assigned to provide the sales solution. And advertising often does! The storyteller becomes mythmaker and the customer, believing the myth, makes it come true.

In evaluating potential agencies or services, know which client description you match, and then evaluate their proposals against your need. Beware of brilliant solutions to the wrong problem. Beware of any solutions until the problems are agreed upon.

AN OBJECTIVE BASIS FOR SELECTING AN AGENCY

Any competent agency can produce innovative and pictorially striking concepts. But even when competing products are essentially the same—e.g., hamburgers, beer, women's jeans, men's athletic shoes, telephone service, credit cards . . . the list is endless—creativity alone is probably not enough. Rather than asking for speculative *creative* presentations, pay the competing agencies to research the reasons for the advertising problem, and then make that the basis for a competition among them based on their proposed solutions.

Do what many of the most successful direct marketers do: Recognize that you do not know what may work until you try it. Within specified parameters of good taste, good policy, and good law, give each of your finalists a chance with its solution to its analysis of the best way to reach your audience. Any good media-buying service can work with you in structuring a fair trial. If budget is a problem, limit your search to just two finalists. And if you must select one only, take comfort in the fact that they are almost all competent and practically everyone else does it that way, too. The fact that they are wrong as often as right is what makes the "agency business" so competitive . . . and so much fun!

Index